Phasal Analysis

Also available from Continuum

Working with Discourse Second Edition
J. R. Martin and David Rose

Discourse Analysis
Brian Paltridge

Phasal Analysis

Analysing Discourse through Communication Linguistics

Karen Malcolm

continuum

Continuum International Publishing Group

The Tower Building
11 York Road
London SE1 7NX

80 Maiden Lane,
Suite 704
New York, NY 10038

www.continuumbooks.com

British Library Cataloguing-in-Publication Data
A catalogue record for this book is available from the British Library.

ISBN: 978-1-4411-4540-6 (paperback)
ISBN: 978-1-4411-4164-4 (hardcover)

Library of Congress Cataloging-in-Publication Data
A catalog record for this book is available from the Library of Congress.

Typeset by Newgen Imaging Systems Pvt Ltd, Chennai, India

Jaya gurudeva amala avinasi
jnanarupa antara ke vasi
Paga-paga para dete prakasa
jaise kirane dinakara ki.

Contents

List of Texts

Examples of Analysis

Acknowledgements

There are many people to whom I am indebted for their support of this project. Many of the analyses introduced in this text were first developed in my studies and research with Michael Gregory in the early 1980s when we first introduced Communication Linguistics to the linguistic world. Since then Michael Gregory, Michael Halliday, Elissa Asp, Jim Martin, Lynne Young, Murray Evans, Jessica De Villiers and many others have encouraged me to complete this text. I have always been grateful for Michael Halliday's interest in phasal analysis, and his support of those systemicists who are interested less in the systemic aspect of his work so much as its functional aspects. None of these linguists is responsible, of course, for the decisions I have made in this book. Many of these are a consequence of my teaching experience over the last several years. I am most grateful for the feedback of research assistants and countless students who have worked with drafts of this book. I am always searching for the simplest, most expedient and interesting way of introducing students, with little or no linguistic background, to a wealth of analytical tools, so they, too, may engage in the exciting process of linguistic research. My special thanks to Zbigniew Izydorczyk for his support over the years of its writing.

I am grateful to the following for Permission to Copy various texts used in this textbook and on-line:

Chrysler Group, Hyundai Auto Canada Corp., Jaguar Cars Ltd., A. Prest, S. Northfield, M. Dawes, J. Ray and M. Hummel, A. Epp, M. Waft, the Winnipeg Free Press, The Uniter, The Globe and Mail, Pitney Bowes Canada, The Exchange District Biz, Handgun Control Inc., The Bradey Campaign to Prevent Gun Violence, Dundurn Press Ltd.

Special thanks to my yoga community for their continual support, and to my sons Eku and Jyota, who *let* me write this text when I could / should / might have been playing with them.

Introduction

Have you ever read a book, a pamphlet, an article or a billboard and delighted more in *how* the words were conveyed than in *what* exactly they said? Have you ever taken part in a conversation that failed, and wondered what happened? Have you ever read a particular literary passage that evoked a strong emotional response in you, but not known how to explore your reactions or communicate them? Have you ever heard someone talk about a text in a way that felt very 'wrong' to you, but not had a way of proving his / her interpretation was less valid than yours? Have you ever been misunderstood in a way that had serious consequences? Have you ever simply wondered why a particular author / producer, style or register of discourse held such fascination for you? If any of these situations sound familiar, you are reading the right book.

Although you are masters of the language you speak and know how to use it effectively in a great variety of communicative situations, most of you are on a sort of communicative 'autopilot'. You have figured out how to negotiate the communicative demands of your daily life, but you are not consciously aware of how you do so. As a consequence, the moment some communicative event takes an unpredictable turn, if a mutual understanding has gone amiss, you may be at a loss of how to rectify matters, or wonder how to proceed if the way has become overly complicated and / or indirect. Communication can be very simple and straightforward or very complex and subtle.

Generally speaking, the purpose of this book is to support you in becoming more aware of the intricacies of communication, and more conscious of the communicative resources and choices you make over and over throughout your day. The manner this is accomplished is by introducing you to several different ways of making meaning through sounding, drawing / writing, wording, arranging, connecting and correlating. If you learn how to analyse a variety of texts from several different perspectives, you will gain not only a better appreciation of the sophistication of your communicative 'autopilot', but also a detailed understanding of how communication works. You will have tools with which to explore your own questions and come up with answers.

As the Table of Contents reveals, each chapter introduces a form of analysis that reflects the different patterns through which language choices make meaning. Chapter 1 provides an overview of the entire theoretical framework known as Communication Linguistics. As such, you might skim it initially to get a sense of the foundation of the other chapters. However, with its great wealth of technical language, you should not expect to understand it completely (particularly the ideas of phase and phasal strings) until you have become familiar with a few of the forms of analyses described in Chapters 2–6. Once you have become acquainted with the metalanguage appropriate to each form of looking and analysing in the individual chapters, you might review the theoretical orientation to see how each perspective 'fits together' in Communication Linguistics. It is important to become familiar with the entire theory before reading Chapters 7 and 8 of the textbook in which all forms of analysis are combined to come up with the new tools of analysis and new ways of looking and thinking about spoken and written discourse called rhetorical strategies and phasal analysis.

There are five fundamental methodology chapters in the book entitled: graphology, phonology, lexis, syntax and semology. These are traditional 'ways of looking' in the worlds of linguistics and discourse analysis; however, in each chapter, there are innovations to the individual form of analysis and / or ways of reporting the findings that go beyond what is currently available. Chapter 2, **Graphology**, deals with the *seeing* aspect of language, its visual meaning. Chapter 3 focuses on **phonology**, the *sounding* aspect of language. In Chapter 4 the focus is on **lexis**, the *wording* aspect of language. Chapter 5 explores **syntax**, the *sequencing* or *arranging* aspect of language. Chapter 6 deals with **semology**, the *meaning* aspect of language. These various types of patterns are not the only types of meanings that one could analyse. In the later chapters of the book, other forms of analysis are suggested, and other books recommended that complement phasal analysis.

In each of these methodology chapters, you are introduced to a particular way of looking at language, generally. Then, you will be introduced to a specialized language, or *metalanguage*, that will enable you to describe the language choices that encode that type of meaning more precisely. Each metalanguage is theoretically contextualized in a section called *Metafunctions*. With a technical language that supports you in discerning certain types of language patterns, you will be introduced to a methodology that involves identifying, classifying, describing, contextualizing, summarizing and concluding. Each individual process of analysis is described step by step in prose, then a text is analysed as an example of the suggested method. Ways of tabulating your results and writing your conclusions to both summarize your findings and interpret them are included. Exercises and answer keys, available on the internet, are noted at relevant points in the chapter. Each analytical chapter ends with a review of the methodology detailed in the chapter.

Chapter 7 introduces and exemplifies the linguistic reconceptualization of *rhetorical strategy* while Chapter 8 introduces the analysis of phases which effectively interrelates the findings from all previous analyses in order to describe the dynamic aspect of discourse. Both rhetorical strategy and phasal analysis require the student to combine and correlate the findings from each prior form of analysis. After all, decoders do not interpret one type of meaning, then another. Instead, they interpret all types of meaning together, simultaneously. The analyst, however, focuses on one form of meaning at a time, until s / he is ready to consider how every pattern relates to another, reinforcing or challenging it. The whole, of course, is always greater than the sum of its parts. There is much important research to be done on phase before one can fully understand and appreciate the value of this descriptive tool and form of analysis.

This textbook does not argue theory or methodology, it merely presents and exemplifies it. However, by describing language from a variety of perspectives, you will begin to understand how communication works in everyday situations, how meanings are made, how information is exchanged and how ideologies are maintained and / or transformed.

The title of the book, *Phasal Analysis*, indicates the cumulative focus of the entire book. Phasal analysis is unlike the other forms of analysis detailed in the book. It depends on, and makes use of, all other forms of analyses. Everything in the book leads to phasal analysis and contributes to it. It is a cumulative form of analysis that brings together the results of all the other forms of analysis, shows how they reinforce and challenge each other, and most importantly, shows how a discourse evolves spontaneously as it happens. In this way, phasal analysis is a unique form of analysis. It alone captures the continuous, albeit intermittent, shifts in language that are a consequence of changes in the interlocutors' relationships in the situation and culture. In phasal analysis all the more synoptic, or static, forms of analysis introduced in the early chapters are combined to describe the dynamic aspect of communication.

1 Communication Linguistics

Communication Linguistics is the theoretical orientation of the descriptive framework and methodology known as *phasal analysis*. It was introduced in the mid-1980s by Michael Gregory and Karen Malcolm (Gregory, 1985; Malcolm, 1985*a*) as a development of Michael Halliday's systemic model (1978, 1994), and as influenced by Ilah Fleming's stratificational communicative model (1988) and Ken Pike's tagmemics (1982). In Communication Linguistics, language is considered from both a social and cognitive perspective. Socially, language is an intentionally communicative behaviour that enables language users to exchange meanings, negotiate status, maintain cultural values and beliefs in a particular situation and culture. Cognitively, language involves both what the encoder knows and intends and what the decoder knows and interprets. To capture both the social and cognitive aspects of communication, Communication Linguistics differentiates between *planes of experience* and *language's realizatory code* (Figure 1.1).

PLANES OF EXPERIENCE	LINGUISTIC REALIZATORY CODE
SITUATION	**SEMOLOGY**
Communicator's Communicating Context	Non-instantial Register (experiential,
Generic Situation	interpersonal & textual resources:
Referential Realm	processes, speech function, etc.)
Referential Plot	Non-instantial Rhetorical Strategy
GNOSTOLOGY	
DISCOURSE	**MORPHOSYNTAX**
Cultural Dialects	turn, sentence, clause, group, word,
Instantial Register & Rhetorical Strategy	morpheme (systems, structures, classes)
Discourse Plot	
Phase & transition	
MANIFESTATION	**PHONOLOGY/ GRAPHOLOGY**
Audible Sound Waves	tone groups, foot, syllable, phoneme etc.
Visible Marks	verbal & non-verbal graphs

Figure 1.1 Malcolm (2005 Linguistica; cf. Malcolm, 1985*a*, p.137).

Before the framework of Communication Linguistics is discussed, a few more basic concepts will be introduced.

Communicative event

A **communicative event** is an event in a *situation* and *culture* in which *language* (spoken or written) and / or visual images are *manifested* by someone (the *encoder*) to communicate something (the manifested message or *discourse*) to someone else (the *decoder*).

Encoder and decoder

The terms *encoder* and *decoder* refer to the ***real-life* interactive participants** in the situation that produce and receive images. **Encoder** refers to the writer, speaker or visual artist who chooses, consciously or unconsciously, what language and / or visual alternatives to communicate. Her choices are based on both her *intentions* to communicate a particular message and her familiarity with the various linguistic and visual systems of options that are available to her in the particular situation and culture that will enable her to fulfil her communicative intentions. A **decoder** is the person who reads, hears or sees the message and who *interprets* it through her own experience and knowledge of the communicative options available in the situation and culture. **Represented participants** are those people or things represented in the discourse and / or in the visual images included in the text: they may be fictional or representations of *real* people, as in photographs or written memoirs.

Message, discourse and text

Message refers to the meaning that is exchanged in the communicative event between the encoder and decoder. The message is ***manifested*** as visible marks on a page or in audible sound waves. The word **discourse** refers to the product of the intentionally communicative event: the message that has been manifested in the situation. The word *discourse* is used in contrast to the word *text*. **Text** refers to the *written* record of the verbal (spoken or written), visual or multimodal discourse. A text generally forms a unified whole that exhibits an internal connectedness or coherence. If the discourse were *written*, the text would be equivalent to the same written document as the discourse. However, if the original discourse were *spoken*, manifested in audible sound waves, the text would be the written transcription of a recording made of the spoken discourse. The distinction between discourse and text, then, is particularly important when analysing spoken discourse, where the written text is different from the original discourse and is subject to possible errors and omissions made by the transcriber when transcribing the communicative event. In this textbook, the word *text* is used more than *discourse* because, for the purpose of analysis, all discourses, whether originally manifested in speech or writing, are presented as written / transcribed texts.

Marked and unmarked

The notion of *marked* language versus *unmarked* is useful to analysts who compare one text to another. Very simply, **unmarked** tests are typical, *predictable* and often somewhat stereotypical, while **marked** texts are unusual, *unpredictable*, differing from language users' expectations. The value of using a cline between highly marked texts and very typical unmarked texts will become much clearer as you follow the analyses of marked and unmarked examples of texts included in this book.

To the analyst, unpredictable marked examples of discourse may seem more interesting than the many texts which are unmarked and culturally predictable. Marked texts are more likely to exemplify a new range of stylistic possibilities which enable the analyst to make new discoveries about the linguistic choices used either to encode complex and indirect intentions or to decode subtle readings and interpretations. However, much of language is necessarily unmarked and predictable in order to facilitate clear and easy interpretation. Whether focused on marked or unmarked texts, linguistic analysis is *descriptive* rather than *prescriptive* or evaluative: one text is not valued more than another.

Planes of experience

The **planes of experience** of Communication Linguistics describe the actual *communicative event* as a dynamic process that happens in a 'real' instance of time and space. The three planes of experience relevant to the communicative event are *situation, discourse* and *manifestation*. The central discourse plane represents the communicative event itself in which the language / discourse is manifested in its situation. You might think of it as the *product* of communication. More specifically, the **discourse** plane is defined as the linguistic realization of what the encoder has selected as communicatively relevant to the decoding receiver. It is the manifested message which is simultaneously an instance of, and evidence for, our linguistic and cultural knowledge. The plane of experience entitled **manifestation** refers to the intentionally communicative speech sounds, visible marks on a page, gestures and / or facial expressions that are manifested in the communicative event as the discourse. You might think of it as the *process* of communication. The upper most plane, **situation**, describes the contextual features of the situation and culture that are relevant to the communicative event described in the manifested discourse. You might think of it as the *context* of communication.

Situation

The culture and situation relevant to the communicative event are described using four variables: *referential realm*, *referential plot*, *communicator's communicating context* and *generic situation*. In Communication Linguistics we define **referential realm** as the real or imagined persons, things, events and interactional intents and attitudes that are *available* in the world (situation and culture) to be encoded in the message. The term was borrowed from Ilah Fleming. '[Referential realm] involves anything a communicator wishes to talk about in his message', no matter whether it is factual, hypothetical, mythical, concrete or abstract (Fleming, 1988, p. 298). More simply, referential realm refers to everything and anything that could be talked about in a situation and culture. From the referential realm of possibilities the encoder selects her *referential plot*. The **referential plot** refers to the 'real' sequence of persons, things, events, intents and attitudes and so on that are actually *selected* from the referential realm of possibilities to be included in the message of the communicative event (Gregory, 1985, p. 203). More simply, referential plot refers to the specific sequence of the events that the encoder chooses to communicate.

The **Communicator's Communicating Context** (CCC) describes the comparatively *permanent* cultural context of the interlocutors' situation in terms of their temporal, geographical, social and individual provenance. Throughout the textbook, the word 'culture' refers, more generally, to these aspects of the CCC. **Generic Situation** (GS) describes the more *impermanent* and immediate relationships that characterize their communicative situation. The user's and receiver's relationships to the experience is called the interlocutors' *representational relationship*. Their relationship to each other is called the *interactional relationship*. Their relationship to the medium of transmission of the discourse, be it spoken or written, is the *medium relationship*, and to the purpose of the discourse is their *functional relationship*. These various relationships are referred to as *field, personal tenor, mode* and *functional tenor*, respectively, by systemic linguists. In the textbook, 'situation' is used to describe, more generally, the relationships of the GS.

The interrelationships between culture, situation and language have been studied for much of the twentieth century, particularly by those involved in anthropologically oriented research. Both Boas, in his research on the language of Baffinland, and Malinowski, in his work on the discourse of Trobriand Islanders, realized that discourse could not be translated without an understanding of cultural and situational contexts (cf. Dinneen, 1978, pp. 213, 300). These ideas were further developed by Firth, who talked about the importance of the *context of culture* and *context of situation* in describing the communicative event (ibid.). In the 1970s Halliday and other systemicists developed these ideas more fully by relating the systems of language to the functions of language and to the field, mode and tenor in situation (1973, p. 99). Insights into *context of culture* led to the CCC of Communication Linguistics; whereas the development of *context of situation* led to GS.

Communicator's Communicating Context

The CCC captures and classifies those features of the **culture** that are relevant to any communication. If you step into a new country, travel back in time, or even walk across town to where people from a different socio-economic or ethnic group live and communicate, you become acutely aware of the cultural specificity of language when familiar points of reference disappear, and you find yourself in unfamiliar terrain, perhaps even unable to communicate (cf. 'communicative competence' Bonvillain, 2003, Chapter 10). In different **geographical** **provenances** only a few miles apart, Northern Germany and Southern Denmark, for example, inhabitants use an entirely different language to communicate. Trying to interpret the meaning of Early Modern English Shakespeare, not to mention the Old English of several centuries earlier, makes the difficulties of interpreting the language and culture of a different **temporal** **provenance** very clear. Languages change over time, from place to place, and even from group to group. Age, gender, ethnicity, social class, level of education, economic status, religious affiliation and political ideology are some of the factors that determine an interlocutor's **social** **provenance**, which also affects communicative choices. Each configuration of temporal, geographical and social provenance convey different belief systems, different assumptions, different customs and different values, each with its repository of communicative resources available to language encoders and decoders alike. When an encoder from one social group communicates to a decoder from a different social group, even man to woman, grandparent to grandchild, communication may prove challenging.

Many linguists over the past century have noticed that language and culture interrelate in a mutual dialectic (Sapir–Whorf hypothesis, cf. Bonvillain, p. 49). The beliefs and values held by the people of a particular culture determine the breadth and variety of linguistic resources that are created or acquired to communicate them. While, at the same time, the range of linguistic possibilities constrains the way language users are willing, and able, to think and communicate.

Cultural dialects, in the Discourse Plane, are the linguistic reflection of the *temporal*, *geographical* and *social* provenances of the CCC in the Situation Plane. There is also a fourth dimension of the CCC: **individual provenance**. Have you ever noticed that one of your friends speaks in a unique style? Or, at some point in your life, have you deliberately cultivated a personal style or voice, that transcends, or even challenges, the temporal, geographical and social norms of your cultural dialect? In your writing and speaking, your communication will inevitably be affected by the range of linguistic resources that reflect your beliefs, attitudes and values. In other words, your individual provenance is bound to affect your personal dialect as well as the time, place and society in which you live.

Generic Situation

Just as the variety in our *cultural provenance* influences the communicative resources we bring to each communicative event, so do the *relationships* that capture the different aspects of the communicative **situation**. In the 1960s, systemicists coined the words *field, mode* and *tenor* to describe these relationships. Generally speaking, *field* refers to the relationship between communicators and the experience they are representing in their discourse. *Mode* refers to the relationship between the interlocutors and their chosen medium of transmission in the communicative event. *Personal tenor* refers to the relationship between the encoder and decoder involved in the communicative interaction. And *functional tenor* refers to the purposeful relationship between the interactants involved in the communicative event (cf. Gregory and Carroll, 1978; Halliday, 1978).

Field is the aspect of the situation that describes the focus of the activity or experience represented in the message. Eggins writes that field can be glossed as the 'topic' of the situation that varies in terms of *technicality* (1994, pp. 67–74). In *everyday* situations, common knowledge is sufficient background for communication. Everyday language uses ordinary terms that most people can understand to share experiences. However, in *technically specialized* situations, where there is an assumed knowledge of, and expertise in, a specific activity, there is a greater likelihood of a technical jargon, understood by 'insiders' only, people who share the same technical expertise. Acronyms like *DNS*, *VPN* and *DHCP*; abbreviated syntax like *ping it*, and technical action processes like *virtualize a PC* are signals of technical computer jargon, which is sometimes called 'field-restricted' because its interpretation is restricted to those in the field.

Mode, the relationship between interlocutors and their medium of transmission, describes the contrast between spoken and written discourse. Eggins suggests that both spoken and written discourse be considered in terms of spatial / interpersonal distance and experiential distance (1994, pp. 53–4). By **interpersonal distance** she refers to the proximity between the interlocutors that affects their communication. Language users might be face to face, in which case there is the possibility of both visual and aural contact and immediate feedback. Or they might communicate from afar, like a novelist and her reader, without the possibility of either contact or immediate feedback. By **experiential distance**, Martin means the relation between language and the action or social process involved. Children converse as they build a Lego ship together. Adults read an instruction manual to assemble a chair (*language as action*), or use language as a social process when they write a personal journal (*language as reflection*) (1984, p. 27).

Personal tenor refers to the interactive relationship between interlocutors in the discourse, which is a function of the particular social role each interactant plays in the communicative event. Eggins uses three different continua to assess personal tenor: *power, affective involvement* and *contact*. In terms of **power**, interactants manifest either the *equal / symmetrical* power of intimate friends, the unequal *hierarchical / asymmetrical* power of employer / employee, or something in between these two extremes (Eggins, 1994, p. 64). In terms of **contact**, interactants may have *frequent* contact like spouses, *infrequent* contact like distant acquaintances, or something between (ibid.). **Affective involvement** refers to the extent to which the interactants are emotionally involved in, or committed to, the situation (ibid.). Close friends have a *high* affective involvement; work colleagues, a *low* affective involvement, and others a middle level somewhere between. These various aspects of tenor influence the choices that are encoded in the discourse, and the way they are interpreted.

They also clarify the definition of, and distinction between, formal and informal situations. In *formal situations,* like meeting with your professor or employer, typically there is an unequal or hierarchical power relationship between the interactants, infrequent contact and low affective involvement. In *informal situations* like meeting with friends at a pub on a Saturday night, the reverse tends to be true: power is more likely to be shared equally among interactants who have frequent contact and are emotionally highly involved (high affective involvement) (Eggins, 1994, pp. 63–6). The language used in formal and informal situations often differs in predictable ways. In informal situations, there is a greater likelihood of slang, abbreviations, contractions, swearing, tag questions, interruptions, overlap, certain types of modals, vocatives involving first names, nicknames and terms of endearment and evaluative lexis, or appraisal, that carries positive or negative judgement. In formal situations, titles plus surnames are more typical as vocatives, and the lexis is more likely to be neutral and formal, without slang or swearing. People go out of their way to be polite, turn-taking is done carefully and modals are of a specific sort (cf. Eggins, 1994, pp. 67–8).

Functional tenor describes the relationship between the interlocutors and the purpose or goal of the communicative event. In each culture there are many possible communicative purposes which affect communication. In North America, encoders wave to greet one another, put a finger to their lips to ask someone to be quiet. They say "*I'm sorry*" when they want to apologize. Within a classroom, teachers speak clearly, comparatively slowly, glossing their terms as they go, giving examples, asking questions that they already know the answers to, repeating key concepts, to help their students learn. Students participate by listening, taking notes, asking questions that they do not know the answers to, and responding to the teacher's questions when they can. Advertisers, politicians, public relations employees employ a variety of tactics to persuade the public to follow their suggestions: buy the products they endorse, vote for them, agree with their point of view. They teach, entertain, illustrate, exemplify, humour, criticize, inform and more.

Message and manifestation

Until discourse is manifested in the 'real' world, there is only a *message* in the *encoder's* mind, something the person is thinking of communicating.

Communication linguists differentiate between three types of messages: the *encoder's intended message*, the *decoder's interpreted message* and the *actual manifested message* which is the same as the discourse. The **intended message** represents the encoder's experiential, interpersonal and functional choices from those available in the field, personal tenor and functional tenor of the referential realm. The encoder's choice of mode of discourse, whether spoken or written, determines the nature of what is manifested in the communicative event as discourse. **Manifestation** transforms the encoder's communicative intentions into real discourse which can be seen or heard and interpreted by the decoder.

Intentions or thoughts are transformed into the 'real-life' physical attributes of the communication: the audible sound waves, written graphs, movements, facial expressions, and / or gestures that encode the intended message as the **manifested message** or discourse. Once the message has been manifested, the *decoder* uses her knowledge and experience of communicative resources to interpret the manifested message. The decoder's **interpreted message**, the meaning she draws from the manifested message, is affected by the cultural, situational and linguistic knowledge she brings to the communicative event. In theory, the degree to which the intended, manifested and interpreted message are similar or different depends on the degree to which the encoder and decoder share similar cultural, situational and linguistic experience and understanding. In practice, the intended and interpreted messages often prove quite different as illustrated by the children's game where a message is passed around a circle of friends, and everyone laughs as they hear the disparity between the final interpreted message and the original manifested one. How seldom their interpretations match what was intended is something all language users would do well to remember.

Analysts who have a more objective perspective on the discourse because they were not involved in its production or reception and a greater linguistic awareness of the communicative event and of the registerial constraints and cultural ideologies behind it than most encoders and decoders, analyse the *manifested message* or discourse. They do not have complete access to either the intended or the interpreted message.

Discourse

Discourse is the product of the communicative event once the message has been manifested in the situation. The Discourse Plane forms the central plane of experience concerning communication and language operating within a situation once manifested. The discourse reveals the **cultural dialect** of the encoder that reflects the temporal, geographical, social and individual provenance of her CCC. The language of today would be unrecognizable to language users a hundred years ago, and words like *togue, serviette, biscuit,* and *boot* mean something quite different in other Englishes of the world (British, American, Australian, for example) than in Canada. Teenagers laugh at their parents' dated vernacular, and parents roll their eyes as their daughter says *like* for the fifth time in a single sentence.

Discourse is the 'real-life' plane that provides both evidence of the encoder's communicative intentions and knowledge, and incentive for the decoder to access her linguistic knowledge when interpreting. The discourse plane is central, then, in that it is the plane that 'assumes' the static linguistic realizatory code. Discourse does not, and cannot, happen without language users' communicative and linguistic knowledge, which guides both encoders and decoders in their selections within the communicative event. Like the other planes of experience, situation and manifestation, discourse captures the dynamic aspect of communication as it happens. All planes of experience are considered *instantial* in that they only exist in the moment in which the communicative event occurs in its situation.

Differentiating an instantial, dynamic real-life social communicative event from the non-instantial, static cognitive linguistic knowledge which realizes it, has brought to light new ways of looking at language and communication. Concepts like **discourse plot, phase** and **phasal strings** are not even part of the linguistic realizatory code, but only emerge in the actual communicative event. Even **register** has a completely instantial aspect to it which belongs in the discourse, aside from its non-instantial function in the linguistic realizatory code.

Discourse plot

Whereas the *referential plot* describes the real life chronology or sequence of events from which the encoder makes her communicative choices; **discourse plot** reveals the way the encoder has chosen to arrange the same events in her discourse. A real-life, linear chronology of 'first this happened, then . . . , and finally . . . ' may not be the encoder's choice at all. She could choose to talk about what happened most recently, then return for some background details at some point, then return to the present moment. In other words, her discourse plot could start with events taken from any point of the real life sequence, and then move backward or forward in time whenever she wants. In literature, authors play with time through flashbacks that move back in time and prophetic dreams that move forward. In such situations, the discourse plot, the organization of the persons and events in the discourse, may be quite different from the 'real' life version as it happened chronologically in the referential plot which inspired it.

Phase

It was their discovery of *phase*, in the early 1980s, that led Gregory and Malcolm to consider communication both dynamically and statically, socially and cognitively, and to differentiate the planes of experience from the realizatory linguistic code. Back in the early 1980s, Gregory was analysing Shakespeare, while he and Malcolm were also investigating children's discourse (cf. Gregory, 1995; Gregory and Malcolm, 1995). In both studies, they recognized the same phenomenon, more clearly in the children's discourse than in Shakespeare. Through analysing each text phonologically, lexically, syntactically, semologically and cohesively, they discovered that each text was organized or 'structured' in 'chunks' of tri-functional consistency (cf. *metafunctions* to understand tri-functionality) (Gregory, 1985; Malcolm, 1985*a*). This means that in a few lines of a text experiential, interpersonal and textual systems were realized in a particular momentarily consistent combination of patterns before shifting to a new, equally consistent chunk of different tri-functional realizations. After exploring numerous registers of written and spoken discourse, literary and non-literary, they realized that this spontaneous structuring of discourse is a feature of all intentionally communicative discourse. In a sense, it is not surprising that the brain 'packages' language in chunks of consistency as this facilitates both encoding and decoding.

These chunks of metafunctional consistency they called *phase*. A **phase** describes a unique chunk of tri-functional and tri-stratal consistency, produced spontaneously and unconsciously, as it happens in all intentionally communicative behaviours manifested as discourse. Gregory and Malcolm described phase as "the dynamic instantiation of micro-registerial choices" (1995 / 1981). Phases are *not* part of the synoptic realizatory code. They cannot be known and remembered because they only occur as the discourse is manifested. Phase is *only* instantial: it occurs simultaneously as encoders manifest their discourse in a communicative event. Hence, phases are represented theoretically as belonging among the planes of experience, and more specifically to discourse. Some phases are quite obvious and transparent to the analyst because they are limited in codal alternatives: the alternatives encoded are simple and repetitive (cf. Chapter 8, Malcolm, concerning children's discourse, 1985*b*). Other phases become apparent only through detailed tri-functional and tri-stratal analyses because of a greater range of resources, involving greater complexity and more internal variation (cf. Malcolm, 1998, concerning adult *non-literary* discourse, and Malcolm, 1991, 1996, 2001, concerning *literary* discourse).

Phasal strings

Phasal analysis does not reveal a homogeneous, continuous and predictable fabric of tri-functional consistency or a random weave that only occasionally 'hangs together'. Rather, it seems that communication is encoded in 'chunks' of tri-functional consistency, where experiential, interpersonal and textual information relate in one way for a moment in time, and then all three shift into a new type of interrelationship captured in the next 'phase' of tri-functional consistency. One of the phenomena that has become evident through phasal analysis is that some phases work together forming larger discoursal structures (cf. Chapter 8). Some phases gradually evolve over time to become something slightly different forming **continuous phasal strings** (Malcolm, 1985*b*). Other phasal consistencies disappear only to reappear some time later in the same discourse forming **discontinuous phasal strings**. Research indicates that children are more likely to shift from one set of phasal consistencies to an entirely new one in their conversation than adults forming **isolated phases** (ibid.). However, if they are engaged in an activity as they talk, the activity talk may return in the same consistency intermittently throughout their conversation (discontinuous phasal strings). Subsequent research has also indicated that interlocutors, who have not shared prior experience with one another, are more likely to structure their discourse in continuous phasal strings than friends' discontinuous ones (cf. Malcolm, 1998). The continuous shifting of phasal consistencies reflects the fluctuation throughout communication of the experiential, interpersonal and textual relationships in the situation. This fluctuation is continual, although intermittent, in spoken and written discourse.

Register

In every different communicative event that occurs within a situation in a specific culture, there is a different configuration of relationships classified as field, mode, personal and functional tenor, which define that situation. These often reoccurring configurations of relationships carry with them a predictable range of language selections. For instance, in a communicative situation in a post office setting, one would expect to hear something like this:

> Buyer - excuse me. could I have two stamps?
> Seller - for Canada?
> Buyer - no, one to England. how much will that be?
> Seller - a dollar fifty
> (Seller hands buyer a stamp)
> Buyer - thanks

In North American culture, in a post office communicative situation, the field of the discourse relates to stamps, letters and mail. The exchange will be spoken, face to face and spontaneous. Typically, the transaction will involve two interactants: a buyer of stamps and a seller of stamps, who have no previous shared experience. This means that their affective involvement is likely low, and their frequency of contact, low. The power relationship between the two is hierarchical since only one of them has the relevant information, and has been designated officially to facilitate the service. The purpose of the communicative event is one of exchanging a service: buying and selling. The situation, both physically and in terms of information exchanged and relationships involved, is recurrent and predictable.

The language used in this reoccurring communicative situation is also predictable. The same could be said about the language that is used in hundreds of communicative situations that occur daily in a particular culture. A language user who has lived within a particular culture for most of her life can predict, with a certain degree of accuracy, both the representational (field), interactional (personal tenor), medium (mode) and purposeful relationships (functional tenor) in a situation at the doctor's office, the grocery, the bank, the workplace, the family dinner table, as well as the type of language that is used in these settings. The language, the configuration of linguistic resources that the members of a culture typically associate with a given generic situation, is called **register** (Gregory, 1985, p. 204).

In Communication Linguistics register is considered in two ways. The predictable post office talk that was just described indicates that register needs to be part of the non-instantial realizatory code for one, stored in the language user's *gnostology*. In a sense, this idea of register is ***non-instantial*** because it refers to the generalized and somewhat stereotypical configuration of relationships and linguistic realizations that interlocutors 'know' and 'remember' from past experiences of similar communicative events in similar settings. As part of an encoder's linguistic knowledge it is a 'potential', a configuration of resources that a decoder has come to 'expect'. A decoder uses this linguistic knowledge comparatively, bringing such expectations to bear on the current discourse she wishes to interpret.

Communication Linguists also think of register in a more instantial way as discourse is manifested in a unique situation. Each instance of post office talk will not be necessarily the same as the one remembered from prior instances. Relationships in the situation might have changed in some subtle way, for instance the post office clerk is a friend and neighbour to the person buying a stamp. The *non-instantial* register of the conversation may be best described as post office talk; however, a simple greeting like *Hi Jane* that precedes the questions and answers of the buyer and seller might make the 'actual' *instantial* version of the register subtly different from its expected version. The instantial version refers to the relationships and linguistic patterns that are unique to that 'real-life' instance in the 'immediate' situation. That is why the instantial notion of register belongs to the dynamic discourse plane of experience where language is manifested in the real time and space of its situation while the non-instantial version belongs to the static realizatory code of potentials stored in the gnostology. To have both an instantial and non-instantial version of register enables the analyst to describe both the predictable and the unpredictable characteristics of the discourse.

Gnostology

People communicate in a wide range of registers applicable to a variety of situations every day. This is possible because they have knowledge of both the relationships and purposes involved in such communicative situations and the codal resources, or registers, that encode them. Both personal experience and / or shared secondary accounts of such experience are stored in the hypothetical construct called *gnostology*, from the Greek 'gnosto' to know. Communication linguists agree with systemicists that language is a social phenomenon, a form of intentional social behaviour (Malcolm, 1985a). They also believe that language is a cognitive phenomenon. **Gnostology** captures the knowing, storing and remembering of information relevant to, and necessary for, communication. Language is considered socially and culturally appropriate (or not, as the case may be) and cognitively informed.

In Communication Linguistics, gnostology acts as an *interface* between the 'real-life' planes of experience (situation, discourse and manifestation) and the 'remembered' realizatory linguistic code. In other words it interfaces with both what happens *instantially* in communication, as described by the planes of experience, and what happens *non-instantially*, as described by the realizatory code.

Consciously or not, language users 'store' in their gnostology knowledge of both the implications of the four dimensions of cultural provenance (temporal, geographical, social and individual) and the relationships (representational, interactional, medium and functional) within particular situations available in communication. In addition, they 'know' all the systems and structures within the linguistic code itself (as well as other communicative codes considered elsewhere), which are used to encode and decode discourse (cf. metafunctions and strata).

The planes of experience describe communication as it happens in a particular time and place. However, there can be no communication without a linguistic code, one of several semiotic codes, that encodes real life happenings. And there can be no communication without people and their knowledge of these codes. All cultural ideologies and the linguistic codes that reflect and create these affect communication, not because they are 'out there' somewhere in the physical world, but because they are in the minds of the culture's encoders and decoders. Language is not just an intentionally communicative social behaviour; it also involves a cognitive process: the cognitive process of *encoders* who pattern their discourse in terms of their knowledge of the linguistic repertoire available to them, and the cognitive process of *decoders* who interpret the message manifested in terms of their shared understanding and memories of past communicative events. Everything remotely related to communication, all options available in the linguistic code itself, all meanings, all registers, all culturally held ideologies that are linguistically relevant: all are stored in the minds of language users. In other words, everything that communicators know of their culture, the situations which are appropriate to it, the linguistic registers that reoccur in these situations, and the entire linguistic code itself is stored in a language user's gnostology.

Linguistic realizatory code

Whereas the *planes of experience* describe instantial discourse manifested in a *real* time and place (situation), the linguistic realizatory code refers to the non-instantial linguistic code of language resources that is *remembered* and known from past communicative events and 'stored' in our gnostology for future potential use (cf. Gregory and Malcolm, 1995 / 1981). The linguistic realizatory code represents the various types of linguistic meanings and resources that are 'retrieved' from the gnostology before encoding and decoding. These resources are further discussed in terms of the *metafunctions* and *strata* of language. In Communication Linguistics the linguistic realizatory code is described *tri-stratally and tri-functionally*. In addition, the linguistic realizatory code includes *non-instantial register* and *rhetorical strategy*.

Metafunctions

One of Halliday's seminal insights into language is his correlation of language *function* and language *system*. From his research in the 1960s on language acquisition among children, he realized that there was a particular correlation between the functions of language and certain systems of language. 'The internal organization of language is the way it is because it has evolved to serve the social functions of language: to relate experience, create relationships and organize information' (Halliday, 1973, p. 34). Following Halliday's ideas, Communication Linguists use three **metafunctions** to reflect the types of relationships that are described in the generic situation and the types of meaning that encode these relationships in discourse.

Experiential meaning represents the interlocutors' relationship to the real life 'content' of their experience with the people, events, things and circumstances of their referential realm as well as the beliefs, thoughts and feelings of our inner world. It reflects the interlocutors' intention to represent and communicate experience. The experiential function of language is realized by choices made from the **system of transitivity** (see also the section called *Metafunctions* in each chapter). Language users fulfil the experiential function of language by selecting actors, processes, goals and circumstances in order to exchange information with one another. The encoder says *I ate the butter tart*, and the decoder recognizes exactly what experience is being shared.

Interpersonal meaning reflects the interactive relationship between the encoder and decoder be it as friends or strangers, close or distant, during their communicative *exchange* whether formal or informal. If you wished to communicate an experience to a close friend in a quick text message, you might not be concerned with spelling errors, incomplete sentences, and using expletives or slang. You rely on your friend understanding, making concessions, unconsciously completing omissions that she is aware of, having communicated with you in the past, all in order to interpret the intended experiential message successfully. If you described the same experience to an authority figure, whom you did not know well, you would likely take greater care with sentence structure, spelling and choice of words. These differences are indicative of the different interactive relationships between encoder and decoder, which carry the interpersonal meaning of the message. The interpersonal function of language is realized linguistically by choices from the **systems of speech function and event mediation** among other things. An encoder could express much the same experiential message in different ways by choosing a statement *He threw her the ball*, a question *Did he throw her the ball?*, or a command *Throw her the ball*. Her interpersonal relationship with the decoder determines which is most appropriate. Not everybody likes to be ordered around; yet parents typically give orders to their kids, and employers to their employees.

Textual meaning reflects the interlocutors' relationship to the medium of transmission of the manifested message or discourse, be it spoken or written. *Spoken discourse* is usually interactive, face-to-face, spontaneous, casual, often using language to accomplish some task. More specifically, it is usually dialogic, organized by turn taking, dependent on its external situation with a dynamic structure and signals of its spontaneous nature (false starts, hesitation fillers, incomplete clauses, interruptions, overlaps). Generally, spoken discourse includes everyday lexis and non-standard grammar; it is lexically sparse and grammatically complex (Eggins, 1994, pp. 55–7). Spoken discourse is often coherent to the situation and the interlocutors' gnostology as well as internally cohesive. *Written discourse*, on the other hand, is more likely to be non-interactive, involving one person at a time, not face-to-face, not spontaneous, not casual, using language to reflect rather than act. More specifically, it is organized monologically, comparatively independent of its context, has a more synoptic structure which is rhetorically staged and finite, represents the final polished draft only, uses prestige lexis and a standard grammar, is lexically dense and grammatically simple (ibid.). Written discourse is usually cohesive internally, but seldom coherent to the situation in which it is manifested. As well as cohesion, the textual function is also concerned with message organization realized by the **system of theme** in the clause. An encoder could choose to begin her sentence with the participant *She ate her meal yesterday* or by the temporal circumstance *Yesterday she ate her meal* depending on what she perceives as most significant thematically.

The non-instantial ideas of *register* and *rhetorical strategy* are considered **tri-functional** in that each register and rhetorical strategy is comprised of the systems and structures which realize the three metafunctions of language: experiential, interpersonal and textual, and which reflect the field, mode and tenor in the situation.

Non-instantial register

As one of the gnostological variables of the realizatory linguistic code, ***non-instantial* register** encodes the predictable relationships in *remembered* recurring situations (described by field, tenor and mode) through the systems and structures which encode experiential, interpersonal and textual meanings in our linguistic code. There is a continuous dialectic between language function and language system: a continuous interchange and interplay between the real life demands and uses of language and the systems of alternatives which realize them in the language code.

Even if language users have not experienced a register personally, they will often have a generalized idea of what it entails simply from being part of the same culture and having heard about it. People extrapolate from their own relevant experience, form hypotheses, and make assumptions based on media reports, friend's experiences, culturally accepted stereotypes and hearsay. And so when they do experience a register, even for the first time, they have a comparative body of hypotheses from which they can formulate new hypotheses, and refine their knowledge of the linguistic configurations of the register. After several experiences of the same register, language users gain a sophisticated understanding of non-instantial register choices.

There are numerous registers of *non-literary* discourse that are part of our daily lives and are potentially of interest to the analyst: instructional manuals, newspaper articles, reports, recipes, reviews, editorials, lectures, essays, interviews, buying and selling transactions, stories, gossip, casual conversation, interviews and more. There are also numerous registers, or genres, of *literary* discourse: mysteries, science fiction, thrillers, romances, horror stories, autobiographies, memoirs, fantasies, tragedies, comedies, war stories: written in prose and sonnets, haiku, villanelle, sestina, lyric, ballad, open form: written as poetry.

Some literary genres and non-literary registers are quite formulaic and predictable from instance to instance because the relationships in the situation do not change appreciably over time. If, however, a variable in the situation changes, for example the encoder recognizes the cashier at the grocery as an old friend rather than the predictable stranger, the entire register might change incrementally or entirely. Whether the interpersonal shift merely interrupts the exchange briefly in a single utterance like *oh, nice to see you* or whether it motivates a shift to another register entirely, such as casual conversation, depends on a variety of features in the unique instantial situation and discourse. Such possible shifts show how valuable it is to have both an instantial and a non-instantial version of register as a descriptive tool. The *non-instantial* register which may evolve over time, but does not change dramatically, captures the repertoire of language choices that is available to, and expected by, both encoders and decoders. The *instantial* version, which is much more susceptible to slight shifts in relationships, describes how such shifts affect the choices made by language users in their actual instantial discourse.

The notions of marked and unmarked can also be used descriptively, especially when describing registers that are open to a certain amount of conscious variation. *Non-instantial* versions of register are all **unmarked** or ordinary in the sense that language users remember what is predictable and consistent. *Instantial* versions of registers manifested in real life discourse may also be unmarked, but they may also be **marked** or extraordinary and unpredictable. In some registers such as classical literature and advertising, *marked* versions revitalize language and appeal to new markets by exploring new topics in new forms and new styles.

Rhetorical strategies

Over the years, analyses have shown that register is not the only non-instantial configuration of tri-functional (cf. metafunctions) and tri-stratal (cf. strata) choices known and remembered by language users. In many registers of both literary and non-literary fiction, stylistic choices used to describe people, places and things are very predictable despite different registerial affiliation. In registers of literary discourse, character and setting *descriptions* are tri-functionally and tri-stratally quite consistent from discourse to discourse, as are *narrative* passages, where the plot is advanced. In some novels, passages of *dialogue* and *interior monologue* also reveal specific strategic configurations of linguistic patterning (cf. Chapter 7). Depending on the register, non-literary discourse employs an even broader range of **rhetorical strategies** than literary discourse each with its **non-instantial** configuration of tri-functional and tri-stratal choices stored in the gnostology. Recipes, for instance, typically include two strategies: first there is a *list* of ingredients, and then there is a *process* passage in which the methodology for making the food is given.

Like register, rhetorical strategies can also be a useful tool for describing **instantial** discourse. *Instantial* examples of particular rhetorical strategies may also be **marked** or **unmarked** in terms of how they correlate to the non-instantial versions stored in the gnostology. A passage from a fictional text might be primarily narrative, for example, but include the odd descriptive element which suggests to the analyst that the text be described as a marked example of narration. Rhetorical strategies have been used effectively in the historical and forensic research of Malcolm and Becker (2008).

The strata

In the definition of register and rhetorical strategy, the term **tri-stratal** refers to the three **strata** in the non-instantial linguistics realizatory code. Communication linguists use *phonology/ graphology, morphosyntax* and *semology* to describe the three different strata of linguistic patterning and meaning available to language users (cf. Halliday's semantics, lexico-grammar, and phonology/ graphology, 1994).

The ***phonological stratum*** describes language's *sounding* potential focussing on the phonological rank scale: phonemes, syllables, foot, tone group; as well as pace, dynamics, silence (Chapter 3). The ***graphological stratum*** describes the *seeing* potential of language using its assortment of 'visual' marks: letters, numbers, lines, paragraphs, punctuation, special effects, pictures, charts (Chapter 2).

The ***morphosyntactic stratum*** describes *wording* potential using the meaningful sequential arrangement of words in groups, clauses, sentences and turns. Morphological affixes (*endings*, for the most part) and the syntactic arrangement of structural elements reveal the encoder's choices of mood, modality, tense, aspect, voice, and polarity as well (Chapter 5).

The ***semological stratum*** describes language's *meaning* potential in terms of its semological roles (like actor, action process, patient), speech function, event mediation, and its lexical/ conceptual fields and taxonomies (see Chapters 6 and 4 respectively). At another level of abstraction, non-instantial registers and rhetorical strategies are also considered to belong to the semological stratum.

Semological choices are realized in the systems and structures of the *morphosyntax*, which, in turn, are realized in *phonological* or *graphological* choices. Each strata of the language encodes experiential, interpersonal and textual meanings in certain systems and structures (cf. the section *Metafunctions* in each chapter). The systems and structures that realize each metafunction might be thought of, and visualized as, a 'vertical' subdivision of each 'horizonal' stratum. The systems included in the following chart are representative examples only.

	Experiential	Interpersonal	Textual
Semology	Transitivity	Speech function	Lexical relations
Morphosyntax	Tense, polarity	Mood, modality	Ellipsis, conjunction
Phonology/Graphology	Phonemes, letters	Intonation, dynamics	Adjacency pair, turns

What this means, practically, is that an encoder could encode the same interpersonal meaning semologically, syntactically, phonologically and/or graphologically. For example, an encoder could ask a semological question by choosing the morphosyntactic sequential arrangement indicative of interrogative mood *Did he throw her the ball* or she could select the declarative mood *He threw her the ball* and then use rising intonation, phonologically, to encode the question. If the text were written, rather than spoken, a morphological declarative could be transformed into and interpreted as a semological question by the graphological indication of question, that is, a question mark '?'. Either way, the choices made by the encoder in the 'upper' semological stratum, in this case 'question', *are realized* by choices made in the 'lower' strata: morphosyntax, phonology or graphology.

In Communication Linguistics, language is described, then, in terms of the semological, morphosyntactic, and phonological/graphological systems and structures that reflect 'language as representation' (ideational/experiential function), 'language as interaction' (interpersonal function) and 'language as enabler' (textual function). These systems of linguistic possibilities, with the conceptual taxonomies used to describe our experience, form the linguistic realizatory code which is stored in all language users' gnostologies, and that is activated in a communicative event in which language users manifest and interpret discourse in a situation and culture.

Phasal analysis

Not all registers are as linguistically predictable and consistent as service encounters or recipes. *Registers*, such as casual conversation, can scarcely be called single registers, because they are so unpredictable, shifting constantly from one combination of registerial consistencies and constraints to another (cf. Malcolm, 1985*b*). The idea of *rhetorical strategy* to describe the shifts within a register is not sufficient to describe what happens on a more delicate level of analysis. *Phases*, sometimes defined as the dynamic instantiation of micro-registerial consistencies, are the perfect linguistic tool for describing the spontaneous, continual yet intermittent, shifts of relationships made evident in the discourse as manifested in the situation. The primary difference between phase and both rhetorical strategy and register is that phase is *only* an instantial 'unit'; there is no non-instantial gnostological version, as there is with register and rhetorical strategy. Phases have no predictable character. They emerge unique each time, with encoders completely unaware of how they have combined different language patterns to form chunks of consistency that facilitate both encoding and decoding.

In Communication Linguistics the descriptive procedure or methodology used to analyse all texts is called **phasal analysis** (see Chapter 8). Once the analyst has analysed the text tri-stratally and tri-functionally she is ready to combine all these forms of analyses in order to search for *phases*, chunks of tri-functional and tri-stratal consistency. More specifically, graphological, phonological, lexical, syntactic, semological and cohesive analyses must be complete before phasal boundaries can be determined. This is reflected in the organization of this book. Chapters 2 to 6 introduce the main forms of analyses that are used in preparation for phasal analysis. The actual procedure which combines all other analyses in order to discern phasal boundaries, transitions, sub-phases, continuous and discontinuous phasal strings in lengthy texts is described in the last chapter of the book.

Phasal analysis is a completely replicable and analytically precise way of unearthing the overall *schematic structure* of even the most complex register. If a particular register of discourse is highly unmarked / predictable, phasal analysis will reveal the **schematic structure**, the series of functional steps through which the particular register unfolds, for example greeting, request, information (cf. Ventola, 1987; Eggins, 1994). In addition, if there is a shift in the relationships in the situation which causes a shift in register, phasal analysis will capture the change. As a moment-by-moment description of the dynamic instantiation of metafunctional consistency, phasal analysis reveals both predictable generic schema and unpredictable fluctuations in the same. Phasal analysis reveals whatever **discourse structure** the discourse manifests in that particular instance, whether an unmarked example of the register or a marked example, or an unpredictable shift from one register to another.

Further reading

Mattiessen, C. (2004), Key Terms in Systemic Functional Linguistics. London: Continuum.

Halliday, MAK . & revised by Mattiessen, C. (2010), An Introduction to Functional Grammar (3rd ed.) London: Arnold.

2 Graphology

Introduction

In written communication the **visual** aspect of a text, the organization of space into recognizable patterns or symbols, encodes the meaning of the text. **Graphology** describes this visual organization in terms of the relationship between *positive* and *negative* space. **Positive** space is 'filled in' by the *graphs* that are selected by the encoder. **Negative space** is empty, blank, untouched by an encoder. Although positive space is often considered the more meaningful of the two, it is, in fact, recognizable only by its boundaries of negative space. Contemporary encoders often use negative space instead of punctuation both on paper and web pages to guide the decoder's reading and interpretation. Negative space is not synonymous with background. The distinction between *background* and *foreground* is a matter of *perspective* that has nothing to do with the distinction between positive, filled-in space and negative, empty space. The background of an image could be positive or negative space or a combination of the two, as when an image of a car is placed against an outdoor landscape.

A **graph** refers to the minimal meaningful visual unit that comprises positive space. Letters, words and punctuation are communicative in a ***verbal*** way; drawings, photographs, mathematical equations, graphs, tables, charts, and maps, communicate in a ***non-verbal* visual** way. Many of the communicative modes commonly used in daily life, such as newspapers, magazines, menus, catalogues, web pages, are multimodal, as they include verbal and visual elements (and sometimes auditory as well). Graphological description analyses the visual component of all and any texts, although the analysis of verbal texts is the focus of this book.

Depending on the register of written discourse, the visual units which make up the ***graphological rank scale*** from least inclusive to most inclusive include: letters, numbers, recognizable symbols and / or punctuation marks; words and multi-digit numbers; lines and sentences (beginning with a capital and ending with a punctuation mark); bullets, stanzas, columns and paragraphs; pages and chapters.

A graph can be *communicative* or *non-communicative* depending on the situation and culture in which it is used. The mathematical symbols that are **communicative**, interpretable, in that discipline might well be **non-communicative**, non-interpretable, in another. And the letters that are communicative in the language of one geographical provenance may be unrecognizable and unmeaningful in another. Visual and verbal graphs are situationally and culturally specific. Visual and verbal information reflects and constrains cultural ideology (and vice versa), so it is not surprising that language users may not be able to encode or decode the visual representations of another language and culture.

Aside from choice of visual graph, both *orthographic convention* and *reading pathway* are culturally specific graphologically. **Orthographic conventions** (spelling) make such cultural information, more specifically the geographical provenance or regional variety of a particular text, visible graphologically. In British English, orthographic conventions dictate that words such as *colour, honour, editing* are correctly spelled; whereas, American English deems the alternative spellings *color, honor, editting* to be correct.

Reading pathway refers to the directionality language users employ to encode or decode language: from left to right or right to left and from top to bottom or bottom to top. The reading pathway of English speakers and writers is left to right and top to bottom. The way decoders read is not just culturally specific, but also *registerially* specific. A reader expects an instructional manual to include not only a sequenced list of steps identified by numerals *1,2,3,* down the left-hand side of a page, but also a series of non-verbal diagrams that reinforce the verbal meanings itemized in the steps. Readers / decoders expect numbers arranged from top to bottom in consecutive order on the left to introduce each new step. Some registers, such as the phone book involve an even more complex reading pathway. It is, therefore, not surprising that web-based phonebooks, where you simply type in a person's name to find his / her number, have all but replaced the paper versions. Multi-modal web pages have transformed the idea of a culturally specific reading pathway, as decoders start reading whatever is of greatest interest to them no matter where it is on a web page, and proceed from web page to web page. Lempke describes the entire communicative event involving the decoder's forming one coherent whole from the interrelationships between a series of web links in a single situation as **hypertext** (Lemke, 2002).

Texts like the following, available on the internet, question more than reading pathway. How much information do decoders actually need to interpret discourse successfully?

> *Olny srmat poelpe can.*
>
>   *Cdn'uolt blveiee that I cluod auclaclty uesdnatnrd what I was rdanieg. The pha-*
> *onmneal pweor of the human mind, aoccdrnig to a scheearcg at Cmabrigde*
> *Uinervtisy, it deosn"t mttaer in what order the ltteers in a word are, the only*
> *iprmoatnt thing is that the frist and lsat ltteer be in the rghit pclae. The rset can be*
> *a taotl mses and you can still raed it wouthit a porbelm. Tihs is bcuseae the human*
> *mind deos not raed ervey lteter by istlef, but the word as a wlohe.*

*Exercise: Culture and Register

Graphological analysis

Preparation

Before you start your analysis it is important to record your first impressions of the text. **First impressions** might take the form of single impressionistic words like *dense, clear, orderly, beautiful, disturbing*. Review your graphological **expectations** based on situation, register, strategy and communicative purpose, and then formulate **preliminary hypotheses** based on your thoughts. Posing the hypothesis as a question might be helpful; for example, *Is this text a typical example of a ten year old female diary entry*? Do not get too attached to your preliminary hypotheses; they are never as interesting as final conclusions where *all* the data are considered.

Analysis

Once you have noted the *general* graphological character of the text, for example, *English graphs, formal sentences, paragraphs, punctuation and font, verbal text only*, it is important to get progressively more specific and detailed. Specifying the type of font, the size, the use of special effects like italics and bolding, the spacing: single or double and the layout: size of margins, justification and other predictable and / or unpredictable uses of positive and negative space is a good way to begin. All communicative graphological choices are meaningful, whether consciously or unconsciously made. In this textbook, italicized words are important terms, while bolded words are followed by definitions. Words and sentences from specific examples are also italicized to separate them from surrounding discourse. Special effects, then, are used to draw attention to, and differentiate, the words they highlight.

Once the graphological character of the text and / or image has been described, the description must be contextualized to be fully appreciated and interpreted. This means considering the *situation and the relationships therein* in which the discourse or image was produced and manifested, the *cultural context* of the encoder and decoder, the *register* of which the text is an example with its experiential, interpersonal and textual meanings, the *strategy* and the *purpose* of the text (see Chapter 1). Because graphological conventions vary situationally, culturally, registerially and strategically, all these contextual matters must be considered in order to interpret the analysis of graphological selections.

Let the characteristics and idiosyncrasies of the text and register you are analysing determine what needs to be described. What is important is that you describe *all* the features which contribute to the decoder's response: those which are predictable in the culture, given the particular register, and those which are not. It is also important to note the graphological features of a register which are predictable although they are *not* realized in the text: these may contribute to the unique flavour of your text also. The **consistency** of each graphological feature in your text is also significant. If there is a change in type, or size, of font at one point in the text, mention it: it is meaningful. Changes in special effects, spacing, layout may also be significant, and must be described. You might begin to consider *What encoder's intentions motivated these changes?* and *How do these graphological choices affect the decoder's interpretation?*

As will be discussed further in the section 'Graphology and the Metafunctions' (p. 32), Kress and Van Leeuwen have come up with a visual grammar that is useful when describing the graphological aspect of visual images. *Experiential meanings* are encoded by choices of narrative or conceptual structure: the shape and positioning of the represented participants in the image, described with or without vectors, signalling action or relational processes, reminiscent of language's system of transitivity. *Interpersonal meanings* are realized by choices of eye contact / gaze, social distance (size of frame, field of vision), perspective / attitude in terms of horizontal and vertical axes, and modality (continuums of colour saturation, differentiation, modulation, contextualization, detail, depth, illumination and brightness). The ways experiential and interpersonal meanings are related, connected and highlighted, fulfilling the *textual function*, are realized by systems of salience, framing, horizontal and vertical information value.

Results

Once the analysis of verbal and non-verbal discourse is complete, it is time to summarize the findings of your analysis. To do so, you **count** the number of instances of each feature that you have described in your text. Frequencies of individual graphs need not be tabulated. Word counts are available on the computer, and numbers of sentences, lines, bullets, paragraphs, and / or stanzas are straightforward. In your results section tally the number of times each special effect is used. Concerning a visual image, decide what features warrant counting: the number of participants making direct eye contact with the viewer, perhaps.

Once the counting is complete determine what are the **major** characteristics of the encoder's **graphological repertoire**, what are of **medium** import and what are the **minor** features. The distinction between major, medium and minor is made in terms of *frequency* and *linguistic context*. If ten words were italicized in a text that was thirty words long, italics would be considered a *major* special effect of the encoder's graphological style; if the text were two hundred words long, ten words would likely be deemed *minor*.

Once you have differentiated major features from minor, the next step is to judge each in terms of its *predictability* or *markedness*. To determine whether a graphological feature is **predictable** or **unpredictable**, unmarked or marked, the analyst recalls her *expectations* of the text given its strategy, purpose, register and cultural context. In other words, the analyst compares the features of her *instantial discourse* and text to similar *non-instantial gnostological* examples she remembers from past experience. In car advertisements, pictures and words pertaining to cars are predictable; pictures of yoga poses are not (see example p. 37). When considering predictability, do not forget to include typical graphological features that may be *missing* in your text. Such omissions would be unpredictable and marked features of the encoder's **graphological style**. For example, a car advertisement without words and images representing cars would be marked, unpredictable.

Conclusions

Once your results are complete, you are ready to *think about, wonder* and *interpret* your findings in terms of register, strategy, cultural context and so on. This textbook suggests two sections to your **conclusions**. In the *first* section you **summarize** your findings / results in *prose* (sentences and paragraphs) using a balance of generalizations, examples and statistics. In other words, you answer the question: *How did the encoder create this particular graphological style?* In the *second* section you **interpret / contextualize** your findings in terms of the variables summarized below. The questions to be considered are: *Why did the encoder use this graphological repertoire? How does it best serve her purpose and intentions?*

The following terms are used in your contextualization / interpretation. The **cultural context** determines the *temporal, geographical, social* and *individual* **dialect** of the interlocutors as well as their belief and value systems (ideologies). Encoders do not always make their graphological selections to *reinforce* registerial constraints and cultural values, but sometimes to challenge existing ones or create new ones. *Intended* decoders are the encoder's targeted receivers; *actual* decoders are the readers of this textbook. Shakespeare's *intended* audience were the people of his day, but his *actual* decoders may be twenty-first century readers. This means that Shakespeare's *intended message* might be quite different from the one *interpreted*.

Situation refers to relationships in the communicative event: the relationships to what is represented / experienced in the discourse; the interactive relationships and the relationship to the mode of transmission (pp. 9–11). There may be two relevant situations: the *interactive* **situation** which involves the encoder and decoder of the communicative event and the *represented* **situation** which might be *fictional* involving imaginary characters or *real-life* involving a photograph or verbal description or narration of 'real-life' people. A **register** is the *linguistic* configuration of these relationships, the metafunctions, that typically occur in a particular situation, for example, instructional manual, rental agreement, advertisement, bank statement, directions, casual conversation (pp. 15–22). **Strategies** are the tri-functional non-instantial choices that comprise description, narration, dialogue, process and the like and are typical of certain registers (cf. Chapter 7). Particular registers of language are usually designed to fulfil certain **purposes** e.g. to inform. Some purposes are expressed directly and explicitly; others, often embedded, are encoded indirectly and implied e.g. to persuade.

While following the recommended steps in completing your analysis, you are advised to record your insights informally as 'comments' throughout the process. Thorough comments lead to insightful conclusions. Good credible conclusions include a thorough balance of generalizations, examples and statistics. Trying to appreciate the intricacies of the communicative event by contextualizing the text in terms of its situation and register, purpose and strategy, cultural context and dialect of the encoder, intended and actual decoder is not always straightforward. Your text is always your *primary* source of evidence; scholarly research on the life and times of the encoder, and scholarly criticism is *secondary*. It is important to remember that analyses of a few passages of text are insufficient evidence for sweeping generalizations about register, encoder, strategy or anything.

Graphology and metafunctions

Language users make graphological choices in terms of the experiential, interpersonal and textual meaning they wish to convey. **Experientially**, encoders make graphological choices that represent the relationships between fictional or 'real-life' people, places and the things they depict. **Interpersonally**, they project relationships between the *represented participants* in the discourse / image, as well as between the represented participants and the ***real-life interactive participants*** encoding and decoding the text. **Textually**, verbal texts and visual images form 'wholes' that connect or cohere to themselves and their situation. Although the focus of this book is *verbal* discourse, because the *visual / graphological* aspect of verbal discourse is the focus of the chapter, Kress and van Leeuwen's visual grammar is considered in some detail (1996). As they write, 'Visual structures realize meanings as linguistic structures do' (1996, p. 2). However, the semiotic code of language has different ways of realizing meanings than the semiotic code of visual images.

Experiential

Experiential meanings are encoded graphologically by the choice of graphs: letters, words and images that refer to the people, events and circumstances involved in the communicative event. Generally speaking, experiential meanings are those that express or encode the 'content' of the discourse: who and what is doing what, how, when, where and why.

In order to describe the experiential meaning of an *image*, Kress and van Leeuwen describe the represented *participants, processes* and *circumstances / setting* (cf. semological roles of verbal communication in Chapter 6). By *participants* they mean the animate or inanimate shapes or volumes which represent people or objects. Squares and rectangular shapes denote mechanical, technological, world order, and they represent honesty; circles suggest that participants are self-contained, complete in themselves, and they denote endlessness, warmth, protection (Dondis, 1973, p. 44; Thompson and Davenport, 1982, p. 110). Kress and van Leeuwen identify the different types of **processes** by analysing the angles or vectors, between various participants. *Action processes* are represented by oblique lines / vectors between participants in the foreground, or between participants in the foreground and objects in the setting / background. The vector starts with the *actor* (the participant who instigates the action or from whom the action emanates) and the vector departs (pp. 32–3) (often marked as the most salient participant with regard to size, place in the composition, colour saturation, sharpness of focus pp. 57–61), and moves to the *goal* (the participant to whom the action is directed, p. 74). *Circumstances* include secondary participants / objects which are not involved in the action, nor related to the main participants by vectors, but instead function as part of the *setting* (represented as less salient: smaller, less focused, less colour saturated, p. 71). A *setting* requires a contrast between *foreground* and *background*. Images including action processes (vectors between participants), creating the illusion of action and drama, are called **narrative representations** (Kress and van Leeuwen, Chapter 2). These images represent transitory spatial arrangements, changing in time as the action continues.

Mental / speech processes, representing what a represented participant is saying or thinking, form a vector between the *process* (communicating participant) and her speech / thought bubbles, as in comic strips (p. 67). **Relational processes are shown as** straight lines relating one participant to another (p. 79). The participants in such visuals may be objectively portrayed, symmetrically arranged to one another, more generalized, and similar in size. Relational processes are often set against backgrounds that are plain / neutral, where depth is reduced or absent. Images involving relational processes, such as maps, diagrams and charts, form **conceptual representations** (Kress and van Leeuwen, Chapter 3). They evoke a dry and conceptual, timeless, stable, static, scientific and impersonal mood.

Interpersonal

The **interpersonal** function of language reflects the *interactive* (between writer and reader of verbal texts; producer and receiver of visual texts) and *represented* (in the discourse / image) participants' relationships in the situation. These relationships are described in terms of *power* (hierarchical asymmetrical or symmetrical), **contact** (frequent or infrequent), *affective involvement* (high or low emotional involvement), and *formality* (informal or formal (with hierarchical power, infrequent contact and low affective involvement)). An encoder could, potentially, select a more personally styled font or write by hand to signal friendship. However, this choice might be affected by geographical and social provenance. Not everyone has computer access, nor the training to use it. Expediency likely determines choice of font more than identity, making generic fonts like *Arial* the unmarked choice despite interpersonal relationship. Cultural trends and tastes in various registers affect interpersonal choices too. Wedding invitations warrant a formal font, business and academic discourse a generic one, family restaurants an informal and sometimes humorous one. The represented participant in a toothpaste advertisement is more likely smiling signalling friendship with the interactive participant than scowling.

Matters such as *contact, size of frame, social distance, field of vision, attitude* and *modality* also encode interpersonal matters in photographs. Concerning **contact**, when the represented participant gazes *directly* at the interactive participant / decoder's eyes through gaze, facial expression, and arm gestures, the visual configuration **demands** the decoder enter into an imaginary relationship with her (Kress and van Leeuwen, pp. 122–7). Pictures, diagrams, maps and charts that address the viewer *indirectly*, where the viewer is not the object of gaze, encode *offers* that are highly valued, objective, dispassionate, free of emotive involvement and subjectivity.

Concerning **size of frame**, participants may be represented: *close-up* (head and shoulders), *extreme close-up* (part of the face), *medium close* (to waist), *medium* (to knees), *medium long* (full figure), *long shot* (human is half of the frame), *very long shot* (human is smaller) with each suggesting a different relationship to the interactive participant (p.130). **Social distance** from the decoder also carries interpersonal information, whether the distance between participants is *close personal distance* where one can grasp the other (intimates); *far personal distance* where two can barely touch; *close social distance* the distance at which impersonal business occurs; *far social distance* the distance people move to when someone says 'stand away so I can see you'; *public distance* for strangers (pp. 130–1).

Another dimension of interpersonal meaning in visual imagery is **perspective**, both *horizontal* and *vertical*. Participants in visual communication may be represented from a *naturalistic* perspective or a *non-naturalistic* one (where the angles of natural perspective are not adhered to). In terms of **horizontal** perspective, images may be represented from a *frontal* angle where the photographer centrally faces the represented participants or an *oblique* angle where the photographer is off to the side of the participants. Kress and van Leeuwen suggest that a frontal angle shows involvement 'what you see is part of our world'; whereas, an oblique angle suggests 'what you see here is not part of our world', so the represented participants are considered 'other' (Kress and van Leeuwen, pp. 143–9). In terms of **vertical** perspective, images may be taken from a variety of angles. If the image is photographed from a *high* angle, it diminishes the represented participants, empowering the viewer (p. 146). Alternatively, a *low* angle 'looks up at' the represented participants, empowering them. An *eye level* vertical perspective suggests an equality in the power held by represented and interactive participant.

The *modality* of an image also encodes interpersonal information (Kress and Van Leeuwen, Chapter 5). Generally speaking, the *higher* the modality of the represented participant, the more naturalistic and credible; the *lower*, the more abstract and less credible. A higher **modality** and naturalism is manifested by more fully saturated, differentiated and modulated colours and a more detailed background with greater depth, realistic illumination and greater brightness. Each of these variables affects the viewer's interpretation of the visual. In many technologically advanced cultures, language users assume the more realistic and measurable, the better.

Textual

The **textual** function is the 'enabler': the function of language that puts experiential and interpersonal meanings together simultaneously in a coherent message appropriate to the selected *medium of transmission* with what has been chosen as most thematically significant as a point of departure. In English-speaking cultures, the way we encode and decode **verbal** texts is influenced by the way we read, from left to right, top to bottom. Titles are positioned centrally at the top of the page, emphasized by upper-case letters and so on. Visual patterns of positive and negative space in verbal texts reinforce other patterns of meaning contributing **graphological coherence** between one part of the text and another and / or to its situation and gnostology. Paragraph indentations reinforce the interpretation of the paragraph as a coherent meaningful whole. Negative space delimits one chapter, one newspaper column, one newsflash on a screen, from another, adding an internal visual coherence to the text and a relationship to the rest of the page at the same time. The textual meaning of language is realized by design layout, format and composition: how one block of positive space relates to, connects with, and highlights, another.

Composition 'enables' and relates experiential and interpersonal meaning through three interrelated systems: *salience, framing* and *information value* (Kress and van Leeuwen, pp. 193–215). **Salience** creates a hierarchy of importance in the text through the most eye-catching participant: the largest, most detailed, best illumined, brightest coloured, sharpest focused and farthest forward in the picture. **Framing** refers to the way elements in the composition are either *disconnected* from each other signifying they do not belong together or *connected* signifying they do. The more a participant is represented as separate and unconnected, the stronger the framing; the more elements are presented as a single connected group, the weaker the framing.

The **information value** of certain spatial arrangements also encodes new and given information. In cultures with a reading pathway from top to bottom and left to right, according to the ***horizontal axis***, what is represented on the *right* side of an image represents 'new' information, while what is represented on the *left*, represents 'given' information, what the reader is assumed to know already. In terms of the ***vertical axis*** of the text, the *upper* section of a visual text encodes the future 'idealized' promise of the product: 'what might be'; while the *lower* section visualizes the 'real': 'what is here and now'.

Purpose

The ***purpose*** or *functional tenor* of *verbal* texts varies from register to register. Generally, textbooks *teach*, newspapers *inform*, comics *entertain*, advertisements *persuade*. However, often several minor embedded purposes work together to accomplish these broader purposes. Certain newspaper articles inform, others critique, some entertain, others teach. And to fulfil these agendas, they may *confirm, justify, explain, exemplify, inform, clarify, promise* and more. Ultimately, albeit indirectly perhaps, the purpose of a text is to foster, maintain, reinforce, manipulate or challenge the beliefs and values of the producers and receivers of the text or image.

Example: A graphological analysis of non – literary discourse

Text

Analysis

1. Preparation / first impressions

– text / advertisement is communicative verbally and non-verbally (includes pictures and words)

– non-verbal is as important as verbal

– *hypothesis* – directed to middle-class, English-speaking North American audience, women in particular

2. Analysis of text

a. Verbal graphs

– English, black print (in analysis, text is often italicized; no italics in actual)

– minimal graphs in *upper two-thirds of page*: real or fictional names of yogic postures beneath each small photo of particular posture, e.g. The Candle, The Bow, The *Spine Twister, The Lotus, The Camel, *The Sonata (Asterisked names are fictional)

– Top left, bolded, upper case, larger font, name of advertised vehicle and year **2001 SONATA**

– Balances photo of car bottom right and below brand name of car in larger font still (but not huge), also in upper case, bolded, with car logo to left of name (**logo**) **HYUNDAI,** and below brand name slogan **DRIVING IS BELIEVING**, in font same size as *2001 Sonata*, bolded

– line of text, separating A. upper two-thirds of page (including pictures of yogic postures) from B. lower one-third of page (image of car to right, verbal text to left), same font size, all caps, bolded as upper *2001 SONATA*: **SUGGESTED DAILY ROUTINE FOR ACHIEVING INNER PEACE**

– verbal text in lower left, not bolded, smaller font (not as small as yogic posture names above)

– most of verbal text in mixture of upper and lower-case letters

– lines of verbal text, double spaced

– two paragraphs of text marked by slightly larger separation than double space, no indentation

– first paragraph following traditional sentence conventions for the most part, mixture of punctuating devices, e.g. quotation and question marks, periods, commas

– second paragraph more like list, still upper and lower-case letters, but also numbers; commas and periods, few slashes too

– last line recognizable phone number *800–826-CARS* and web site address: *www.hyundaiUSA.com*

– small verbal line, price, under front of car photo: *Starting at $15,799* in small font like yogic postures, mix upper and lower, no bolding

– very small, almost unreadable two lines (disclaimer) at very bottom of page left:

See dealer for UNLIMITED WARRANTY details. ** 2001 MSRP for Base model with air and automatic (GLS package shown, MSRP $17,799); excl. freight, taxes, title, licence and options. Dealer price may vary.

- in terms of size then, brand name is biggest
- then specific car (upper left), slogan (lower right), separating line between upper and lower page : all same size, all caps, all bolded
- verbal text: mixed upper and lower, no bolding, much smaller than bolded words
- names of yogic postures up top and price at bottom a bit smaller than verbal text and
- disclaimer at very bottom of text: tiny, unnoticeable, not really part of advertisement

b. Non-verbal graphs

- *design of page* – on actual page of magazine, which is medium gray, the advertisement looks like a notebook page in white placed on top of gray background with gray borders around white text about one half inch – specific car name upper left and slogan lower right printed on gray, with white page cut out slightly – tiny disclaimer at bottom also on gray
- everything else on white background
- photo of car lower left about an inch and a half high and three and a half long, car silver, car on angle to show perspective, front to centre of page
- 6 yogic postures top two-thirds of page – six photos of attractive slim, fit woman in wine coloured sleeveless leotard and tights, long single braided hair, doing yoga poses: two at top, middle three more, and bottom row last pose, centred and emphasized by surrounding negative space *The Sonata* – most poses involve side silhouette of woman, mid-centre one facing front, but meditative so woman's eyes closed – five poses seem like spokes of wheel surrounding centre hub which is the only front facing meditative pose
- all yogic poses: photo of woman's body against white background of adver-tisement's notebook-like page, with slight shadow of figure under each
- white background could be interpreted as negative space, or positive space all white

Contextualization

Situation – Interactive Situation – parent reading *Parenting* magazine; student read-ing this textbook
  – Represented Situation – Hyundai trying to sell a car to people interested in yoga
Register – full page car advertisement taken from *Parenting* magazine 2001

Purpose – overtly – to find inner peace
  – to link peace of yoga to owning and driving the Hyundai Sonata
  – covertly – to sell car to peace loving buyers, specifically women
  – **strategies** – comparison / contrast between yoga and driving Sonata
    cause / effect – yoga causes peace, so by analogy driving Sonata causes peace
    problem / solution – to end worries buy Sonata
    argument – all pro: buy Hyundai, no con; persuasion through other strategies

Metafunctions

i. Experiential

verbal – car brand names (lexis) and logo are largest font, bolded and capitalized to highlight product to be sold through advertising;
– secondary-sized bolding highlights relationship between car and yoga, e.g. *driving is believing* & *suggested daily routine for achieving inner peace*
– price in small print, and disclaimer almost invisible, so small
– use of fictional chant in quotations "*ten years, no worries . . .*" makes it sound sacred, added credibility to yoga students
– phone number and web address culturally recognizable

non-verbal / visual – two primary represented *participants*:
– *woman* (top) in yoga poses culturally valued and idealized slim attractive woman's figure and revealing clothes but closed eyes in a few shots removes overt sexuality
– *car* (bottom) – silver colour deemed culturally sophisticated and tasteful in 21st C North America
– yoga poses and car are represented in static, stable, generalized relational *process* in conceptual representation – no action, goal or setting
– relationship between women / yogi and car suggests relational *process* of possession

ii. Interpersonal

verbal – easy reading, impersonal choice of font,
visual – offer – silhouette, side view of woman, except central pose would be a demand, but direct gaze negated through closed eyes
social distance – yogi and car long shots, hence between strangers
perspective – yogi frontal suggesting involvement; car oblique suggesting detached eye level camera angle suggests equality between represented and interactive participants
modality – muted colours: silver, gray, white, wine (culturally valued as sophisticated, tasteful, car and yogi equally illumined, detailed, decontextualized, bright wine of woman's leotard goes well with rest of ad's colour scheme
mood – from visual information only, top photos give sense of balance, order, but little more info hence: impersonal
Marked – unreal *driving* (yoga pose) position at bottom adds humour

iii. **Textual**

- *written to be seen* (non-verbal: visual) and *read* (verbal) or *read* (as if chanted): part *be read as if chanted*

verbal – *theme* – size of font & bolding emphasizes *Driving is Believing, 2001 Sonata*

- **coherence** positive block of verbal graphs lower left

visual – *salience* – yoga poses together form a larger unit than the single car at the bottom

framing – yoga poses related to one another in overall pentagonal shape with centralfocus; represented participants not overly crowded, balanced with negative space, gray margin to entire ad; verbal text beside car image, beneath yoga

information value – horizontal axis – yoga poses centralized carrying given and new info, car visual on right: new; verbal text on left: given

- vertical axis – yoga poses top of page: ideal; car and verbal lower: real
- circular – various yoga poses around central meditation pose

Linguistic context
(information from other linguistic analyses that relate to graphological)

- the graphological analysis is most closely tied to *lexical* information in this text, e.g. each yoga pose photo is named lexically, the car photo is named lexically; the relationship between yoga and car is emphasized lexically: in slogan and *suggested daily routine* . . . and graphologically, in juxtaposition of yoga poses with car
- *lexical* sets emotional and religious reinforce graphological, and add *safety* set of 2nd paragraph
- *semological* mental processes unusual selling feature for cars with male audience, e.g. *chant, feel, melt, picturing*
- *syntax* – character and contrast of paragraph 1 and 2 of verbal text: first, complete sentences, variety of mood; second, no sentences

Cultural context

a. **encoder / producer**
geographical, temporal, social – English-speaking, North American team of writers / designers / photographers in 2001, who have knowledge of market, specific target audience, particular magazine in mind, specific purpose in mind
- yoga poses in wheel-like pattern has Eastern religious connotations, e.g. Buddhist 'Wheel of Life', Hindu 'Shiva Nataraj'
- predominance of black and white reminiscent of Buddhist ying-yang symbol

b. *intended* **decoder** / target audience
geographical, temporal, social – North American middle-class, middle-aged parent in 2001
- appeals to women's personal interest in health and spiritual matters: peace and balance

- appeals to women as parents – middle-aged, lexis of practical safety
- appeals to women with money to buy this car – middle-class car (not expensive)

***actual* decoder**

English-speaking student in twenty-first century learning how to do graphological analysis

Results

Verbal text – Paragraph one – three lines including five sentences: one with a quotation, two ending with question marks, three by periods, no special effects.

Paragraph two – six lines including no sentences, but fifth line ends with period before last line with phone number and email address.

First line ends with dash, and introduces list of three safety features in next four lines, each separated by a comma.

No special effects.

Special effects (bolding and all upper case) in names and slogans only.

Visual text – see analysis.

Major – non-verbal yogic postures and photo of car dominate ad

– verbal – Brand names and slogans emphasized through size of font and special effects

Minor – verbal – names of yogic postures, details of driver's emotional state and safety features, price, disclaimer

– non-verbal – numbers in phone number and price

Predictable (in terms of situation / register) non-verbal – photo of car, logo, numbers

– verbal – brand names and slogans emphasized by special effects

– small size of price, disclaimer and even details of car

Non-predictable – non-verbal – photos of yoga postures in car ad

– verbal – words pertaining to yoga highlighted, e.g. *daily routine, inner peace, Believing*

Conclusions

Summary

This text takes a full page in a parenting magazine in the summer of 2001. It is an advertisement of the 2001 Sonata, the larger and slightly more expensive family-oriented model of car made by Hyundai, a brand name geared to middle-class buyers in North America. In most contemporary car advertisements I would expect to see a combination of non-verbal and verbal information: likely a picture of the car with a person or family enjoying it, the brand name emphasized, followed by a list of the car's features, the location of a local dealership and some indication of the price. And in terms of many of these expectations, this particular car advertisement is quite predictable. In the lower right is a picture of a brand new shiny silver Sonata with the brand name Hyundai with its logo underneath, and in the top the name of the car Sonata is bolded and capitalized. In the lower left is a block of verbal information pertaining to the car, including a phone number. The address of a local dealership has been replaced by a web address. And not surprisingly, the price is written in small print below the photo of the car.

What is surprising about the text is how the advertising team / producers of the car have decided to make the car appealing to the target audience / buyers. There is no happy family driving off into the sunset, but rather the top two-thirds of the ad show a wheel-like design of six small photographs of a woman doing different yoga poses. There are five poses taken from a side view, and the sixth, in the middle is the only pose with the woman's face to the front. However, her eyes are closed, as if she were in meditation. Under each of the six small photos, on a plain white background, is the name of each yogic posture. The only pose which is not realistic, in terms of culturally valued hatha yoga, is the one at the bottom of the wheel layout. Although presented from the same perspective as the others surrounding the hub of the wheel, it shows a woman in a position as if she were driving a car. But the car seat and steering wheel are not visible, and so she looks as if she were sitting in mid-air.

What is also surprising, although more relevant to a lexical analysis than a graphological one, is the number of words that pertain to yoga and other spiritual practices from the East, and have nothing to do with cars: *daily routine, inner peace, believing, chant, freedom, mind* . The reason why this lexical information is included in a graphological analysis is that each of these words (except *freedom*) is given graphological emphasis: the first three by size, bolding and upper case, *chant* and *mind* by beginning or end of line status (meaning a juxtaposition of positive and negative space, and the emphasis that results from this). The other lexical feature that is not graphologically marked, but certainly reinforces what is graphologically memorable, is the type of feature that has been selected to sell this car. There are very few words referring to the parts of a car like *power steering, power brakes, power windows*; instead many of the words belong more to a 'support' set than a 'car' set: *no worries, relax, tension melt away, warranty, best warranty, advantage, protection, bumper to bumper coverage, roadside assistance*. The focus on spirituality and peace rather than machine and power, both graphologically and lexically, account for the mood created by the text: a soothing sense of peace, balance, symmetry, and goodness. This becomes even clearer if the analyst revisits the advertisement through the more detailed lenses of Kress and van Leeuwen's visual grammar and Malcolm's phasal analysis, descriptive of verbal texts (cf. Chapter 8).

In terms of the **experiential** meaning encoded in the composite yoga image, the ad is *conceptual* in that the various yoga poses of the ***represented participant***, the woman, are photographed as static, stable, generalized, timeless, decontextualized, in symmetrical relation to one another with the same orientation to the horizontal and vertical axis of the picture. These features describe a ***relational process***, where the various poses are classified as belonging to hatha yoga. The car is also *represented* in a *conceptual*, static, timeless way, as a symbolic relational process. The two images: the woman's asanas and the car form a relationship of possession with one another. In one way, the Sonata pose / asana shows that the woman is an appropriate size to own the car; in another way, the Sonata engulfs the driver, and so, possesses her.

Interpersonally, these images realize an ***offer***, in that there is an imaginary barrier between the represented participants (woman and car) and the interactive participant, the viewer: there is no direct eye ***contact*** between the two participants. Interestingly, in the central yoga pose, where the represented participant faces the camera and potentially could make a demand by a direct gaze, she does not do so, her eyes are closed. The implication is that the peace that her meditative pose suggests to the viewer is also one that is offered, not demanded. This is important in that offers invite rather than command, and are thus valued in symmetrical relationships between female friends rather than asymmetrical ones between strangers. However, in terms of ***social distance***, both yogi and car are represented in very long shots, appropriate to the social distance between strangers where the represented participants are 'on display'. Although the yoga poses are photographed from an eye-level frontal ***perspective***, suggesting involvement between equals, the car is photographed from the side, an oblique detached perspective, that is not quite naturalistic. Still the eye-level camera angle suggests an equality in power between the represented participants and viewer. In terms of ***modality***, the images are quite similar: equally illumined, detailed, decontextualized, bright, colour saturated and so on.

Textually, the yoga poses are somewhat more ***salient*** than the car, in that the group of poses is larger than the car. The five individually framed yoga poses around a central figure form a pentagon, although the shape seems circular overall in terms of composition and **information value**. The 'Sonata car pose' at the bottom becomes *salient* by being surrounded by negative, empty space on three sides, and the central pose, the meditative lotus, by its central position carries the dominant message: yoga is a source of peace. All other poses are subservient to this one. One might say they 'still the mind' in preparation for the yogi's meditation. In terms of the **horizontal axis**, while the yoga group is centralized, carrying both *given* and *new* information, the image of the car is on the right side of the page carrying the *new* information. The verbal text is represented as *given*. In terms of the **vertical axis**, the yoga poses represent the top of the page, what Kress and van Leeuwen suggest 'is to come', the idealized goal / dream. The bottom yoga pose: the Sonata, together with the image of the car and the verbal text, on the lower half of the page represent the reality: 'what is'. And in terms of how the entire ad was positioned in its magazine context, it was located on the right, the 'new' side of the magazine, when open.

The **verbal** portion of the text, the 'given' and the 'real' in terms of its compositional arrangement, further develops this argument in three phases. These phases capture unconsciously encoded chunks of spontaneously tri-functional and tri-stratal consistency (see Chapter 8). In the **first phase** the verbal echoes the yogic focus of the top images: *Chant after us, 'ten years, no worries. Ten years, no worries.' Feel your body relax? The tension melt away?* Yoga lexis dominates, with an interesting mixture of mood selections: imperative and interrogative, as if the words were the spoken directives of a yoga instructor. Cohesion is largely a consequence of lexical relations. **Phase two** re-defines the yoga participant, as 'you' the consumer in the context of a car, specifically the Hyundai Sonata, through an introduction of car lexis: *That's the freedom of America's Best Warranty at work. Whether you're driving the Sonata, or just picturing it in your mind.* The mood is declarative. Relational and action processes replace the mental ones of phase one, other than *picturing* which carries cognitive possibilities, and by so doing, binds phase two to phase one cohesively. That phase one and two are graphologically joined in one paragraph is important for developing the analogy between yoga and Sonata. *Picturing in your mind* is syntactically equated with *you're driving the Sonata*. **Phase three**, separated graphologically, from phases one and two, is quite different. Punctuation is rare because there are no syntactic sentences forming this block of text. All yoga words and constructions disappear, as the yoga image has disappeared in the lower portion of the ad, and the phase is realized by a list of car details *America's best Warranty, the Hyundai Advantage, 10 Year / 100,000 Mile Powertrain Protection, 5 Year / 60,000 Mile Bumper-to-bumper Coverage, 5 Year Unlimited Miles 24 hr. Roadside Assistance,* ending with the typical, *for more information* phone number and email.

A phasal analysis of the verbal portion of the text alone would not have done the ad justice. The visual grammar Kress and van Leeuwen have developed, combining features of Halliday's systemic functional model with art theory, is crucial for appreciating how the ad works. In the case of the Hyundai ad, the viewer was not initially attracted by the verbal information at all, not by the bolded and enlarged caption *Suggested Routine for Achieving Inner Peace,* and not by the name of the car itself. The given and new 'dream' of yoga images, symbolically representing peace of mind, were the only reason she did not continue flipping through the magazine. The car image, 'New' and 'real' compositionally, was simply too predictable, in terms of register, to engage the viewer initially.

Kress and van Leeuwen write "Images have the function of illustrating an argument carried by the written word, that is, presenting ('translating') the contents of the written language, in a different medium" (p. 38). In this case the argument presented in the visual information reinforces that encoded in the verbal: buy this car, and you will experience the same peace of mind as meditation and chanting.

Interpretation

The outcome of these surprising juxtapositions is a marked instance of the register of car advertisements. The text may be unpredictable; nevertheless, it is quite likely very suitable, attractive and appealing to its target audience. What kind of viewer / consumer did the producers of the ad have in mind when they made their decisions?" Middle-class, middle-aged, North American women and mothers. The target audience is portrayed as one who values the peace and good health of yoga, as well as the safety, protection, and assistance of driving a new car: specifically the 2001 Sonata Hyundai. By omission, we see that the target audience is also portrayed as having little interest in how the car works: in the new gadgets or sources of power that might break down, and hence require a warranty, powertrain protection plan and roadside assistance.

Although the group of people who function collectively as the ***producer*** of the ad do not know the viewer, who is not physically present during the *context of production,* they are, as Kress and van Leeuwen write 'guided by interest, that complex condensation of cultural and social histories and of

awareness of present contingencies' (p. 11). 'If they want to see their work dis-
seminated, [they] must work within more or less rigidly defined conventions,
and adhere to the more or less rigidly defined values and beliefs of the social
institution within which their work is produced and circulated' (p. 120).
Readers / viewers, who are alone in the *context of reception*, have only the
image in common with the producers, and a knowledge of the communicative resources, the social beliefs and values available in their situation.

Readers may recognize the communicative intentions and purposes of the
producers, and the values and attitudes that have been ascribed to them as
readers. They even have the choice whether to accept them as their own. In
this case the viewer reported that her response shifted from curiosity to
annoyance. Initially the ad attracted her because she values yoga. However
once she realized this value had been exploited by the producers of the ad to
persuade her to buy the product, she was not so interested. In advertising, one
of the most visually creative and ever changing registers of the written mode,
every verbal and non-verbal visual device imaginable is used to capture the
attention of the increasingly sophisticated reader / viewer whose expectations
become ever more demanding. Every font, effect, photograph, chart, diagram,
artwork that the producers can come up with is used to persuade the reader /
viewer to buy the product.

The text has been designated *marked* because it says so little about the
product being sold, but instead uses the interests of the target audience to sell
a completely unrelated product. However, this strategy is quite typical of contemporary advertisers, and in that sense makes the text predictable and
unmarked in its specific cultural context. Had the ad focussed on engine
parts, it is likely the receivers of the ad would have ignored it entirely, and the
whole communicative event would then be considered unsuccessful.

*Exercise: Graphological Analysis

Review of graphological analysis

Analysis

Preparation

Note **first impressions** of the graphological style of the text:

Describe *the obvious generally*.

Is the text communicative to you? Completely? Partially?

What graphological features make this text communicative to you?
Does the text include verbal and or non-verbal graphs? Letters? Pictures? Other?
Where is the text from?

How does the text build on your cultural **expectations?**

Formulate **preliminary hypotheses** based on dialect and register.

Description
Verbal Communication

1.a. Describe the *Verbal* Graphs

If the text is written in English *letters*, does it follow conventions concerning the use of lower and upper case?

Are *numerals* used: Arabic, Roman?

Punctuation – Is it predictable, following conventions, or unpredictable?

Have *special effects* been used: italics, bold, underlining, other?

Is the text *handwritten / printed or typed*? If typed, what *fonts* have been used? *Size* of font?

What is the *layout / composition* of your text (margins, justification, location of text)?

What *spacing conventions* / constraints are used: paragraphing, indentations, double-spacing, stanzas, lists?

Is the verbal portion of the text *consistent* in choice of font, size, tenor, effects?

1.b. Describe how each **metafunction** of language is encoded **verbally**.

i. Experiential function – choice of letter graphs and type of numeral, by the range of punctuation devices, spatial conventions of positive space, and relationship to negative space;

experiential focus may be emphasized by special effects, e.g. bolding, underlining, italicizing and the like.

ii. Interpersonal function – choice of style, font, writing tool, 'paper', legibility, and punctuation as deliberately formal or informal, signalling cline of social distance (friend to stranger)

interpersonal focus may be reinforced by special effects on words and the like that carry interpersonal meaning.

iii. Textual function – choice of visual marks (written discourse) or sound waves (spoken discourse), the medium of transmission is further defined by the composition and coherence of the graphs and blocks of graphs in terms of size, special effects (positive and negative space), punctuation and spatial conventions (above and below, left and right) that specify the type of written discourse (to be read, seen, said, read as thought etc.) by what is made thematically most important by spatial arrangement, size, colour, and by what is given visual prominence over something else (foreground versus background).

Visual Communication

2.a. Identify the **type** of ***non-verbal*** communication: photo, pictures, charts, equations, graphs, and the **elements** that characterize this type of ***visual*** communication.

Photographs – represent what is visible to the naked eye in a moment of time, show naturalistic detail (reality is defined on the basis of the correspondence between the represented participants and what we see in the 'real' world).

Diagrams – may make visible what normally is invisible, may depict a process over time, uses abstract schemata / minimum geometric shapes, may incorporate verbal discourse too. Charts, diagrams, equations etc. give a scientific feel that adds credibility to many registers in this culture.

2.b. Describe how each **metafunction** of language is encoded ***non-verbally / visually***.

i. Experiential function

1. ***Participants*** – animate or inanimate, usually in foreground – in relational processes, participants are more generalized, less objective, decontextualized from setting
2. ***Processes*** – ***Action*** = oblique lines form vectors between participants, or participants and circumstances creating the illusion of action, drama
   forms **narrative** representation
   Mental = speech / thought balloons, e.g. comic strips
   Relational = straight lines relate one participant to another through symmetrical composition, equal distance from one another, same size, same orientation to horizontal and vertical axes, angle is frontal and objective
   – classification relations are created through visual rep, not real life.
   forms **conceptual**, rather than narrative representation
3. ***Circumstances (Setting)*** – background to participants in foreground, often in less detail, less colour saturated, darker / lighter than foreground participants
   – with relational processes setting often plain / neutral background, depth is reduced / absent.

ii. Interpersonal function

1. **contact**: demand (gaze at viewer) or offer (gaze not at viewer)
2. **social distance**: intimate / personal (close shot), social (medium), impersonal (long)
3. **attitude**: involvement (frontal angle) or detachment (oblique angle) or equal (eye level) or represented participant empowered (high angle) / equality (eye level) / represented participant empowered (low angle)

Objectivity: *action* orientation (frontal angle) or *knowledge* orientation (top / down angle)

4. **Modality Scales:** (greater abstraction = lower modality; more natural = higher modality)
   a. full *colour saturation*, to absence of
   b. full *colour differentiation*, to limited palette, to monochrome
   c. naturalistic range of *colour modulation* eg. many shades of red, to flat
   d. absence of background, to full detailed background (*contextualization*)
   e. maximum abstraction, to maximum *representation* of pictorial
   f. absence of *depth*, to maximally deep
   g. *illumination* representation of full play of light and shadow, to its absence
   h. *brightness* degrees of brightness, to just black and white

iii. **Textual function** – how things are connected to one another (composition)
   1. **salience** – most eye-catching element due to foreground placement, larger size, more light, brighter colour, sharper focus
   2. **framing** – elements are either disconnected, marked off from each other, or connected, joined together signifying that they belong together or do not; the stronger the framing element, the more it is represented as separate unit of information; absence of framing stresses group identity
   3. **information value** – *horizontal* axis – right 'new', left 'given'
      vertical axis – top 'dream', bottom 'reality'
      circular – centre 'central info'; margins 'dependent'
      (cf. Kress and Van Leeuwen, 1996)

3. **Describe** the **interrelation** of the *verbal* with the *visual* in a **multi-modal text**, and the implications this has on **reading pathway**, and the possibility of this creating a unique **hypertext**.

Contextualization

Situation – Describe the relevant field, mode, personal and functional tenor of the *interactive* and the *represented* **communicative event**.

Register – Identify the **register** of the text.
Are the graphological features of the text a function of the register?
What graphological nuances make your text unique in terms of its register?

Purpose – to humour, entertain, persuade, inform, confront, argue, confirm, teach (didactic), make a connection (phatic), fill the silence, deceive etc.

Strategy – compare / contrast, argument, classification, process, cause and effect, problem / solution, definition, description, narration, dialogue.

Metafunctions

Describe how the graphological choices highlight particular **metafunctions**.

i. Experiential

Aside from the individual words that are manifested in this text, what verbal or non-verbal graphs add information about the experience that is developed in this text? What elements of the experiential have been emphasized visually by special effects such as bolding, italics, underlining?

Is there a represented situation and culture with represented characters, plot, setting and themes that are distinguished graphologically?

ii. Interpersonal

What visual elements contribute more to the relationship between encoder-decoder than to the experience that is communicated?

Are the special effects used to emphasize certain *evaluations* or *attitudes*, rather than the experience itself?

What *tone / personal tenor* has the author adopted in her choice of font / handwriting style? Is it neat, messy, beautiful, ugly? Casual, formal, or a combination? Identify the *mood* created by these graphological choices: humorous, ironic, serious, etc.

iii. Textual

written to be read, seen, said and so on.

theme – Is there a particular visual *focus* to the text overall? in smaller blocks or patterns?

coherence / composition – Are there *patterns* or *blocks* of positive space that create coherence in the text?

Linguistic context

a. Does the placement of the text in terms of its larger linguistic context (eg. entire magazine, pamphlet, novel etc.) affect, or account for, the text's graphological features and style?

b. Describe the way other linguistic information relates, reinforces and challenges the graphological choices of this text, for example, *lexical, syntactic, semological*. (Since there is an entire chapter devoted to each type of description in this textbook, and you are not expected to read Chapter 5 before Chapter 2, this section of your graphological analysis might be brief; however, if you have studied the other forms of analysis already, do comment briefly on how they relate to your graphological insights.)

Cultural context and dialect

a. Who is the **encoder**? What is her age, ethnicity, gender, nationality? How do her graphological choices reflect her situation, culture, beliefs and values? In other words, how do they create her social identity and construct her social reality?

b. Who is the **_intended_ decoder** (the expected / target audience)? How might her situation and culture, and experience of the register affect her interpretation of the encoder's graphological choices?

Who is the **_actual_ decoder**? How might her situation and culture, and experience of the register affect her interpretation of the encoder's graphological choices?

Note: In most communicative events / situations the _intended_ and _actual_ decoder are the same. However, if you are a student reading _Phasal Analysis_, you are in a rather different situation: you are the _actual_ decoder, but you may or may not be the _intended_ decoder.

Results

1. **Count** the instances of whatever special graphological effects might be noteworthy in your analysis. This does not mean counting every letter and word. But it might mean counting the number of lines, stanzas, sentences, bolded or italicized words and so on.
2. Note which are **major** / important graphological features, and which are **minor** / less important in terms of the size of the text.
3. Decide which of these features and totals are **unmarked / predictable** given the situation, register, encoder and decoder (see conclusions), and which features (omissions as well as occurrences) are **marked / unpredictable**, atypical of the register, and hence potentially significant.

Conclusions

1. **Summary**
   Describe the encoder's **graphological style** in prose, using examples and statistics when appropriate.
2. **Interpretation**
   How do these choices serve the encoder in communicating her message?
   Why did the encoder choose this graphological style to communicate her message?
   a. Describe how this graphological style reinforces or challenges the findings of your **other analyses** (e.g. Linguistic context: lexis, syntax, etc.)
   b. Describe how this style highlights certain **metafunctions**: experiential, interpersonal, or textual.
   c. Describe how the graphological style of this text is, and is not, appropriate for the **strategies** that have been used to develop it, the **register** of which it is a member, and its **purpose**.
   d. Describe how the graphological style of this text reveals the **_encoder's_ situation** and **cultural dialect,** and that of the **_intended decoder_**.

e. Describe how these graphological choices might contribute to the **actual decoder's** interpretation, given her situation, culture, familiarity with the register and so on.

Further reading

Becker, B. and Malcolm, K. (2008), 'Suspended Conversations that intersect in the Edwardian Postcard', in Nina Nørgaard (ed.), *Systemic Functional Linguistics in Use.* Special issue of Odense Working Papers in Language and Communication, Institute of Language and Communication, University of Southern Denmark.

Kress, G. and Van Leeuwen, T. 1996. Reading Images: The grammar of Visual Design. London: Routledge.

3 Phonology

Introduction

Phonology is the study of the phonic substance that language users manifest in their spoken discourse in order to communicate by *sounding*. Phonic substance includes the sound waves that decoders recognize as patterns of consonants and vowels that form words, utterances and turns. Patterns of stress, rhythm, pitch and silence also encode and organize communication. In the countless registers of *spoken* discourse, where there are no visual / graphological clues to indicate meaning, the phonic substance encodes every aspect of meaning in the discourse. If an encoder commands *Read the book,* the decoder, from her gnostological awareness of meaningful sounds in the situation and culture, can interpret the relevant experience: participants, events and circumstances; the interpersonal relationship as asymmetrical, and the mode of communication as verbal spoken discourse.

In *written* texts too, phonological choices carry meaning. Certain registers of discourse like plays and speeches are written with sounding in mind. However, even when we read texts that are written to be read only, we recognize their phonological character at a certain level, often sub-vocalizing the words we read. Advertisers often highlight the phonological resources of written discourse with titles like *Just click, crack and cook*, echoing the sounds of preparing an egg for breakfast (Canadian Living). And when decoders read *Few artists capture the majesty, mood and unique charm of each season with the breathtaking vision of the Painter of Light, Thomas Kincaid*, the repeated *m* sound reinforces the soft, gentle effect of the painter's representational style (Good Housekeeping, p. 136). The hard *g*'s in the following advertisement energize, rather than subdue: *Start your career in golf. SDGA gives graduates the extra edge needed to obtain a great job in the golf industry. Our Associate Degree Program prepares you for all aspects of a challenging golf position, whether as a golf professional, golf facility manager, or with one of the many other golf related businesses* (Golf Digest, p. 128).

Phonological analysis is considered an integral part of analyses for transcriptions of both spoken and written discourse.

Transcription

In order to describe the phonic substance manifested by language users accurately, analysts **transcribe** the discourse into symbols which comprise the **International Phonetic Alphabet** (IPA). 'This is an internationally recognized set of symbols for designating the phonetic characteristics of (theoretically) all the distinct sounds in the world's languages' (Ladefoged, p. 85). Each symbol in IPA provides a concise description of the way the sound it represents is formed. IPA includes 113 symbols, 84 that represent the formation of various consonant sounds and 29 that represent the formation of different vowel sounds (Ladefoged, p. 177). Some African languages have over a hundred contrastive sounds; however, English includes only about forty contrastive sounds (phonemes), depending on which dialect is being considered. This book includes the symbols for describing English only.

Whereas the *graphological* alphabet introduced in elementary school describes the contrastive *graphs* used to encode written discourse, IPA describes the contrastive *sounds* available to encode and analyse discourse. In English the five *graphs* representing vowels *a, e, i, o, u* signal at least eleven vowel *sounds*, each with its appropriate symbol in IPA. The *i* graph, for instance, represents the two different vowel sounds in both *bit* and *bite*. Twenty-one consonant *graphs* signal at least twenty-four consonant *sounds*. In the words *ceiling* and *cat*, the single graph *c* represents two different sounds /k/ and /s/. On the other hand, in the word *wish* two graphs *s* and *h* represent only one sound symbolized by / ʃ / in IPA.

Phonetics

Phonetics is the study of how sounds are produced. As Finegon and Besnier write in *Language*:

> Human beings have no organs that are used only for speech. The organs we use for producing speech sounds have evolved principally to serve the life-sustaining process of breathing and eating. Speech is a secondary function of the human vocal apparatus and in that sense it is sometimes said to be parasitic on the organs used for these other functions. (p. 38)

In the following drawing the various parts of the mouth and vocal tract that are involved in the production of speech are labelled.

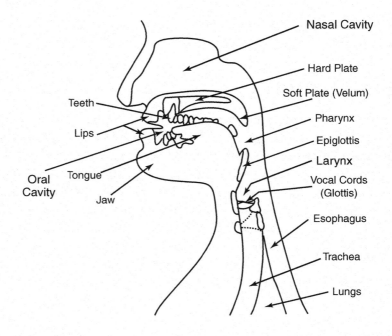

The production of speech begins with the exhalation of air from the lungs causing the *vocal cords*, two skin-covered flaps of muscle, to open and close across the passage to the lungs and oscillate with a wave-like motion. 'In making sound, the vocal cords operate like the open end of a blown-up balloon, which buzzes rapidly if pulled tight so air can escape more slowly' (Rist, p. 25). This vibration releases an energy that the ear and brain interpret as sound. The vocal cords are in the larynx, the tip of which forms the Adam's apple. In humans, the position of the larynx is relatively low, allowing the tongue greater freedom to move and thus shape sounds. The rest of the human vocal instrument consists of the throat, tongue, mouth, lips and, of course, the respiratory system. 'Although the pitch depends on the number of times per second the vocal cords collide – ranging from as few as 55 times per second for a low A sung by a bass to 1,047 times per second for a soprano's high C – the refinement and articulation of speech takes place in the throat and mouth. The human throat is remarkably short – just six or seven inches from larynx to lips which shape vowels ranging from a mellow U to a sunny E' (Rist, p. 26).

Consonants

Consonants are produced by partially or completely blocking air in its passage from the lungs through the vocal tract. They are described in terms of how they are produced in terms of (i) *voicing* (ii) *manner of articulation* and (iii) *place of articulation*. **Voicing** refers to whether the vocal cords vibrate as a consonant is produced. The **manner of articulation** describes what is happening to the flow of air as it passes through the vocal tract: is it stopped at some point, for example, the teeth; is it continuous; does it flow through the nasal cavity as well as the oral cavity? **Place of articulation** describes the part of the mouth involved in the production of the particular consonant and the part that is touched by the tongue. When considered in isolation, slashes distinguish the units of sound called *phonemes* from mere orthographic *graphs*, for example /t/.

i. The position of the lips and tongue remains the same when saying *sip* and *zip*. However, these two words, known as **minimal pairs** because they differ in one contrastive feature, are different in terms of **voicing**. The phoneme /z/ of *zip* is **voiced**; whereas the /s/ of *sip* is **unvoiced / voiceless**. As the stream of air comes from the lungs up through the vocal tract, the air forces two folds of muscle known as the vocal cords to vibrate as it passes through the narrow aperture known as the glottis. This vibration, or voicing, enables speakers to differentiate two otherwise identical sounds. The voiced consonants are: /b, d, g, v, z, ʒ, m, n, ŋ, w, r, l, j, dʒ, ð/. The voiceless consonants are: /p, t, k, f, s, ʃ,h, θ, tʃ/.

ii. Although /s/ and /z/ in *sip* and *zip* are different in terms of voicing, **the manner of their articulation** is the same. In both, the air is somewhat obstructed by the position of the teeth and alveolar ridge, being forced continuously through a narrow opening. Consonants produced in this way are called **fricatives**. The phonemes that are fricatives are: /f, θ, s, ʃ,v, ð, z, ʒ/ (the first four are voiceless, the last four are voiced).

When producing the consonants /t/ and /d/, the air is completely stopped behind and above the upper teeth at the alveolar ridge, and then released or exploded in a small burst of air. As a consequence /t/ and /d/ are called **stops**, produced at another place of articulation. The phonemes that are stops are: /p, t, k; b, d, g/. Of these, each is produced at a different place of articulation; the first three are unvoiced, the others are voiced.

Nasals are consonants produced by lowering the velum (the muscle between the nasal cavity and the mouth), allowing the stream of air to pass out through the nasal cavity instead of the oral cavity. English has three nasal stops /m/ as in *mad*, /n/ as in *ten* and the last pronounced sound in *sing* /ŋ/ (where the 'g' is silent unlike the two separate sounds /n/ and /g/ in *finger*). The nasals are called *bilabial* /m/, *alveolar* /n/ and *velar* /ŋ/, determined by the place of articulation (where the tongue touches the upper part of the mouth). The velar nasal occurs at the end of a word only. Other than these three nasal phonemes, the rest of the consonants are produced in the oral cavity with the nasal cavity closed off.

The two **affricates** in English, represented orthographically by the consonant cluster *ch* in *chin* and the single 'soft' *g* in *gin*, phonemically by / t ʃ/ and / dʒ/ , are produced by a build up of air formed by a complete closure of the vocal tract at some place in articulation, which is released like a stop, but then continued like a fricative. So, the affricate is a stop-fricative. The / t ʃ / is voiceless; the / dʒ / is voiced.

There are five phonemes in English known as **approximants**: /h/, /j/, /r/, /l/, /w/. /h/ is the voiceless counterpart of the vowel that follows as in *history* and *here*. /j/ is a *palatal* approximant in *you*; the word *cute* begins with the consonant cluster /kj/. The difference between /r/ and /l/ is that the /r/ is pronounced by channelling air through the central part of the mouth, and /l/ is pronounced by channelling the air on either side of the tongue: /r/ is therefore called a *central* approximant, /l/ a *lateral* approximant. In the pronunciation of the /w/, the lips are rounded, as in *wild*. When /w/ is the second element in a consonant cluster, as in *quiet*, the initial phoneme /k/ is rounded in anticipation. /j/ and /w/ are also considered semi-vowels by some. And finally, there are a few examples of the voiced alveolar **flap** in Canadian English: the phoneme /ɾ/ represented by the *tt* graphs in the words *butter* and *Ottawa*. The sound in both these words is more relaxed than the single stop /t/.

iii. Once the air passes through the vocal folds, it is shaped primarily by the **place of articulation**, the position of the tongue and the lips. There are three major places of articulation for the English *stops*: the alveolar ridge, the lips and the soft palate. The /p/ and /b/ in the words *pit* and *bit* are both produced at the lips, where air is built up behind the two lips and then released. Because the greatest point of closure is at the lips, /p/ and /b/ are called **bilabial** stops. /k/ and /g/ in *kick* and *get* are pronounced where the tongue reaches the roof of the mouth at the velum, so they are called **velar** stops. The third pair of stops /t/ and /d/ in *to* and *do*, articulated at the alveolar ridge, are called **alveolar** stops. In addition, there is evidence of a voiceless glottal stop /ʔ/ in Canadian English when we say *oh oh*.

The *fricatives* and *affricates* are pronounced in other places. The *th* represented by /θ/ in *thin* is a fricative pronounced with the tongue between the teeth; hence, it is called an **interdental** fricative. The *th* is unvoiced in *thin* /θ/, but voiced in *the* /ð/. Both the *sh* of *wish* /ʃ/, the final consonant in *measure* /ʒ/ (fricatives) and the first sound in *chin* / t ʃ / and *gin* / dʒ / (affricates) are pronounced with near closure at a place in the mouth between the alveolar ridge and the velum / palate. Hence, these sounds are called **palatal-alveolar**. The /f/ in *fish* and the /v/ in *vote* are produced by a continuous stream of air passing through the bottom lip and top teeth; these sounds are called **labiodental** fricatives.

The approximants and nasals are produced in a variety of places of articulation: /m/ and /w/ are bilabial produced with both lips; /n/, /l/, /r/ are alveolar; /j/ and /ŋ/ are velar (some call the former palatal); and /h/ is produced at the **glottis**.

The *Summary of Canadian English Consonants* in the *IPA* chart shows how the voicing of the vocal folds, the manner of complete or partial obstruction of the air flow and the place of articulation interrelate in the following symbols:

Summary of Canadian English Consonants in IPA

Consonants	Stops		Fricatives		Affricates		Approximants			Nasals
	Voiced	Unvoiced	Voiced	Unvoiced	Voiced	Unvoiced	Unvoiced	Voiced central	Voiced lateral	voiced
Bilabial	b *by*	p *pet*						w *wit*		m *mitt*
Labiodental			v *vet*	f *fit*						
Interdental			ð *that*	θ *thick*						
Alveolar	d *do*	t *to*	z *zoo*	s *sit, city*				r *red*	l *lit*	n *no*
Palatal Alveolar			ʒ *beige*	ʃ *show*	dʒ *jump*	tʃ *chin*				
Velar	g *gift*	k *king*						j *yes*		ŋ *sing*
Glottal		ʔ *oh-oh*					h *hat*			

+ voiced alveolar flap /r/ *Ottawa*

Many of the symbols used in the IPA resemble the same orthographic graphs that you use when spelling. However, there is no IPA symbol for the graph *c* or *q*: the symbols used are either /k/ in *car*, /s/ in *cease*, /kw/ in *quick* . In addition, the IPA symbol for the consonants *sh* is /ʃ/, *th* is /ð/ or /θ/, *ch* is / t ʃ /, *dge* is / dʒ /, *ph* is /f/, *ng* is /ŋ/ and *ge* in *beige* is /ʒ/. The other unfamiliar IPA symbols are /ɾ/ to represent the alveolar flap, and the glottal stop /ʔ/. Otherwise, all the IPA symbols are written using the same sized font; there is no distinction between upper and lower case.

Note: IPA symbols may be downloaded to create a phonetic keyboard from the Summer Institute of Linguistics web site: html, or more specifically:

http://scripts.org/cms/scripts/page.php?site_id=nrsi&item_id=DoulosSIL_download
http://scripts.sil.org/cms/scripts/page.php?site_id=nrsi&id=UniIPAkeyboard

Once the Doulos SIL font and the IPA Unicode Keyboard are downloaded, for the most part, the phonetic symbols are available by pressing '=' or '<' followed by the letter graph most closely related to the symbol.

Consonant clusters

In each language there are certain consonants that form clusters and others that do not, for example, in English: *tree, stream, ground, milk*, but not /hl, dn/. In each language there may also be constraints concerning what consonant clusters can occur initially and finally. For example, the clusters /tr, str, gr/ are acceptable initially only, while /lk, nd/ are only acceptable in final position.

Vowels

Whereas consonants are produced by a constriction or narrowing of the vocal tract, **vowels** are produced by a smooth unobstructed airflow through the vocal tract. The position of the tongue and lips determine the shape of the oral cavity and the type of vowel that is produced. Vowels are more resonant than consonants. The different vowel sounds produced in English are characterized in terms of (i) **height**, (ii) **position**, (iii) **tension** and (iv) **rounding** (in elementary school, simplistic distinctions between 'long' vowels and 'short' vowels were the only distinctions made). Among vowels, *phonemic symbols* are not the same as *visual graphs*. For example, the symbol /i/ represents the vowel in *feet*, not *fit*.

    i. When the tongue is **high**, the vowel sound /i/ in *feet* is produced. The other vowels produced with the tongue in high position are /ɪ/ in *bit*, /u/ in *pool* and /ʊ/ in *foot*.

When the tongue is in **low** position, the vowel /æ/ in *fat* and the vowel /ɑ/ in *father* are produced. When the tongue is in between these two positions, in a **middle** position, the vowel sound /e/ of *fate* is produced. Other mid-vowel sounds are /ɛ/ in *bet*, /o/ in *boat*, /ɔ/ in *hot*, /ə/ (schwa) in *but*, *herd* (in this text, no distinctions between stressed and unstressed variants are made).

ii. When the tongue is at the **front** of the mouth, the vowel sounds /i/ in *beat*, /ɪ/ in *spin*, /e/ in *pay*, / ɛ / in *pet*, /æ/ in *pat* are produced. When the tongue is at the **back** of the mouth, the vowel sounds /u/ in *mood*, the /ʊ/ in *could*, the /o/ in *loan*, /ɔ/ in *cot, caught, cord*, and the /ɑ/ in *hard* are produced. When the tongue is in a **central** position, the vowel sound /ə/ (schwa) in *above, earn*, and *the* is produced.

iii. When the musculature of the tongue and mouth is tight, or **tense**, the vowels /i/ in *field*, /u/ in *food*, /e/ in *ate* and /o/ in *goat* are produced. When the musculature is more re**lax**ed, the vowels /ɪ/ in *rid*, /ʊ/ in *hood*, /ɛ/ in *head*, /ɔ/ in *on*, /æ/ in *fad*, /ə/ (schwa) in *unkind* and /ɑ/ in /*father*/ are produced. (Some do not make a distinction between tense and lax.)

iv. When the lips are **rounded**, or closed, the sounds /u/ in *cute* are produced. In English, only the back vowels are rounded, and the high back vowels are rounded the most (Delahunty and Garvey, p. 84). When the lips are unrounded, open, or spread, all the other vowel sounds are formed.

The *Summary of Canadian English Vowels* in the *IPA* chart shows how the height, position and tension of the tongue and vocal tract and rounding of the lips interrelate in the following symbols:

Summary of Canadian English Vowels in IPA

Vowels		Front	Central	Back
High	Tense	i *deed*		u *duty*
	Lax	ɪ *did*		ʊ *wood*
Mid	Tense	e *date*	ə *upon*	o *cold*
	Lax	ɛ *debt*		ɔ *torn, cot*
Low		æ *dab*		ɑ *calm*

Note: In some dialects the distinction between /ɔ/ and /ɑ/ is non-distinctive (different textbooks use the same words to exemplify each of these two sounds).

Diphthongs

When the tongue, lips and oral cavity are held constant in the production of a vowel, we call the resulting sound a **monophthong**. When there is a change in the configuration of the mouth, diphthongs result. In English **diphthongs** the tongue starts by producing one vowel and ends by producing another vowel within a single syllable. Generally speaking, the distinction between different dialects of English (Canadian, Australian, British, American etc.) lies beyond the scope of this textbook; however, the distinction between American and British diphthongs is considered briefly (each is described somewhat differently). Canadian diphthongs are: /ɑi/, /ɑu/, and /oi/.

American English /ɑy/ in *bite, I, pie*; /ɑw/ in *pout, cow*; /oy/ in *boy, coil*. American English speakers sometimes use a weaker set of diphthongs: /iy/, / ey/, /uw/, /ow/.

British English /ei/ in *may, made*; /ou/ in *go, hole*; /ɑi/ in *bite, I*; /ɑu/ in *pout, cow*; /oi/ in *boy, coil* (all but the first diphthong are the same as the American diphthongs; however, they are written using a second vowel rather than a semi-vowel / glide).

British English speakers sometimes use the centring diphthongs: /iə/, / ɛə/, /uə/ instead of articulating an r, for example / ɛ ə/ for air, /puə/ for poor

Canadian English diphthongs resemble those of the Northern United States. However, as soon as Americans hear Canadians say 'about' /əbɑut/, they know they're Canadian, because Canadians hold the latter part of the diphthong a fraction of a second longer than Americans.

*Exercise: IPA Transcription
* Discovery Exercise

Phonology

Phonology is the study of how sounds are organized in speech, each sound in its linguistic environment. The speech sounds that are significant carry meaning in a particular language. For example, the difference in the consonant *t* in *team* and *steam* is not noticeable to most English speakers although the *t* in first position is pronounced with an exhalation of air and the *t* following *s* is not. These two *phonetically* different sounds cannot replace one another in the same environment in English: they cannot contrast or distinguish one utterance from the other, so they are considered a single *phonological* unit or phoneme symbolized by /t/ in the IPA. The sounds which distinguish minimal pairs, however, are contrastive. They do distinguish different meanings, and hence are called two separate phonemes, for example *mat* and *sat*. A **phoneme** is the minimally contrastive unit of sound. In other words, it is the smallest sound that can change the meaning of a word.

Phonological Rank Scale (phoneme, syllable, foot, tone group)

In the same way that a letter, number or punctuation mark is the minimal *graphic* substance in written communication, the **phoneme** is the minimal *phonic* substance. Once whole texts are transcribed, slashes no longer surround each phonemic symbol.

When an encoder speaks several phonemes together, a decoder hears a certain *rhythm* emerging from a pattern of strong and weak **beats**. In *above*, there are two beats or syllables: *a* is the first and *bove* is the second. In the word *obliterate* there are four syllables *o-bli-ter-ate*. A **syllable** is comprised of one or more phonemes (minimally, a single vowel, or a vowel surrounded by optional consonants (C)V(C)). A *syllable* is considered more inclusive than the phoneme in the phonological rank scale. Graphological *words* may be classified as monosyllabic, disyllabic, trisyllabic and so on according to the number of syllables they contain. In this chapter, syllables are separated by a hyphen, for example *bro-ken*.

In each word certain syllables are spoken with greater force or **stress** than others. The syllable that carries the greatest force is called *strong* (and is bolded in this chapter); other syllables are called *weak*. (Some texts distinguish intermediary levels of stress.) In the word *a-bove*, *bove* is the strong syllable carrying the primary or salient stress, *a* is the weak syllable. In the word *o-bli-ter-ate*, the primary stress is on *bli*. Halliday writes, 'the rhythm of speech derives from the marked contrast between strong and weak syllables. [Interestingly] the strong syllables tend to occur at roughly even intervals' (1994, pp. 7–9). Generally, the strong syllable in a word does not change. However, in some words a change in stress may indicate a change in syntactic class: *pro-ject* is a noun, *pro-ject* is a verb.

A **foot** is the rhythmic unit of language that begins with a strong syllable followed by a number of weaker syllables. The strong syllable carries the beat. A *foot*, including one or more syllable(s), is the next, more inclusive, unit in the phonological rank scale. A foot (phonological unit) does not necessarily correspond to word boundaries (graphological unit). In this chapter each foot is surrounded by a pair of slashes.

In order to analyse the phonological feet in a sentence: (1) divide the words into syllables, (2) mark the strong syllables, (3) begin each foot with a strong syllable.

E.g. Lila wanted some water.
1. Li-la wan-ted some wa-ter   syllables
2. **Li**-la **wan**-ted some **wa**-ter   + stress
3. / **Li**-la/ **wan**-ted some / **wa**-ter/   +feet

This sentence could be spoken in three feet; however, it could also be spoken and described in four feet if *some* were also stressed. E.g. / **Li** la/ **wan** ted/ **some** / **wa** ter/

In a *spoken* text, determine the feet by what is stressed: each strong syllable begins a new foot. This is not so straightforward when analysing written discourse. In *written* texts, decide what is stressed based on how you would say the entire sentence if unmarked. If a sentence begins with an unstressed syllable (for example: *the*), place the stress on a silent syllable preceding the unstressed syllable and mark it with a caret '^'. E.g. / ^ the/ **child**/ **spoke**/ **soft**-ly/

*Exercise: Stress and Feet.

Beats of *rhythm* are described in *feet*; while rising or falling pitches and *melodies* are described in **tone groups**. A **tone group** is the *melodic* unit of language; a foot is the *rhythmic* unit of language. Each tone group may include several feet, but only one in which there is a notable change in pitch that falls or rises. The *foot* in which this change in pitch occurs is called the **tonic**, and its *strong syllable* is known as the **tonic prominence** or **nucleus** of the tone group. All naturally spoken discourse in every language is made up of an unbroken succession of tone groups. The boundaries of each tone group are often indicated phonetically by a pause, a rhythmic break, a syllable lengthening, or a shift in the pitch of unstressed syllables. Double slashes // distinguish one tone group from the next. The tonic foot is underlined, and the stressed (bolded) syllable within it is the tonic prominence.

> E.g.   //<u>**Lunch**</u> / **is** / **rea**-dy // ;
> //^ In -/ **struc**-tions are in / <u>**clud**-ed in the</u> / **pack**-age //;
> //**She** / **went** to the / <u>**store**</u> //.

Delineating tone groups in *written* discourse is more challenging than in *spoken* discourse. In spoken discourse, the encoder's choice of tonic prominence is clear; in written discourse, the analyst has to assume the unmarked way of saying a sentence will capture the encoder's intonation patterns. Halliday writes 'generally one or a small number of these possible intonation patterns will stand out as more natural and more likely' (Halliday, 1994, p. 9). In written discourse, graphological lines and punctuation, and syntactic clauses and sentence elements reinforce phonological decisions. E.g. // <u>Eku,</u>// ^ will / **you** come / <u>**here**</u>?//

* Exercise: Phonological Rank Scale
* Exercise: Tonic Prominence and Tone Groups

Phonological analysis

Preparation

Before beginning your phonological analysis, reread your text, and for a moment think about your **expectations** in terms of situation, register and purpose of the text. Do the sounding features seem ordinary or extraordinary? Are they consistent throughout the text, or are there changes? Find a few words to describe your **initial responses** to the text: *soft, harsh, gentle, dense, choppy, smooth, lyrical, melodious, memorable, fast, slow, exciting, sad* and so on. Develop **preliminary hypotheses** concerning how the phonological style of the text contributes to its meaning.

Analysis

The first step in phonological analysis is to **transcribe** the text into IPA symbols accurately, including all communicative sounds like *mmhm* and *uh* from a tape or transcription. If spoken, the analyst transcribes the encoder's choices; if written, she transcribes according to her own unmarked assumptions. The latter, of course, may limit her ability to capture the phonological details of a regional dialect.

Once the IPA transcription is complete, analyse the text in terms of stress, feet, tone groups, tonic prominence, and New and Given information units (cf. p. 71). When the analyst has completed working with the rank scale (phonemes, syllables, foot, tone group), she comments on the text's dynamic range, tempo, evaluative colouring, pacing, and use of silence. Throughout the analyses, the analyst looks for patterns of consistency and moments of change. Changes in phonological patterning may reveal shifts in strategy or experiential focus, for example. It is important to note relevant insights throughout the process of analysis on a comments sheet, so they will not be forgotten.

Results

As in other results, the first step is to **count** the instances of each phonological feature. Tabulating frequencies of individual phonemes is easiest using the consonant and vowel charts provided online. Totals are translated into percentages after tabulating the total number of consonants or vowels. If a text is phonologically consistent in style throughout, frequencies of the different types of patterns can be tallied for the the text as a whole. If, however, a close rereading of the text reveals a shift of phonological patterning from one section of the text to another, it might be preferable to total the instances of features for each section separately. Otherwise, the totals of one section might 'neutralize' and misrepresent the phonological character of another, obscuring the uniqueness of each. In the following chart, the frequencies of each feature are recorded in a way to reflect the four different phonological sections in a hypothetical text. The numbers tallying the high front tense vowel /i/ can be interpreted as follows. The first number, from the left, is the total of instances in the first section (6); the second number, is the total from section two (3); the third number, is from section three (1), and the fourth number, from section four (10). Even if you have divided the frequencies of different sections to reflect phonological shifts in the text, it is easy enough to come up with totals for the entire text by adding the instances in each different section Eg. 6 + 3 + 1 + 10 = 20.

Vowels		Front	Central	Back	Diphthongs
High	tense	i **6,3,1,10**		u 3201	
	Lax	ɪ 5702		ʊ 1001	

Once frequencies are totalled, phonological features are first evaluated as **major** or **minor**. The frequency of the feature, given the length of the document, decides which. If there were five instances of rising tones (cf. p. 69) in a single prose paragraph, it might be considered major; whereas, in a text several pages long, it would be minor. Once phonological features are assessed as major or minor, they are further judged in terms of predictable / **unmarked** given the strategy, register and situation, or unpredictable / **marked**. In a doctor–patient interview, the analyst would expect questions and answers manifested in phonological rising and falling tones. If their results indicated falling tones only, this result would be considered marked. Similarly, a mixture of questions and answers in dialogue is predictable; in narration and description, it is not. Deciding what classification of consonant type is unmarked is not so straightforward. For the purposes of this textbook, several unmarked texts have been analysed in order to come up with unmarked ranges of stops, fricatives and so on.

In *unmarked* discourse:

consonants:			*vowels*:	
stops occur	30%		50%	appear to be front vowels
fricatives	20–25%		20%	back vowels
affricates	1–2%		17–25%	central vowels
approximants	25%		9%	*diphthongs*
nasals	15–19%			

If the frequencies in your results fall within those ranges, the text is considered *unmarked* in that feature.

If the analyst discovers that a text she thought was marked is not, she should not automatically assume she was wrong. A consonant may be unmarked in usage, but marked through repetition or positioning. If the analyst 'hears' a text as 'choppy' or 'harsh', she should keep looking for explanations. Choice of consonant is just one possible option. Also, watch for phonological features that depart from gnostological expectations. Stops might be typical in a description of a gruff, black-bearded tycoon, whereas they would be marked in the description of 'a willowy winsome slender slip of a girl'. In addition, silence can be meaningful. There is no evaluation attached to the distinction between marked and unmarked. Unmarked does not mean 'boring' or 'bad'. In some registers of doctor–patient talk, for example, phonological markedness might confuse decoders and lead to misunderstanding. In many situations, for many purposes, clarity is paramount, and clarity is best achieved by a predictable unmarked style.

Conclusions

Begin your conclusions by **summarizing** your results / findings in paragraph form (prose). What are the patterns of vowels and consonants that have been used in the text? How many feet are there in each tone group, and how many tone groups are there in a sentence? Does the New come before the Given in information structure, or vice versa. Are there rhetorical figures which affect your phonological response to the text, for example alliteration, assonance, consonance, dissonance, onomatopoeia? Is the positioning of such rhetorical highlighting towards the beginning, middle or ending of the passage? How consistent is the phonological style throughout the text? Can you find chunks of different sounding choices in the text? What is their relation to changes in strategy, speaker, and so on? From a consideration of all these questions come up with a statement that summarizes the phonological style of the text. Throughout the summary section of your conclusions use a balance between generalizations, examples and statistics in your description of the encoder's phonological style.

Once the style has been amply described, in the **interpretive** section of your conclusions examine *how* the encoder's phonological style has affected the decoder's response. One of the ways of doing this is by contextualizing your findings. This is done by considering how various contextual matters such as situation, register, purpose, strategy, metafunctions, cultural and linguistic context explain the encoder's phonological choices. For example, if the situation included someone yelling at another, the analyst might expect various phonological resources that encode that anger. If the register of a text were a sports commentary of a hockey game, the analyst would expect numerous consonants, short tone groups, an evaluative colouring of excitement, as the commentator yells *He shoots, he scores!* If the purpose of the discourse were to scare you, the phonological selections are bound to be quite different than if the purpose were to apologize. In some cultures, people speak naturally and normally somewhat louder than in other cultures. By thinking about such contextual matters, the analyst speculates *why* the phonological style of the text best serves the encoder's intended message.

When you have interpreted your findings by thinking through what they mean, and why they have been chosen, it is advisable to return to your *first impressions* to ensure that all have been addressed and explained in your conclusions. It is easy to miss something that might have been quite important in evoking your response to the text. In addition, it is always a good idea to be on the lookout for new forms of analyses that enable you to see and understand more. The theory and methodology of Communication Linguistics develops from the insights of analysts engaged in practical research.

Phonology and the metafunctions

Experiential

In *spoken* discourse all the patterns (experiential, interpersonal and textual) that encode the meaning of the text are manifested in sound waves. A phonemic transcription will be most accurate if taken directly from the recording device. Although primarily visual, *written* discourse also carries with it a record of the sounding choices made by the encoder that can be described phonemically. Experiential phonological choices encode the participants, events, and circumstances of the situation in phonemes, syllables, feet and tone groups.

Interpersonal

There are a variety of phonological / prosodic features which carry the information that describes the interlocutors' interpersonal relationship in *spoken* discourse: melody, evaluative colouring, dynamic range, pacing / rhythm, tempo and pause. Melody, described in tone groups, is interpersonal because the choice of tone encodes the language users' relationship. Halliday links phonological tune with speech function (choice of statement, question, command) when he connects a *rising* tone (tone 2) with questions, and *falling* tones (tone 1) with statements (1994, p. 305). Rising tones manifesting questions indicate an *asymmetrical* relationship between encoder and decoder. Sometimes the person in power asks the question; sometimes the person without power. A teacher, who already 'knows' the answer, asks a student a question to check her comprehension. An interviewer is also institutionally sanctioned to ask questions, although she is unlikely to know the answers. Alternatively a student might ask a question or a pedestrian might ask for directions, neither in the position of power or 'knower'. Commands are not realized by a particular tone, although they too indicate asymmetrical relationships. However, it is quite possible that commands carry a more intense evaluative colouring than statements. In **written** discourse, graphological punctuation marks guide analysts in determining speech function: a question mark signals a rising tone 2; a period, a falling tone 1.

Some feel that melody carries more interpersonal information than speech function. Certain American intonologists discern four different **keys** or *levels of pitch*: 1. extra-high, 2. high, 3. mid, 4. low. They suggest that a falling terminal contour from pitch level 1 to level 4 is more contrastive than a fall from level 3 to 4, and potentially carries an element of surprise (Pike, 1945, pp. 26–47). Sounding choices also encode interpersonal matters of politeness, indifference, irony, sarcasm, arrogance and more, although research has not determined how. In *spoken* discourse, **evaluative colouring** is carried by a shift in stress, pace or pitch in the encoder's voice. In **written** discourse, such interpersonal colouring is encoded lexically rather than phonologically, for example *'Get out of here', he said sadly* (see Chapter 4).

Variations in **dynamic range** or volume may also carry interpersonal meaning. An encoder may increase her dynamic range in order to encode relationship. People with or without power might resort to shouting or yelling if they get angry or frustrated. A higher volume manifested in their discourse encodes a greater asymmetry in their relationship than if their normal voice were used. Still, such choices are registerially constrained. An employee is less likely to yell at her employer than at a misbehaving child. Increasing the volume in formal professional situations is frowned on in this culture; while it is more predictable in informal situations. Decreasing the volume can also indicate hesitancy, fear and the like in some situations. In *spoken* discourse, such interpersonal decisions are carried phonologically by unpredictable phonological tones and stresses. In *written* discourse, this type of phonological meaning is also encoded lexically, for example *She answered* **quietly***, 'No'.*

Interpersonal meaning can also be communicated by *tempo.* **Tempo** refers to the number of beats or accents per time unit, and **speed** is the number of syllables per time unit. People are more likely to *speak* quickly to friends with whom they have shared prior experiences than to strangers who do not share the same points of reference. In *written* discourse, tempo is lexicalized, for example, *She said* **quickly** *and fearfully 'let's get out of here'.*

While listening to a story, a decoder is also affected interpersonally by the encoder's artful *pacing.* **Pacing** refers, not to speed or tempo of speaking, but to how an encoder varies slow passages with faster ones to achieve certain effects: to create suspense, humour, and to sustain a decoder's interest. Pacing evokes emotional responses in language users. In *spoken* discourse, similar effects are encoded phonologically by choice of consonant and vowel, rhetorical repetition of certain sounds, unusual patterns of stress, changes in tempo and momentary increases in dynamic range or volume. In *written* discourse such effects are encoded tri-stratally.

A predominance of *stops* slows the decoder's reading of a text while *approximants* and *fricatives* enable her to read more smoothly and quickly. There may also be a correlation between *pacing* and *strategy.* Descriptive passages seem to slow a passage down; while narrative passages speed it up (see Chapter 7). Although the analyst may not be able to afford the expensive equipment to document such matters, at least, she can begin to become conscious of them while exploring different ways of mapping them (cf. Couper-Kuhlen and Selting).

Silence is also a means of encoding interpersonal meaning phonologically. In *spoken* discourse silence can express affiliation or disaffiliation, intimacy or enmity. In *written* discourse, phonologically marked silence may be encoded in graphologically marked negative or empty space.

Textual

Textual meaning describes those features of the discourse pertaining to mode of transmission. As mentioned, when discourse is *spoken*, it is the phonological patterning that encodes all experiential and interpersonal meaning. It is also phonological information that contributes to the distinction between spontaneous (monologuing and dialoguing) and non-spontaneous speech. Generally speaking, spontaneous speech is realized by overlapping, interruptions, and a greater variation in pacing and dynamic range.

The phonological tone group contributes to the textual meaning of a text in its capacity to carry the speaker's assessment of the relationship between the message and its audience. In this sense, the tone group acts as an *information unit* highlighting *new* information over already known, or *given*, information. The **information unit**, realized by the single pitch contour of the tone group, consists of a single *new* element (obligatory) as well as a *given* element (optional), for example, // *She* / *went* to / *France* // Given-New. The tonic prominence, in this case *France*, carrying the information focus, marks the end / culmination of the **New** element. Often it coincides with the last functional element in clause structure. The **Given** information *she went to* precedes the New information in this information unit. (Although the end of the New is marked by tonic prominence, there is nothing that marks the beginning. Hence, New is written under the tonic prominence while Given is written before it, under the beginning of the tone group.) In ordinary situations, Given-New is the *unmarked* sequence in the information unit; however, occasionally, in *marked* situations, the New may come first, for example, // *This* / *news* pa per is / *yes* ter day's //. New-Given (see Halliday, 1994, p. 297).

In texts that are *written to be read as spoken*, even *written to be read*, phonological meaning still contributes to the cumulative meaning of the text. In addition, in *spoken* and *written* discourse the rising tone of questions connects to the falling tone of answers (questions and answers are **adjacency pairs**, one follows the other) adding phonological coherence to a text. In *written* discourse, phonological highlights may be carried graphologically by a repetition of certain consonant graphs at the beginning of consecutive words (alliteration) or vowel graphs in the middle of words (assonance). Reoccurring patterns of consonant and vowel sounds also contribute to the coherence of a text to itself.

Example

Text

C – (giggle) what do I need I need colour black
J – we're doing black we're doing red remember?

C – red head? I didn't say red head

J – then what did ya say? bed? bed or head? do you think we will go to bed at school? I need a triple

C – I need a tripled bum trippley trippley pippley

J – bum bum bada bum dumdum dum (walks figure on table) I'm so beautiful see I'm so I'm I brags I'm so pretty see . . . see?

C – wanna see me?

J – I looks so tidy

C – (walking with finger) me got blond hair go over my eyes me got blond hair me got blond hair look at the back I think that's should go the other way around don't you? I got blond hair

J – hey put your hand on for goodness sake

C – where? on what?

J – on his arm he doesn't even have a hand

C – look at this look Jacqui

J – what?

C – now what do we need? we need a I know what we need

J – me I'm a really old man eh eh eh eh

C – we need this this is what should happen this is what we need this is a boy I think it should go the other way

J – do you think this is a good touch?

C – do you think this is better? do you think this is better? (giggle) mm mm now I know how to do it

Analysis

Preparation

First Impressions: fun, child-like, rhyming, rhythmic, varied, nursery rhymes

Hypothesis – Children's talk while playing Lego is not only practical, but also playful. The children seem to relish the phonological possibilities of their language.

Note – The analyst divided the text into four chunks, which sounded somewhat different to her, to see whether the phonological style of the text was inconsistent as she suspected.

Description – (steps 1 & 2)

1. C – (giggle) // **hwət** du ai / **nid?** // ^ ai / **nid** kə-luər / **blæk** //   2 tone groups: 2 feet, 3 feet

J – // ^ wir / **du** iŋ / **blæk** // ^ wir / **du** – iŋ / **rɛd** // ^ ri-/ **mɛm** – bʊr //   3 tone groups: 3 feet, 3 feet, 2 feet

C – // **rɛd** hɛd // ^ ai / **dɪ** – dənt / **se** / **rɛd** hɛd //   2 tone groups: 1 foot, 4 feet

J – // ^ ðɛn / hwət / dɪd ja / <u>se?</u> // <u>bɛd</u>? // bɛd or / <u>hɛd</u>? // du ju / θɪnk wi wɪl go tu / bɛd æt / <u>skul</u>? //

    4 tone groups: 4 feet, 1 foot,
    2 feet, 4 feet
    11 tone groups

2. J – // ai / <u>nid</u> ə / trɪ – pəl //

    1 tone group: 3 feet

C – // ai / <u>nid</u> ə / trɪ – pəld / bəm // trɪp – li / trɪp – li / <u>pɪp</u> – li //

    2 tone groups:
    4 feet, 3 feet

J – // bəm bəm / <u>ba</u> – də bəm // dəm – / dəm / <u>dəm</u> // (walks figure on table) // aim / so / <u>biju</u> – tɪ – fʊl // <u>si</u> // aim so / aim ai / <u>brægz</u> // aim so / <u>prɪ</u> – ti // <u>si</u> // <u>si</u>?

    8 tone groups: 1–3 feet
    11 tone groups

3. C – // wa – nə / <u>si</u> mi ? //

    1 tone group: 2 feet

J – //ai / lʊks / so / <u>tai</u> – di //

    1 tone group: 4 feet

C – (walking with figure) // mi / gɔt / bland hɛr go / o – vər mai / <u>aɪz</u> // mi /gɔt / bland / <u>hɛr</u> // mi /gɔt / bland / <u>hɛr</u> // lʊk æt ðə / <u>bæk</u> // ^ ai / <u>θɪnk</u> // ðætz ʃʊd go ði / ə – ðʊr we ə – / <u>raund</u> // dont / <u>ju?</u> // ai / gɔt / bland / <u>hɛr</u> //

    8 tone groups: 2–5
    feet

J – // <u>he</u> // pʊt jor / hænd / <u>ɔn</u> // ^ for / gʊd – nɪs / <u>sek</u> //

    3 tone groups: 1
    foot, 3 feet, 3feet

C – // <u>hwer?</u> // ^ ɔn / <u>hwət?</u> //

    2 tone groups: 1
    foot, 2 feet

J – //^ ɔn hɪz / <u>arm</u> // hi / də – sənt / i – vən / hæv ə / <u>hænd</u> //

    2 tone groups: 2
    feet, 5 feet

C – // lʊk æt / <u>θɪs</u> // lʊk / dʒæ – ki //

    2 tone groups: 2
    feet, 2 feet

J – // <u>hwət?</u> //

    1 tone group: 1 foot
    20 tone groups

4. C – // nau / hwət du wi / <u>nid?</u> // wi / <u>nid</u> ə // <u>ai</u> / no / hwət wi / nid //

    3 tone groups: 3f, 2f, 4f

J – // <u>mi</u> // aim ə / ri – li / old / <u>mæn</u> // e / e / e / e //

    3 tone groups: 1f, 4f, 4f

C – // wi / nid / <u>θɪs</u> // θɪs ɪz / hwət ʃʊd / <u>hæ</u> – pən // θɪs ɪz / hwət wi / <u>nid</u> // θɪs ɪz ə / <u>boi</u> // ^ ai / θɪnk ɪt ʃʊd / go ðə /ə – ðər / <u>we</u> //

    5 tone groups: 3 feet,
    3 feet, 3 feet,
    2 feet, 5 feet

J – // ^ du ju / θɪnk θɪs ɪz ə gʊd / <u>tətʃ?</u>//

    1 tone group: 3 feet

C – // ^ du ju / θɪnk θɪs ɪz / <u>bɛ</u> – tər? // ^ du ju / θɪnk θɪs ɪz/ <u>bɛ</u> – tər? // **(giggle)** //
mm / <u>mm</u> // nɑu ɑi / no / hɑu tu / <u>do</u> ɪt //   4 tone groups: 3 feet,
3 feet, 2 feet, 4 feet
16 tone groups

Step 3 – no noticeable evaluative colouring, changes in dynamics, tempo, pacing, or silence
Step 4 – no rhyme scheme or specific metrical pattern like a poem;
however, rhyming words section 1: *red, hed, bed*, and 2 *tripley pipley*
rhythmic play section 2 with sound words, e.g. *bum, dum*,
in section 3 repetition of *I got blond hair* acts as rhythmic refrain
Step 5 – see tone groups and feet and tonic prominence (underlined) in description of text
Rising tones indicated by ? : section 1: 5 of 11, section 2: 1 of 11, section 3: 5 of 20, section 4: 4 of 16
Usually Given then New, except a few instances eg. *Look Jacqui* where *Look* is New; *Jacqui*, Given.
In section 4 child adopts 'old man voice' when saying *e e e e*; later *mm mm* (rhymes and rhythms (Step 4) add phonological coherence of text to itself)
Non-verbal behaviour accompanies verbal sections 2 and 3: *walks Lego figure on table*
section 1 and 4 – non-verbal *giggle*

Contextualization

Situation – two children talking as they play Lego, specifically Lego people
Register – casual conversation accompanying non-verbal Lego activity
Purpose – at times to entertain each other; at other times, play Lego together
        Strategy – mixed assortment

Metafunctions

Experiential – All the sounds, consonants and vowels recorded in the results chart go together to form the feet and tone groups that encode the experience, the field of the discourse.
Interpersonal – Many clauses are statements encoded as falling tones;
rising tones encoding questions are used in each section of the text: section 1 – 45%, 2 – 9%, 3 – 28%, 4 – 25%
several commands: *remember, see, put your hand, look at*, (1 or 2 examples per section)
Textual – Endophoric cohesion – examples of alliteration and assonance, (lexical repetition contributes to repetition of same consonants and vowels)

Exophoric coherence – rhyme and rhythm contribute to phonological coherence, as do rising and falling tones of adjacency pairs (Q & A)

Linguistic context

syntax 'errors': *I looks, me got, you got* (3x), sentence level elements

semology: action, mental and relational processes

lexis – sound play: *tripley, trippley, pippley; e e e e; mm mm*

conceptual sets relevant to Lego play: colour, parts of the body

Cultural context and dialect

Encoder – 6-year-old dyad: J is a girl, C is a boy; Toronto, 1980s

Intended **decoder** – each other, as the two children alternate turntaking

Actual **decoder** – reader of this text and analyst

Results

Consonants	Stops		Fricatives		Affricates		Approximants			Nasals
	Voiced	Unvoiced	Voiced	Unvoiced	Voiced	Unvoiced	Unvoiced	Voiced central	Voiced lateral	Voiced
Bilabial	b *by* 4,7,5,3	p *pet* 0,7,1,1						w *wit* 6,0,5,10		m *mit* 2,11,6,7
Labiodental			v *vet* 0,0,3,	f *fit* 0,1,1,						
Interdental			ð *that* 1,0,4,2	θ *thick* 1,0,2,11						
Alveolar	d *do* 19,8,12,14	t *to* 6,6,12,11	z *zoo* 0,1,3,6	s *sit, city* 2,6,6,5				R *red* 9,7,11,3	l *lit* 5,8,8,2	n *no* 5,4,16,10
Palatal Alveolar			ʒ *beige*	ʃ *show* 0,0,1,3	dʒ *Jump* 0,0,1,0	tʃ *chin* 0,0,0,1				
Velar	g *gift* 1,1,7,2	k *king* 5,0,8,4						J *yes* 2,1,3,3		ŋ *sing* 2,0,0,
Glottal		ʔ *oh-oh*					h *hat* 5,0,13,7			

Consonants Results

Section	Stops (30%)	Fricatives (20–25%)	Approximants (25%)	Nasals (15–19%)
1	33s of 73 c = **48%** +	3f of 73c = **4%** –	27a of 73c = **37%** +	9n of 73c =**12%** –
2	29s of 62c = **47%** +	8f of 62c = **13%** –	16a of 62c = **26%** +	15n of 62c = **24%** +
3	45s of 127c = **35%** +	20f of 127c =**16%** –	40a of 127c = **31%** +	22n of 127c = 17%
4	35s of 109c = **32%** +	27f of 109c = 25%	25a of 109c = 23%	8n of 109c =**7%** –
Totals	142s of 371c = **38**% +	58f of 371c = **16%** –	108a of 371c = **29%** +	54n of 371c = 15%

Note: plus and minus indicate greater than or less than average

Vowels		Front	Central	Back
High	Tense	i *deed* 8,10,11,13		u *duty* 7,1,2,8
	Lax	ɪ *did* 4,5,4,20		ʊ *wood* 1,0,8,3
Mid	Tense	E *date* 2,0,4,4	ə *upon* 3,14,11,19	o *cold* 2,3,7,5
	Lax	ɛ *debt* 10,0,4,4		ɔ *torn, cot* 0,0,7,
Low		æ *dab* 4,1,8,2		a *calm* 1,1,6,

Diphthongs	ɑu 0,0,0,3	ɑi 3,7,6,1	oi 0,0,0,1

Vowels Results

Section	Front (50%)	Central (17–25%)	Back (20%)	Diphthongs (9%)
1	28f of 48v = **58**% +	3c of 48v = **6%** –	11b of 48v = 23%	3d of 48v = 6%
2	17f of 43v = **37**% –	14c of 43v = **33**% +	5b of 43v = **12%** –	7d of 43v =**16%** +
3	31f of 77v = **40**% –	11c of 77v =14%	30b of 77v = **39**% +	6d of 77v = 8%
4	43f of 80v = 54%	19c of 80v = 24%	16b of 80v = 20%	5d of 80v = 6%
Totals	109f of 248v = 44%	47c of 248v =19%	62b of 248v = 25%	21d of 248v = 8%

Conclusion

Summary

In this passage the four sections of the text thought to be distinct truly are.

Section 1 is quite marked phonologically, with its high percentage of stops (48% compared to 30%), its low percentage of fricatives (4% compared to 22%), and its high per cent of approximants (37% compared to 25%). In terms of vowels, it has more than average front vowels (58% compared to 50%) and less than average central vowels (6% instead of 20%). The repetition of the rhyming words red, head, bed accounts for many of the stops (especially /d/), and many of the front vowels (especially /ɛ/). Section 1 is distinct interpersonally with its high percentage (45%) of rising tones encoding questions, many of which are encoded phonologically rather than syntactically, for example remember? (rising tone, imperative mood).

Section 2 has almost as many stops as Section 1 (47%), and more fricatives (13%) although it is still marked in both types of articulation (the former greater than average, the latter lower than average). It is also marked by the number of nasal phonemes (24% compared to 17%), almost twice the percentage of Section 1. In terms of vowels, Section 2 is marked by its paucity of front vowels (37%) and its excess of central vowels (33%), making the front and central vowels quite balanced in number. The repetition of the sound play words *bum bum bada bum dum dum dum* account for many of these results both of consonants and vowels. Section 2 has fewer back vowels than usual (12% compared to 20%) and more diphthongs than predictable (16% compared to 9%). The sound play already mentioned is not the only sound play. In this passage a version of *triple* or *tripley* is repeated four times and rhymed with *pippley*. Compared to Section 1, the stops in this section are more equally balanced between bilabial and alveolar, voiced and unvoiced consonants (/b,p; d,t/). Both examples of repeated sound play account for the high number of high front vowels /i/ and mid-central vowels /ə/. Because *I* is repeated in a series of False Starts *I'm so, I'm I brags I'm so* the diphthong /ai/ is most frequent in this section.

Section 3 is still marked by its excessive stops (35%) and fewer fricatives (16%); however, it is much less marked in both than Sections 1 and 2. Section 3 is somewhere between the two, however, in it markedness concerning approximants. Much of these statistics are a consequence of the repetition of the phrase *me / I got blond hair* four times. This accounts for the bilabial /b/ and velar /g/ voiced consonants as well as the /h, r/ approximants. In terms of vowels, the same phrase accounts for the lower percentage of front vowels (40%), and the markedness of its high percentage of back vowels (39%), particularly lower ones. Section 3 is also distinct in its high percentage (28%) of rising tones encoding questions. However, these rising tones are reinforced syntactically by choices in mood: WH and polar interrogatives (WH questions involve situational exophora, connecting the discourse to its physical situation and setting).

Section 4 is the only section that is comparatively unmarked phonologically, with most of the percentages falling close to unmarked frequencies. It does include, however, the least number of nasals of all the sections (7%). In terms of vowels, Section 4 is also the only section that is unmarked in terms of the frequencies of vowels. Interestingly, this unmarked section is the one that is closest to ordinary casual talk, including little sound play, and no more repetition than usual. The most interesting feature of this section phonologically is the girl J's brief role-playing, speaking as the old man Lego figure she builds with her *eh eh eh eh*. In Section 4, one-quarter of the tone groups are rising, signalling questions. Although there is not as much repetition as in other sections, there is some: *we need* (4x), and *I / you think* (4x).

When all the instances of each phoneme are combined, the text is still high in stops (38% compared to 30%), and low in fricatives (16% compared to 22%). Much of the sound play involves stops: *red, bed; bum bum bada dum dum; tripley pipley*. However, it is quite unmarked in numbers of approximants and nasals overall. In vowels, the text is low in front vowels and high in back vowels compared with unmarked averages. The text is quite varied in terms of rising and falling tones. Many of the rising tones are reinforced by choices in interrogative syntactic mood. In each section of the text there is some relevant nonverbal action that accompanies the talk – either kinesthetic: *walks Lego figure on table* (Sections 2 and 3), or the phonologically communicative, but nonverbal: *giggle* (Sections 1 and 4).

Although the text is interesting overall, marked with its sound play, analysing it section by section tells a much more extreme tale than the combination of all features. Each section is marked by its particular form of sound play that seems to dominate, and account for, much of the section's most marked characteristics. The section that is least marked with sound play, Section 4, is the only section that comes anywhere close to being unmarked in terms of frequencies of particular consonants and vowels. And even this section is phonologically interesting for its role playing speech and its consistent alternation of rising and falling tones.

Interpretation

In a sense, in terms of statistical norms, as the frequencies show, this text is quite marked in terms of its phonological makeup. However, considering the contemporary cultural context and situation, the text, produced by two six-year-old children playing Lego as they chatted casually, is not so unusual. Adults would never have created this text. It is full of wonderful childish sound play: rhyming words *red, head, bed*; rhythmic words *bum, bum, bada bum, dum dum*, role playing sounds *e e e e*, miscellaneous sounds *mm mm*, singsongy refrains *me got blonde hair* and non-verbal *giggles*. And Section 4, that is least marked by this sound play, is the one that fits most closely with the averages of consonant and vowel frequencies documented in the text, and taken from several instances of unmarked phonological analysis.

The experience that the children explore in the discourse, one that is dominated by Lego lexical sets and a variety of semological processes and rhetorical strategies, is important to the text in that it is the reason for much of what is encoded, for example, *what do I need I need colour black*. And the greater experiential specificity revealed by the lexical 'part of body' set: *head, arm, hand, hair* is important phonologically, in that it accounts for the sounds of the Jacqui's personified role playing *me I'm a really old man eh eh eh eh*. The boy Christopher is also affected by the Lego characters he manipulates in his chorus of *me got blond hair me got blond hair*. In addition the whole *tripley pipley* rhyming and repetitive word play is initiated by the children needing a Lego piece that has three knobs *I need a triple*.

As important as the experience is to the phonological style the children have manifested, so is their interpersonal relationship. They are playing together in a very familiar setting interacting in a familiar activity. They are friends who converse together easily and naturally. As six-year olds, they are relatively unfettered by social standards. Sound is a dimension of meaning that is part of their world, from the songs they sing at school to the nursery rhymes they chant and hear. They interact as peers, participating equally in a cooperative activity and the talk that accompanies it. The register of Lego talk and the casual relationship between the two also account for the variety and plethora of falling and rising tones. Casual talk, particularly that of children, abounds with both polar and WH interrogatives which encode a rising tone. Both are typical of the cooperative interactive play of friends.

The phonological choices also reflect textual ones. Because the text is a transcription of a spontaneous spoken discourse, tone groups are easily accessible to the analyst. The spoken mode also accounts for the brevity of the turns, and often, the coherence between the children's discourse and their immediate physical situation. Coherence comes as a consequence of the numerous adjacency pairs, where the question is connected to the answer. However, in children's discourse this is not always the case. At times one child asks himself or herself a question and never answers it, at other times when the encoder asks a question of the other, the decoder might not feel compelled to answer at all. Information is unmarked for the most part with the New information at the end of the tone group.

In terms of purpose, the children's phonological choices make it clear that engaging in cooperative Lego play is not the only reason for sounding words that carry meaning. Often they speak, they articulate sounds, just for the joy of it *bum bumbada bum dum dum.*

Review of phonological analysis

Analysis

Preparation

Find a few words that describe your **first impressions** of the phonological character of the text, write them down, and put them aside for later. Make notes about any **preliminary** thoughts, **hypotheses** concerning the phonological character of the text.

Description

1. Make a **phonemic transcription** of the text using the IPA symbols. Transcribe the discourse as the encoder manifests it, if *spoken*. If *written*, transcribe the discourse as if you were the encoder.

2 **a**. Mark the *strong* and *weak* **syllables** in the text (bold the strong syllables, or use an accent).

   b. Divide the text into phonological **feet** (strong beat comes first – use a single slash between feet).

   c. Divide the text into **tone groups** (use double slash), remembering that punctuation often signals tone group boundaries in prose, and line spacing often signals tone group boundaries in poetry.

3 **a.** If the text is spoken, or written to be spoken (dramatic dialogue), note any **evaluative colouring** given to the text, e.g. *irony, sarcasm, angry*, etc.

   b. Note variations in **dynamic range** and **tempo,** e.g. *softly, quickly.*

   c. Try to describe, and map the **pacing** of the text; explain how phonological choices have created this pacing, and begin thinking about the effects of such phenomenon. See prosodic mapping #6.

   d. Note any meaningful use of **silence** in the text.

4. If appropriate, particularly if the text is a **poem**, or resembles one, as is sometimes the case in advertising. This step may be omitted if the text has no resemblance to poetry.

a. Describe any noticeable **rhymes** or **rhythms.**

b. Note any **rhetorical devices** pertaining to phonology, e.g. alliteration (a repetition of consonants), assonance (a repetition of vowels).

5. **Information structure, coherence, mode**

a. Underline the **tonic prominence** in each tone group (strong syllable in the foot where there is greatest pitch change).

b. Identify the **tones** as rising, falling or other.

c. Under tonic prominence in each tone group write **New**, and write **Given** under earlier part of tone group (if the information unit is *marked*, reverse this order).

d. List the phonological features of the text that add **coherence** to it.

e. If the text is *spoken* list non-verbal sounds that characterize this **mode**.

6. **Prosody**

a. Attempt to construct a prosodic map of the entire text, following the guidelines of conversational analysts (cf. Couper-Kuhlen, E. and Selting, M. 1996).

Contextualization

Situation – Describe the relevant field, personal and functional tenor and mode of this communicative event between interactive participants and any represented participants.

Register – Identify the **register** of the text, whether literary or non-literary.

Are the phonological features of the text a function of the register?

What phonological nuances make your text unique in terms of its register?

Purpose – Identify the purpose of this text.

How does phonological information develop this purpose?

Strategies: Does the phonological style have any relationship to the strategies chosen?

Metafunctions

Describe how the phonological choices highlight particular **metafunctions.**

i. **Experiential** – What phonemes, feet, tone groups add information to the experience that is developed in this text?

ii. **Interpersonal** – Describe how the encoder's choice of tone, dynamic range, pacing, and evaluative colouring reveal the relationship between encoder and decoder.

iii. **Textual** – Is the text *spoken* spontaneously or non-spontaneously as monologue, dialogue or multi-party talk; or *written* to be spoken; to be read as if spoken / heard, or just to be read.

What experiential information is encoded as **New** in this text? as **Given**?

coherence – What repetitions and patterns of sounding create phonological coherence in the text?

Linguistic context

a. Does the placement of the text (beginning, middle or end) account for the phonological style?

b. Describe the way other linguistic information relates, reinforces and challenges the phonological choices of this text, for example *lexical, syntactic, semological, graphological.*

Cultural context and dialect

a. Who is the **encoder**? What is her age, ethnicity, gender, nationality? How do her phonological choices reflect her situation, culture, beliefs and values? In other words, how do they create her social identity and construct her social reality?

b. Who is the ***intended* decoder** (the expected / target audience)? How might her situation and culture, and experience of the register affect her interpretation of the encoder's phonological choices?

Who is the ***actual* decoder**? How might her situation and culture, and experience of the register affect her interpretation of the encoder's phonological choices?

Results

1. Complete the following transcription summary sheet, and total the frequencies of particular types of consonants, vowels and diphthongs. Count whatever else is countable, for example various types of tone groups, the number of rhetorical devices pertaining to sounding, the number of examples of evaluative colouring, dynamic range variations and the like.

Consonants	Stops		Fricatives		Affricates		Approximants			Nasals
	Voiced	Unvoiced	Voiced	Unvoiced	Voiced	Unvoiced	Unvoiced	Voiced central	Voiced lateral	Voiced
Bilabial	b *by*	p *pet*						w *wit*		m *mitt*
Labiodental			v *vet*	f *fit*						
Interdental			ð *that*	θ *thick*						
Alveolar	d *do*	t *to*	z *zoo*	s *sit, city*				r *red*	l *lit*	n *no*
Palatal Alveolar			ʒ *beige*	ʃ *show*	dʒ *jump*	t ʃ *chin*				
Velar	g *gift*	k *king*						j *yes*		ŋ *sing*
Glottal		ʔ *oh-oh*					h *hat*			

+ voiced alveolar flap /r/ Ottawa

Vowels		Front	Central	Back
High	tense	i *deed*		u *duty*
	lax	ɪ *did*		ʊ *wood*
Mid	tense	e *date*	ə *upon*	o *cold*
	lax	ɛ *debt*		ɔ *torn, cot*
Low		æ *dab*		ɑ *calm*

Diphthongs	au	ai	oi

2. Note which are **major** features of the encoder's phonological style, and which are **minor,** given the size of the text.

3. By comparing your results with the frequencies given below, decide which of these features and totals are **unmarked / predictable** given the register, encoder and decoder (see conclusions), and which features (omissions as well as occurrences) are **marked / unpredictable**, atypical of the register, and hence potentially significant.

Among ***consonants***: | **stops occur** | **30%** | of the time in typical unmarked discourse,
| | **fricatives** | **20–25%** | of the time,
| | **affricates** | **1–2%** | of the time,
| | **approximants** | **25%** | of the time,
| | **nasals** | **15–19%** | of the time.

Among ***vowels*** about **50% appear to be front vowels** typically,
20% back vowels,
17–25% central vowels,
9% *diphthongs*.

4. review your first impressions and initial hypotheses of your text (see Preparatory Notes), and comment on them.

Conclusions

1. **Summary** – Describe the encoder's **phonological style** in prose, using examples and statistics when appropriate.

2. **Interpretation** – Discuss how this particular phonological repertoire best serves the encoder, given her cultural and situational context, communicative purpose, and register, in communicating her experiential and interpersonal message to her intended audience in this particular mode.

Further reading

Halliday, MAK and Greaves, W. (2008). *Intonation in the Grammar of English*. London: Equinox.

Couper-Kuhlen, E. and Selting, M. (1996), 'Towards an interactional perspective on prosody and a prosodic perspective on interaction.' In *Prosody in Conversation*. Ed. Couper-Kuhlen, E. and Selting, M. Cambridge: CUP.

Watt, D. (2001) 'Intonational Cohesion and Tone Sequences in English' In *Communication in Linguistics* de Villiers, J. and Stainton, R. (eds.) Toronto, Canada: Editions du Gref. pp. 361–378.

Lexis 4

Lexis is the study of the organization of the meanings of words. Communication works because people share meanings. Meanings are organized into taxonomies / groups of relatedness. If someone says the word *cat*, not only do numerous attributes of cats come to mind like *animal, tail, paw, whiskers, fur, meow*, but so do several related words such as *gray, white, stray, tabby, scratch, purr, pet*. The former **denotative meanings** of a word like *cat* include the attributes of cats that are held more or less universally. These meanings are the ones used in dictionary definitions like '*a small furry domesticated animal often kept as a pet*' (*Oxford English Dictionary*). The latter **connotative meanings** are more general, associated with *cat* more by proximity than exclusivity. Connotations are more likely to be situationally and culturally specific. When children talk to friends about their pet cat they use words like *Mukti* (name), *cuddly, purr, gray, Persian*. Professional cat breeders, however, use a very different group of words to discuss cats at cat shows: *Koret, registered (not purebred), lilac point, locket, bracelet, ticking, dam, sire, altered, spay*. Such specialized, technical words are called **field-restricted words** or **jargon.**

Language users understand the meanings of words in terms of the beliefs, values, expectations and stereotypes associated with their culture. Despite the common **referent** (thing in the world), each language has its own **referring expression**: in English, *cat*; in French, *chat*. Communicators also understand the meaning of the present instantial discourse by comparing it to their non-instantial memories of past linguistic experiences of such meanings. Although individuals can easily misinterpret the meaning of a word that is emotionally charged for them, it seems that people share enough meaning to understand one another more or less. However, the disparity between the word a child first whispers to a friend in the game 'telephone' and the word that emerges after being reiterated from user to user, makes clear the precarious nature of communication.

Language users know and remember an enormous range of lexical taxonomies of words that are encoded in the registers of language reflecting recurring situations. In a post office situation, **lexical items** (words that carry meaning) like *stamp, send, mail, courier, registered, special delivery* are predictable; in a grocery, words like *vegetables, milk, meat, eggs*. When reading about cars, decoders expect to see **lexical sets** or **taxonomies** pertaining to *driving, parts of a car, types of cars* and so on, depending on the particular register involved. Mechanics' manuals would include a different range of lexical items than car advertisements, because the decoders' shared knowledge and rhetorical purpose, among other things, is so different.

By dividing the lexical items in a text into lexical sets or conceptual taxonomies, analysts become very clear about the *experiential* meaning of a text: what participants are doing, how, when, where, and why. *Interpersonal* meanings become clear too, as analysts sort out lexical items that carry not only experiential meaning, but also, a subjective slant that reveals interpersonal relationship. If a lexical item like *jerk* or *sweetie* is used, rather than the more objective *Chris*, the encoder has encoded more than a participant, but also a subjective relationship through lexical evaluation or *appraisal*. Some lexical items encode *textual* meanings as well concerning the medium of transmission. Instant Messaging gave birth to acronyms like *lol* (*laugh out loud*), which would have made little sense before the advent of this mode of transmission.

A lexical analysis of a text tells the analyst not only what the discourse concerns experientially, interpersonally and textually in the register and situation, but also much about the cultural ideology of the text producer and the target audience or receiver. Cultural beliefs and values reflecting temporal, geographic and social provenance (age, education, socio-economic, political, and religious background, ethnicities, class and gender) are also encoded in language. Lexical choices reveal how language users use language to construct not only their personal identity, but also more broadly, their entire social reality.

Conceptual lexical analysis reveals not only the experiential, interpersonal and textual meanings that are most obvious and accessible to the decoder, but also meanings that are much less accessible in the discourse. A single lexical item or word from a particular religious orientation, for instance, might add an entirely new sub-text, or secondary reading, to a text. In addition, in some situations, among some interlocutors, *indirect* meanings are intended and interpreted, despite being barely visible in the overall lexical description of the text. The point is, however, that lexical analyses make such meanings clearer and more visible. Certain registers of language promote lexical ambiguity, some for the sake of politeness, some for the sake of manipulation and persuasion. Other registers eschew any secondary reading that might confuse or distract the decoder from interpreting the primary meaning.

Contextual lexical analysis shows how encoders can change the predictable meaning of a lexical item by taking it out of its normal lexical context and juxtaposing or collocating it with lexical items from another quite unpredictable lexical context. For writers of advertisements and literary works in particular, communicating predictable meanings is not enough; they seek to revitalize the language by collocating 'old' words in 'new' ways. Some seek to manipulate meanings by doing the same. Research on courtroom discourse has shown how lawyers can affect outcomes by the lexical choices they make in their questioning.

By choosing words very precisely, an encoder can virtually guarantee that the decoder's **interpreted meaning** will closely resemble her **intended meaning**. That is, unless the decoder is from a different linguistic community, or the encoder's communicative purpose is to confuse rather than clarify; in which case, vague, ambiguous words might be preferable.

The lexical analysis of verbal communication

Despite the sophistication of our lexical memories and expectations, experience has shown how little we know and appreciate the nuances of any particular text. Because lexical meaning is more accessible than others and less abstract, the analyst needs to ensure that she does not assign a greater significance to lexical meaning than the findings from other analyses (see other chapters). In addition, she needs to ensure that she attends to 'all' the lexical information that she gleans from the analysis, and not just what supports a preliminary hypothesis. Intuition is important in the way it guides the analyst's thinking about her lexical findings. If an analysis does not explain all the analyst's first impressions, the analyst needs to reconsider her analysis, whether it has accurately described the lexical meanings in the text as a typical decoder would interpret them. There is a subjective element to lexical analyses, one the analyst needs to acknowledge and minimalize. Accurate, exhaustive, objective analysis is crucial. Lexis' accessibility can lead to simplistic and partial interpretations that either do not account for all the data or misinterpret it.

There are two kinds of lexical analyses. **Conceptual analysis** captures the way hearers or readers (decoders) find meaning in, or interpret, a text based on their own shared knowledge of the culture and the registers of language used in various situations within that culture. **Contextual analysis** describes how encoders confirm or challenge a decoder's cultural expectations through the way they juxtapose different conceptual meanings and the taxonomies of lexical items associated with them. Both forms of analysis are designed to shed light on the communicative process: to illumine how the encoder selects and juxtaposes certain meanings that the decoder then interprets as predictable and insignificant or unpredictable and significant.

Conceptual analysis

Conceptual analysis reveals the actual subject matter of the communicated message selected by the encoder and interpreted by the decoder. It is *decoder-oriented*, in that it reveals the linguistic expectations and interpretations of the reader / hearer in her culture. The objective of conceptual analysis is to discover how the decoder forms taxonomies (sets of related conceptual meanings) in a way that supports her interpretation.

Preparation

In preparation for conceptual analysis, first reread the text, noting both: your *first impressions* of it (e.g. *dense, confusing, provocative, descriptive, exciting, ordinary, educated*), and the *expectations* you bring to bear on it based on (a) the register (e.g. legal discourse, advertisement, mystery), (b) the strategy of development (e.g. description, dialogue, argument), (c) the linguistic context, or the position of the text in a larger document (e.g. first page, last page, middle), and (d) your purpose in analysing this particular text (e.g. first description of protagonist, climax of plot, humorous, randomly selected) in order to come up with *preliminary hypotheses* that will guide, not predetermine, your analysis.

Analysis

Once you have carefully recorded your first impressions and expectations of the text, you begin the analysis. First, you distinguish between *lexical items* and *function words*. **Lexical items** are words that carry meaning. They are italicized in the sentence: The *child* who is *three* does not *likely know* how to *read.* Lexical items are usually nouns, verbs, adjectives or adverbs. Because personal pronouns like *s / he, I* refer to, or substitute for, lexical items, they are considered the same. The non-italicized words in the sentence are **function words** which carry little meaning, but are important in grammatical function, introducing or connecting one word to another. Function words are ignored in lexical analysis. Function words are usually realized by auxiliary verbs, articles, conjunctions, prepositions and certain pronouns.

In the analysis, start at the beginning of the text and **list** all lexical items across the top of the page. (Writing across the longer / landscape side of a page helps.) As you list each lexical item, you may notice that some words are very close in meaning to others. When this happens, list the related word underneath the first instance of the set, in the same conceptual taxonomy or lexical set. For instance, in a car advertisement, every time you come to a new car related term add it below the former, in a column of the *car* lexical set. As you continue, lexical item by lexical item, you **build** your **lexical sets** into vertical columns of words related in meaning. Classify all individual lexical items into one lexical set or another, based on your interpretation of them as an *ordinary member* of your culture (not one with certain areas of expertise). The ordinary person would, for instance, add the lexical item *bracelet* to a *jewelry* set, not a *cat* set as the cat expert might be tempted.

A single lexical item may be added to more than one lexical set if appropriate. For example, the item *soldier* should be included in both a *person* set and a *war* set. As you further develop some lexical sets while beginning others, you will find some lexical sets becoming longer, while others include a single lexical item only. Sometimes it is useful to sub-classify items in a lengthy lexical set. For instance, a long *people* set might become *family, officers, parts of the body,* and *servants* subsets. If the same lexical item is used several times, keep track of the number of instances beside your listing of it, for example *river* (4x). The more a lexical item is repeated, the more significant it becomes potentially.

Once you have classified every single lexical item, check through each lexical set to ensure that each set is *internally consistent*. Sometimes, in the early stages of analysis you might not know how specific a set will become, so an item classified early might no longer belong in the set. Also, double check your *single item sets* to ensure that they do not belong in some of the lexical sets you developed later in your analysis. In the early stages of an analysis many items look as if they belong in a separate set; however, once you have the complete picture of the text, you will see this is not true. For instance, if originally you added *water* to a *river* landscape set as well as leaving it on its own as a potential *drink* set, by the end of the analysis you might see that *drinks* have no relevance to the text, in which case leaving *water* in the *river* set, and deleting *water* as a single item *drink* set is appropriate.

The next step in conceptual analysis (which may be done after, or during, your classification of words into sets) helps maintain *internal consistency*. As soon as you have determined the primary focus of each lexical set, use this focus as a **label** or title of the set. Be as precise as possible when labelling each set. A label like *description* is too vague: are the lexical items pertaining to size, colour, etc.? The label *actions* is equally vague: are they the actions of an animal, human, arm, leg? If you are considering labelling a set *emotions* check your list of items to see whether there is another quality they share: are they all 'negative emotions'? If so, make your label specific: *negative emotions*. In addition, avoid syntactic sounding labels like *adjectives* or *modifiers*: lexis is not syntax. Sometimes, one of the items in the lexical set best describes the entire set. If this is the case, simply underline that item as the label for the entire set. Precise labels are crucial, for it is these labels that you use to describe your analysis in your results and conclusions. Think how misleading it would be if you over-generalized by labelling one set *emotions*, when, in reality, it was limited to *negative emotions* only. What if you gave a lexical set a label that was relevant to only half of the items included in the set, and then compounded the problem by suggesting this set challenged a central theme in the book, which a more accurate label would not have?

Conceptual analysis can be very revealing if it is done precisely, or completely misleading and uninterpretable if it is not. Once the labelling is done, **re-examine**: single item sets, internal consistency and *cultural predictability*. Another analyst from the same culture should agree with your analysis, even if hers is somewhat different. Two conceptual analyses of the same text are seldom exactly the same; but they are not that different either. An analyst with an interest in spiritual matters might be more likely to see a *spiritual* set than another without that interest. However, it is important that the analyst not let her personal interests misrepresent the encoder's lexical choices. If the analyst is from a culture other than the encoder and decoder, it is important she do what she can to gain access into their world. After all, a conceptual analysis is to capture the decoder's point of view, as much as possible. If you are analysing a text written in a different century (temporal provenance), look up the lexical meanings in the Oxford English Dictionary, so you can be sure you are decoding the meaning the encoder intended. Meanings of words change over the centuries. Similarly if there are lexical items that are foreign to you because they are from a language from another geographical prove-nance, you might want to list them separately and note them in your results. If you can ascertain their meaning, great, add them to the appropriate lexical sets in your analysis. If you are working on a text that has been *translated* from another language, remember you are analysing the translator's version of the text, not the original author's. Always do what you can to tune into the encoder's intended meanings by being aware of their temporal, geographical and social provenance, but after that, be clear and open about analysing the text from your own cultural perspective.

There are a few more matters to take note of once you have completed your conceptual analysis. For one, are the lexical items in the text primarily mono-syllabic, polysyllabic, or a mixture? In other words, how complex is the lexis used? The length of words used in a text says a lot about the intended decoder as well as the purpose of the discourse. Books intended for beginning readers, children or adults with little education are going to be much simpler lexically than those intended for highly educated adults. And books intended to inform, like textbooks, may be simpler than books intended to challenge, like scholarly critiques and editorials.

Another lexical matter to consider once your conceptual analysis is com-plete is the *interpersonal* effect of the lexis. It might be useful to make a sepa-rate list of evaluatively coloured lexical items as you are completing your conceptual analysis, as well as including them in the appropriate sets. Then, analysing these items in terms of *appraisal* will follow (cf. the section 'Lexis and the metafunctions'). In some texts, experiential meanings are the most important in interpretation; in others, interpersonal meanings are.

In lengthy texts which measure in pages not paragraphs and which involve shifts in the lexis from one combination of conceptual sets to another, it is useful to maintain the original *sequence* of the lexical items while doing the conceptual analysis. This is particularly important if a phasal analysis is to be made of the text combining all forms of analyses into one coherent whole (cf. 'Sequential Lexical Analysis', Chapter 8).

Results

Once you have completed your conceptual analysis, you are ready to record your **results**. To do this, count the number of lexical items in each lexical set using the *label*, or descriptive title, to record each total. When you have tabulated your results, you are then ready to classify them in terms of frequency (major and minor) and predictability given the situation, register and period of the text.

Generally speaking, lexical sets of more than eight items are called **major**, four to seven items **medium**, and sets with one to three items **minor**. However, these numbers are not absolute, and should be reconsidered given the particular analysis. For instance, if you had two sets with over twenty items, to call ones with five medium would be inappropriate. Some texts are conceptually quite limited in range and develop no more than three major conceptual / lexical sets throughout; other texts may cover a wide range of conceptual groupings, none in great detail. Conceptual analysis reveals the experiential predilections of the encoder, and not just in the major sets. Sometimes by adding no more than a word here or there the connotations of the text can enter whole new arenas of meaning. Hence, minor conceptual sets can often be as revealing as major sets in terms of thematic significance.

Before the results are assessed in terms of predictability, the analyst needs to contextualize them in terms of situation and register. Ten items in a lexical set labelled *car* is quite **predictable** in a car advertisement, but **unpredictable** in a family restaurant menu. Once the situation and register is noted, sets can be classified as culturally predictable and *unmarked* in that context or unpredictable and *marked*. Do not forget what sets *should* or *could be* present, but are **missing**. For example, if the text were describing a person, but there were no lexical sets describing the person visually (*clothes, parts of the body, colour*), it would be quite unusual in most contexts, and therefore, unpredictable. Recording the analyst's lexical expectations of the text before the analysis helps the analyst evaluate the results as marked or unmarked once the analysis is complete. Lexical sets can also be unpredictable in size too. There might be a minor lexical set pertaining to cars in advertising a breakfast cereal, but a major set? The *slant* of the encoder's lexical choices might also affect their predictability. Was the purpose to be *sarcastic, humorous*? If so, expect the unexpected. It is important to record your thoughts concerning your analysis in a *Comments* section.

Comparing your results to those describing other texts of a similar register / genre that you are familiar with is one way to proceed. In your conclusions, you continue this process of contextualizing and comparing in order to arrive at an appropriate interpretation of your text and an appreciation of its intricacies.

After you have completed your conceptual analysis, **reread** your passage and make sure that your conceptual sets describe *all* the lexical meanings that you have intuitively gathered. If they do not, there is a problem with either your analysis or the labelling of your groups. For example, if intuitively you felt a 'religious' tenor to your text, and you have not come up with a religious lexical set, check your lexical items again. Sometimes the most obvious literal meaning has dictated your classification, but there are some culturally acceptable secondary connotative meanings which may carry the religious overtones you detected. At times a significant set might be so scattered about in different minor sets, that you could miss it, if you had not gone back and realized that an important element of your response to the text's lexis was unaccounted for. Your lexical analysis should account for all your intuitive hypotheses and more.

Conceptual analysis reveals the most superficial and accessible response to the question 'what is this text about?'. However, because it includes all lexical items in the analysis, it also reveals the more subtle and perhaps 'covert' secondary meanings encoded in the text. Once the analyst has completed her *conceptual analysis* including analysis, results and preliminary conclusions; she is ready to continue with her *contextual analyses* (Type A and Type B).

*Conceptual Analysis Exercise

Contextual analysis

Contextual analysis is *encoder-oriented* rather than decoder-oriented. Rather than being based on the culturally constrained interpretations of the audience / decoders as conceptual analysis, contextual analysis reveals how an encoder reinforces or challenges cultural norms by the way she orders her lexis. By placing a predictable lexical item near another, she reinforces or confirms the decoder's linguistic experience and expectations. For example, when an encoder writes *queen* next to *reigned*, the decoder barely thinks about it because *queen* and *reigned* naturally belong together: both are from the same conceptual set. However, by placing an unusual lexical item next to *reigned*, like *silence* in *silence reigned*, the encoder challenges traditional meanings and gives the new meanings added significance. In other words, the meaning of each lexical item is coloured by its *context*, hence *contextual analysis*. **Contextual analysis** describes the encoder's conscious or unconscious manipulation of meaning in the way she brings together, or co-locates, lexical items and meanings.

There are two types of **contextual analysis**: Type A involves a very specific process; Type B is more random. Both can be useful.

Type A

In the first type of contextual analysis the analyst begins by choosing a lexical item as a *node*. A **node** is a word or entire lexical set that interests you because the frequency with which it is developed indicates that it is of special interest to the encoder. The node could be a participant, a setting, or a theme that seems significant in the text. The node need not be the word that is repeated the most in the text. Instead, the node is a word that both you the analyst / decoder and the encoder consider important. If you want to understand a participant better, choose the participant's name as your node, with its synonyms and pronominal substitutes. If you want to understand a theme more, choose a node that refers to that theme. Two instances of a node in a paragraph will tell you little; five to seven instances are preferable. So if the word you have chosen as node is not repeated several times, you might use an entire lexical set as the node.

Once you have selected a node, bold each instance of it in the text. Then decide on an appropriate-sized *span* for your analysis. Most analysts use a **span** of three to five lexical items on either side of the *node*. The size of span depends on the size of text, and how far apart each instance of the node is from the next. If your text is a long paragraph, and each instance of the node is far apart, use a span of five lexical items before and after the node. If you are working on a shorter text and each instance of your node is quite close, use a shorter span of three lexical items on either side of your node. This will help you avoid overlap. *Overlap* refers to places where the analyst has used the same lexical items twice in her span: *after* one instance of the node and *before* the next instance of the node. If your analysis involves one overlap, it will not skew your results; however, if it involves several overlaps, your results might misrepresent the encoder's contextual choices.

Write each node in the centre of a line, with 3–5 spaces for the lexical items in the span, on either side, for example:

_____ _____ _____ **node** _____ _____ _____.

Then, return to the text and fill in the three lexical items (not the function words) which immediately precede and follow each instance of the node, maintaining the encoder's sequence of lexical items in the way you record the span. You want to discover what lexical items the encoder placed immediately before the node / focus, and what lexical items are farther removed.

Once the span is complete, make a *conceptual* analysis of it. The goal is to *compare* the conceptual analysis of the *span*, with the conceptual analysis of the *entire text*. This comparison will show you how the encoder has developed the node (e.g. a particular character) through lexical juxtapositions.

Contextual analysis Type A is useful in determining the target / focus of an encoder's humour or sarcasm. If there is negative appraisal in the text, does it surround the character you are interested in, or does it surround and potentially ridicule something else in the text? Once the conceptual analysis of the span is complete, the analyst records **results** as before, as well as her thoughts about them in a *Comments* section.

Sometimes Contextual analysis Type A adds little to an analyst's understanding of the text, particularly when the conceptual analysis of the span mirrors that of the entire text. So much depends on the choice of node, the frequency of its repetitions, and the size of the text. The *second* type of contextual analysis is less systematic, but it is not limited to examining the collocations of a single node. As a consequence, Type B captures interesting collocations that do not show up in contextual analysis Type A. It is not limited by the selection of a single specific node. The analyst should complete Type A and B to understand the encoder's lexical choices, no matter whether one type proves more interesting than the other.

Type B

Authors who rely on a variety of rhetorical devices of ornamentation frequently use interesting lexical *juxtapositions* throughout the passage (lexical items placed beside each other). To capture these *collocations*, the analyst simply lists all the 'unusual' or unpredictable lexical juxtapositions from start to finish in the text. Such collocations may be unusual, in that the two lexical items juxtaposed by the encoder normally do not occur in proximity because they are from two unrelated lexical sets, for example. *silence reigned, the air whispered softly.* When complete, add a 'comments' section to your list where you note any patterns you observe in the unusual collocations. Perhaps, they all refer to a particular participant or setting. Also note whether such collocations can be described as a particular rhetorical figure like personification, and if so, speculate how such figures affect the decoder's response to the text. These details are then recorded in *Comments*.

Conclusions

Once you have completed both *conceptual* and *contextual* analyses (including Analysis, Results and Comments), you are ready to bring all your lexical findings together in a final lexical conclusion. As in other final conclusions, the first section is simply to **summarize** the findings / results from each form of lexical analysis. Sometimes it is helpful to organize the summary of lexical sets into broader generalizations: participants / characters, events / plot, setting / circumstances (temporal, geographical, social). For example, a river, nature and building set may be grouped together as lexical sets that develop setting; while a part of body, profession, emotion, clothing and people set might be grouped together as lexical sets that develop character. As in other chapters, your results are best communicated in a blend of generalizations, frequency counts and specific examples. Your summary should make what the text is about very clear. In addition, it will uncover subtle secondary meanings if they are encoded, as well as subjective positioning (cf. appraisal).

In the second section of the conclusions, the analyst **interprets** her findings in terms of contextual matters like register and purpose. While the original *conceptual* analysis of the text reveals the primary and secondary experiential meanings of the text available to the decoder from her cultural context, the *contextual* analyses (A and B) reveal how the encoder has manipulated these by lexical collocation in order to either reinforce the conceptual meanings by predictable collocations or challenge them by unpredictable juxtapositions. The predictability of the encoder's lexical choices may relate to the register and purpose of the discourse among other things. Books and articles that are designed to teach are likely to include predictable collocations that do not distract or confuse decoders. In opinionated reviews, stand-up comedy sessions and advertisements, unusual juxtapositions may encode sarcasm or humour, or simply revitalize the language so the decoder pays attention. Predictable lexical collocations are often interpreted literally, while unpredictable collocations may illumine a whole sub-text of secondary meanings that extend or undermine the literal interpretation.

Example

Text

'*Wanted: Men who can handle a real road machine. Dodge Challenger Rallye.*
There are special men who develop an almost spiritual attachment to their cars. They want a no-nonsense road machine that grabs a rough, winding stretch of road and holds on. One that stays low and close to the road like a snake. For these men, Dodge builds Challenger Rallye. A trim, taut, tough car that hugs every inch of road it goes over. Why? Because of Challenger's torsion bar suspension. No mushy coil springs for this car – only responsive torsion bars and leaf springs will do. They combine to give you a firm, honest ride all the time' (Chrysler, 1973).

Conceptual analysis

Wanted2	men3	handle	road5	machine2	dodge2	challenger3		special
	They2	grabs	Rallye	cars3		cars3		*violence*
	you	holds	cars3			torsion2		grabs
			ride			suspension		handle
			goes			bar2		holds
						springs / they		rough
								challenger3

	quantity		*romance*				*shape*	*measurement*
develop	almost	spiritual	attachment	no-nonsense	rough		winding	stretch
builds	every		hugs	real	taut		coil	inch
combine			mushy	honest	tough		*muscles*	
			responsive		firm		develop / build	
			give				tough	

position		*question*			*nature*			firm
low	snake	why		no	leaf	do	time	taut
close					springs			mushy
over								
on								

masculine values: rough, tough, taut, firm, honest, real, no-nonsense, men, special, challenger3
sex: handle, grabs, holds, attachment, hugs, mushy, responsive, give, men, special, wanted2, snake
car driving: road 5, rallye, cars3, ride, goes, machine2, dodge2, torsion2, suspension, bar2, springs 2, challenger3

Note: **Labels** are *underlined* if a lexical item in the set, or *italicized* if not a lexical item in the text.

Results

> **Major** (8–24): ride11, car12, car driving24, masculine values12 , sex13
> **Medium** (4–7): men6, tough4, romance5, machine5, muscles6, violence7, position4
> **Minor** (1–3): snake, question, no, do, time, nature2, spiritual, special, shape, measurement, quantity2, builds3, wanted2, holds3, challenger3, honest3
> *Situation* – car ad
> **Predictable** / unmarked: ride, car, car driving, people, machine, dodge, shape, measurement, quantity, position, men, special
> **Unpredictable** / marked: masculine values, sex, tough, attachment, snake, question, nature, time, no, honest, spiritual, builds, holds, wanted, challenger, violence, romance

Contextual analysis

Type A

Handle	Real	Road	**Machine**	Dodge	Challenger	Rallye
Real	Road	Machine	**Dodge**	Challenger	Rallye	Special
Spiritual	Attachment	Their	**Cars**	They	Want	No-nonsense
Want	No-nonsense	Road	**Machine**	Grabs	Rough	Winding
Stretch	Road	Holds	**One**	Stays	Low	Close
Road	Snake	Men	**Dodge**	Builds	Challenger	Rallye
Trim	Tough	Taut	**Car**	Hugs	Every	Inch
Road	Goes	Over	**Challenger's**	Torsion	Bar	Suspension
Mushy	Coil	Springs	**Car**	Only	Responsive	Torsion

Wanted2	men	handle	road6		dodge	challenger3	special	*violence*
	They2	grabs	Rallye3		torsion2			grabs
		holds	ride		suspension			handle
			goes		bar2			holds
					springs			rough
								challenger3

	quantity		*romance*			*shape*	*measurement*
	every	spiritual	attachment	no-nonsense2	rough	winding	stretch
builds			hugs	real	taut	coil	inch
			mushy		tough	*muscles*	
			responsive		taut		

position   tough
low   snake   mushy
close   builds

masculine values: rough, tough, taut, real, no-nonsense, men, special, challenger3, violence7

sex: handle, grabs, holds, attachment, hugs, mushy, responsive, men, special, wanted2, snake

car driving: road 6, rallye3, cars3, ride, goes, machine2, dodge1, torsion2, suspension, bar, springs, challenger3

Note: only items in span are included (not in node).

Comments – some frequencies are greater in span than complete text because of a few overlaps.

Range of lexical sets much the same as in conceptual analysis of entire text, because span of node *car* is almost the same size as the entire text – this is predictable in a car advertisement.

Results

Major: ride11, car9, car driving24, masculine values12, sex13
Medium: men3, tough4, romance4, machine5, muscles7, violence7
Minor: wanted2, holds3, shape3, real3, builds, quantity, snake, position2, measurement2, spiritual
Predictable: rides, car, car driving, people, machine, dodge, shape, measurement, quantity, position, men, special
Unpredictable: masculine values, violence, romance, sex, snake, muscles, spiritual,

Type B: real road, spiritual attachment cars, no-nonsense road machine, grabs rough . . . road, road holds on, one . . . road snake, trim car, car hugs, leaf springs, firm honest ride.

Comments – car items seem unusually juxtaposed to items pertaining to sex or male values.

*Exercise: Conceptual Analysis
*Exercise: Contextual Analysis.

Conclusions

Summary
There is much that is experientially predictable about the conceptual taxonomies in the Dodge car ad. There is a very large *car driving* set (24 items) which can be sub-classified in major sets of *ride*(11) and *car*(12) and medium and minor and minor sets of *men, machine, shape, size, quantity, position, measurement*. However, there are several unpredictable lexical sets too: *masculine values*(9) like '*tough, rough, honest, real, no-nonsense*' and so on; *sex*(12), *muscles*(6), *romance*(5), *violence*(4) and minor sets: *snake, nature, honest, spiritual, builds, challenger, wanted, time*. Many of these unpredictable sets, particularly those associated with values, encode interpersonal evaluation through appraisal.

Contextual analysis Type A is not that valuable in analysing the lexis of this ad because the span of the node *car* is almost the same size as the entire text. Hence, that the range of lexical sets in the conceptual analysis of the span is quite similar to that of the original conceptual analysis is not surprising, nor unpredictable in a car advertisement. A few frequencies of lexical sets were actually greater in the span than the original because of the occasional overlap in the analysis. Contextual analysis Type B is more useful here. It makes the experientially unpredictable, yet culturally predictable, juxtaposition between *car* sets and *male value* and *sex* sets very clear.

Interpretation

In some ways, then, this text is quite predictable. In the verbal portion of the car advertisement, the predictable experiential meaning of the text is encoded lexically by several items: *car* (2x), *ride, machine, coil springs*. The *car driving* set (24 items), including several smaller related sets, makes the focus of the ad very clear, as is important in a register whose communicative purpose is to sell a product. That the name of the car, Dodge Challenger Rallye, is repeated several times in the text, including the title of the text (which is graphologically highlighted by bolding and a larger size of font), is also predictable experientially. The type of car, as well as **the field-restricted items** *torsion bar suspension, leaf springs* which describe it, identify the cultural context of the text as North American, 1970s. At the same time the technical jargon used limits the targeted decoder to those who value such automotive technicalities. The market is further specified by the lexical item *men* which is repeated.

There are other major, medium and minor sets, however, which are not predictable given the experiential focus on cars: *romance, spiritual, real, violence, muscles, male values, snake, sex*. These collocations are interesting in terms of what they say about the interests and values of the target reader of the ad. The lexical appraisal of items like *trim, taut, firm, not mushy, rough, tough, grabs, responsive, no-nonsense* seems gender specific, and brings to mind other intertextually relevant texts of the time. While naming the car in the title is predictable, forefronting and theme marking it with *Wanted: Men who can handle a real road machine* is not. It brings to mind posters from American westerns: *Wanted Dead or Alive*. There was also a book title by Bruce Feirstein that became a popular slogan that seems relevant *real men don't eat quiche*. Although the book came out in 1982, a few years after the Dodge ad was produced, it captures the stereotypical views of masculinity that middle-aged decoders still remember: views that idealize cowboys and even criminals as 'real' men.

The lexical collocations, while unpredictable given the experiential focus on cars, are quite predictable in its cultural context, given the gender of its target audience: men. In a culture where market research is assumed, it is not unusual to sell a product by juxtaposing the product's characteristics to the values of the target audience. In Chapter 2, car advertisers attempted to sell a car to women by juxtaposing car lexis with yoga lexis; here, they use masculine values, sex, muscle and violence to persuade. Although such sets would be unpredictable in a register such as a car manual with a communicative purpose of informing, in a car advertisement designed to persuade (and manipulate?) they are unmarked. *Spiritual* and *romance* sets seem unusual. However, in North America, men's 'special relationship' to their cars is part of our cultural heritage. In a poem called *she being brand* American poet E. E. Cummings also collocates *car, female* and *sexual* lexis, and in a personal birthday message in a local newspaper as recently as 2002, the encoder did the same.

Lexical analyses, both conceptual and contextual, show how the lexical style of the encoder contributes to the decoders' interpretation, given their cultural context, the register of the text and the encoder's communicative purpose. And this particular analysis reveals how certain cultural beliefs, values and assumptions are created, maintained and reinforced by the way lexical items are arranged and juxtaposed. This text paints a clear picture of how a man's social identity and social reality may be constructed lexically by producers with an ulterior motive.

Lexis and the metafunctions

Experiential

Experiential meaning is often the most accessible to decoders, encoded in the words pertaining to the participants, events and circumstances. When someone responds to the question *what is the text about?* her answer will include a representative selection of experiential lexis. In certain specialized situations and registers, though, the experiential meaning of the text may be less clear. This may be a consequence of an overabundance of field-restricted words that can be interpreted by specialists only, or it may result from how the words are put together in long and unwieldy sentences. In the financial section of a newspaper, the *experiential* meaning is still too 'field' restricted to be interpretable by the general public. Still, readers can tell the experiential realm of the text is *finance* by the presence of words like *market, stock, percent, company.*

> Nortel Networks was the story of the TSE last year, soaring 272.7 per cent, driving up the stock of affiliate BCE Corp. and accounting for the lion's share of the Canadian market's advance. The Brampton, Ont.-based telecommunications giant rode higher in tandem with other telecom companies worldwide. Ottawa-based Corel Corp. emerged from the market's doghouse and rode a frenzied wave of excitement over Linux, an alternative computer operating system for which the company has developed software.
>
> (S. Northfield, 2000)

Interpersonal

It is not so much the field-restricted terms that prove difficult to interpret in the financial text, but the *evaluative* words, slang and metaphors: *soaring, market's doghouse, rode a wave, telecommunications giant, market's advance.* In addition, the emotional words are unpredictable in a text pertaining to finances: *frenzied, excitement.* Such evaluative and emotional meanings reflect the **interpersonal** function of language: the interactants' personal attitudes towards their world. The journalist encoder sets himself up in an asymmetrical relationship of authority with his readers when he writes *Corel Corp. emerged from the market's **doghouse** and road a **frenzied** wave of **excitement**.*

Subjectively evaluated lexis is classified as *involvement* or *appraisal*. **Involvement** offers language users a way of constructing various levels of intimacy and affiliation by using slang, vocatives (names), swearing, technical and jargon / field-restricted words (e.g. *byte, web, mouse* in the computer world) as a means of showing the interpersonal relationship between interlocutors (Eggins and Slade 1997, pp. 124–43). **Appraisal** reflects the personal attitudes of language users towards the world, and is measured along a range of dimensions including: certainty, emotional response, social evaluation and intensity (ibid.).

The system of *appraisal* has been further classified into *engagement, graduation* and *attitude.* **Engagement** refers to the use of certain words like *perhaps, seems, surely, alleged, suggest* to 'adjust the arguability of propositions and proposals' (Martin and White, 2005). **Graduation** refers to words like (1) *slightly, somewhat, very, completely* through which speakers increase or decrease the 'interpersonal impact' of their utterances, and (2) *kind of, effectively, pure, true* through which speakers blur or sharpen the focus of their experience (ibid.). For example, when someone says 'she is *kind of* my friend', they are adding an interpersonal graduation that is different than 'she is my *true* friend'. **Attitude** refers to the speaker's positive or negative assessments of an experience in terms of emotional response or social norms and values. For example, words like *interesting, love, hate, sadly, frightened, hero, scoundrel* indicate attitude.

Attitude is further classified into *affect, judgement* and *appreciation.* **Affect** refers to words coloured by an individual's emotions: *pleases, worried, proud, enrage.* **Judgement** refers to words like *hero, greedy, unreasonable, bravery* which assess human behaviour in terms of social norms and ethics. **Appreciation** refers to the evaluation of objects, processes, and states of affairs using words such as *beautiful, good, great, simplistic, exhilarating, horrible, fascinating.*

Textual

One of the important ways that **textual** meaning is encoded in discourse is through *cohesive devices* that connect one sentence to another. In Halliday and Hasan's seminal book on cohesion, they describe **lexical relations** as the cohesive ties that form between sentences including repetitions, synonyms and collocations of a single lexical meaning (1976, Chapter 6). Because function words are not lexical items, they are not involved in lexical relations. Repeated personal pronouns are considered reference rather than lexical relations.

There are three types of lexical relations: reiteration, synonymy and collocation. Although cohesion is defined as those relationships that connect different independent clauses, the analyst need not attend to syntax and clause boundaries when describing lexical relations.

Reiteration (Lr) – Reiteration is a lexical relation which involves the repetition of a single lexical item in subsequent clauses. Each time the word, or a form of the word, is repeated a cohesive tie is formed between that instance and the original lexical item. Different morphological forms of a word, for example *servant, serve* are considered the same lexical item.

E.g. The *servants* wanted higher wages. *Serving* people is not easy.

Lr

Synonymy (Ls) – Instead of repeating a lexical item, some encoders use *synonyms* of the lexical item. These synonyms form cohesive ties with the original lexical item. Different types of synonymy depend on the nature of the lexical relationship between the two words: synonymy (virtually same meaning, e.g. *shut* and *close*), super-ordinate (general and specific, e.g. Honda and car), hyponymy (general words like *person, girl, child, thing, object, idea, fool, place* and their unique referent like *Catherine*), meronymy (part-whole, e.g. *car* and *tire*), antonymy (opposites, e.g. *black* and *white*).

E.g. My *Audi* just had a brake job. I have had that *car* for two years.

Ls

Collocation (Lc) – When different words from the same lexical set are used in different clauses, the lexical relation that creates cohesion is called *collocation*. The word *ground* is not synonymous with *tree,* yet its co-occurrence with *tree* is not unusual, so it generates a cohesive force when used in subsequent sentences. Lexical collocation does not form as strong a cohesive tie as lexical repetition.

E.g. My *car* just had a brake job. Now, ***driving*** feels much safer,

Lc

Chains of identity

When there is a chain of repetitions, synonyms or collocates that *identifies* the same participant or object as the first instance of the lexical item, it is called a **chain of identity.**

*Exercise: Lexical Relations
*Exercise: Lexis and the Metafunctions
*Exercise: Lexical Appraisal and More

Review of lexical analysis

Analysis

Preparation
In a few words, describe your **first impressions** of the lexical character of the text, write them down and put them aside until later. Make notes about any **preliminary** thoughts, **expectations, hypotheses,** concerning the lexical character of the text.

Description
Conceptual analysis

1. **Classification:** Start at the beginning of the text and write one **lexical item** at a time across the top of a page. When you come across a lexical item that is in the same conceptual realm as one already listed, include that lexical item in the appropriate set. In this way you begin to form lists of related items: the lexical sets which represent the conceptual cultural taxonomies interpreted by the decoder. Continue until you have classified each lexical item in the entire text.
2. **Label** each of the lexical sets (graphological lists / columns) with the most precise and representative word you can come up with.
3. **a. Check** the *internal consistency* of each set to ensure that all items belong in the set as labelled. Remember your conceptual taxonomies are to reflect the decoder's stance, the typical native-speaker's linguistic expectations.
   b. Re-evaluate the *single item sets*. Do they really belong on their own, or would they be represented more accurately as a subset of another lexical set?

    c. If your sets are lengthy, sub-classify. If they are too small, further generalize.

4. Note foreign words, field-restricted jargon, evaluative lexis, monosyllabic / polysyllabic tendencies.

5. After you have completed your conceptual analysis, **reread** your passage and make sure that your conceptual sets describe *all* the lexical meanings to which you have intuitively responded.

Contextual analysis

Type A

1. Decide on a **node** (a significant character, theme etc.)

2. Determine an appropriate-sized **span** (3–5 lexical items on either side of your node), and make a table of your node with all the lexical items in the span. Maintain the encoder's sequence.

3. Do a **conceptual analysis** of the lexical items in the span.

4. **Compare** the conceptual analysis of the *span* in your contextual analysis with your original conceptual analysis of the *entire* text.

Type B

Make a list of all the **unusual lexical juxtapositions,** or collocations, in the text, from first to last.

Contextualization

Situation – Describe the relevant field, personal and functional tenor and mode of this communicative event. Is there a ***represented* communicative event** in the text, as well as the ***interactive*** one?

Register – Identify the **register** of the text, whether literary or non-literary.
Are the lexical features of the text a function of the register?
What lexical nuances make your text unique in terms of its register?

Purpose – Identify the purpose of this text.
How does the lexis further this purpose?
Strategies: How does the lexical style make sense given the rhetorical strategy of the text.

Metafunctions – Describe how the lexical choices highlight particular **metafunctions**.

    i. Experiential

      What conceptual sets communicate the experience that is developed in this text?
      What do they reveal about the participants, events and circumstances / setting?
      What themes are encoded in major or minor lexical sets?

    ii. Interpersonal

      To what extent is the encoder's lexis *evaluative*?
      What type of **involvement** or **appraisal** does the encoder rely on?

What does this say about the interactants' relationship in terms of frequency of contact, power, affective involvement, and formality or informality?

iii. Textual

    Cohesion – Lexical relations: repetition, synonymy, collocation.

Linguistic context

a. Describe the way other linguistic information relates, reinforces and challenges the lexical choices of this text, for example *phonological, syntactic, graphological*.

b. Note where in the entire text, the analysed text is found (first page, middle, end etc.)?

Cultural context and dialect

a. Who is the **encoder**? How do her lexical choices reflect her situation, culture, beliefs and values? How do they express her social identity and reality?

b. Who is the ***intended* decoder** (the expected / target audience)? How might her situation and culture, and experience of the register affect her interpretation of the encoder's lexical choices?

Who is the **actual decoder**? How might her situation and culture, and experience of the register affect her interpretation of the encoder's lexical choices?

Results

a. Frequency counts and totals of various conceptual taxonomies / lexical sets.

Once your conceptual analysis is complete, the frequencies must be tallied for each set (including all instances of each item) and tabled in the results.

b. Distinction between major / minor sets, and if analysis warrants it, **medium sets**.

Decide which lexical sets will be classified as major, minor and medium according to frequencies in results. The numerical cut off point for one or the other is arbitrary. The analyst has to have the ultimate discretion, but if there are several borderline cases, feel free to note that in your comments. You need to begin to consider the encoder's lexical style: Is there a single lexical focus or several? Is the focus related to setting, theme, character, plot? What does this say about the register (speech, invitation, recipes, advertisements etc.), strategy (description, narration etc.), decoder, purpose?

c. Which results are predictable given the situation, register, strategy, audience, purpose, or **unpredictable**, atypical of the register, and hence, potentially significant (*omissions* and *subjective slants* too)?

d. Review first impressions and initial hypotheses from preparation to analysis.

e. Make notes concerning your thoughts on the findings in a ***Comments*** section.

Conclusions

It is in your final lexical conclusions, where you bring all lexical information together and contextualize it. In the first part of the conclusions you *summarize* your findings; in the second part you interpret your findings in terms of situation, register, strategy, cultural and linguistic context, encoder and decoder and the metafunctions. The following questions support the analyst in considering how writers mean what they mean, write what they write, or say what they say.

1. **Summary – *What*** *lexical choices, what **lexical style** did the encoder deem best to create her meaning?*
   How *did she create meaning using lexical resources?*

2. **Interpretation – *Why*** *did the encoder choose this lexical style to communicate her intended meaning?*
   How do considerations of situation, register, purpose, strategy, linguistic context, and the metafunctions explain and justify the encoder's lexical choices?
   How do the encoder's graphological, phonological, syntactic etc. meanings reinforce or challenge her lexical choices? (relevant if you are completing all forms of analysis)
   How might the positioning of the text in its broader context / discourse explain its lexical choices?
   Why do you think the writer made these selections and not others?
   How has the encoder's situation and culture affected her intended message?
   How do these selections affect the actual readers? What is their response to these choices?
   How might the decoder's situation and culture affect her interpretation?
   *To what extent do you think the actual reader's **interpreted meaning / reading** will compare to the **intended reading**?*

Further reading

Martin, J. and White, P. (2005). *The Language of Evaluation: Appraisal in English*. New York: Palgrave Macmillan.

5 Syntax

Introduction

The following seven sentences are quite similar in meaning:

1. The boy threw the old plastic bucket into the pond.
2. The boy threw the bucket which was old and which was plastic into the pond.
3. He threw it there.
4. The old plastic bucket was thrown into the pond by the boy.
5. The boy is throwing the old plastic bucket into the pond.
6. Did the boy throw the old plastic bucket into the pond?
7. Boy, throw the old plastic bucket into the pond.

Graphologically, they are much the same length, each beginning with an upper-case letter and a period (except #3 and 6). Phonologically and lexically, they cover much the same range of sounds with the same lexical items *old, plastic, bucket, throw, boy, pond*. Each sentence expresses much the same semantic meaning: *Someone threw something somewhere*. More specifically, *The boy threw the old plastic bucket into the pond* (#1). It is rather like a mini-narrative with a character *the boy*, an event *throws*, a goal *old plastic bucket*, and a setting *in the pond*. Yet, despite these similarities, the specific meaning of each sentence is different.

Sentence 2 is more complex than sentence 1 in that the *old plastic bucket* has become *the bucket which was old and which was plastic*. In sentence 3 all the information of sentence 1 is present, but less specifically. In sentence 4 the participant has been moved to the end of the sentence, and the goal has been moved to the front which appears to give *the old plastic bucket* greater emphasis. In sentence 5 the participant comes first, but the time of the event has changed from the past *threw* to one that continues in the present *is throwing*. In sentence 6 the truth of the event has been called into question. And in sentence 7, the event has not taken place, but rather an unknown encoder is demanding the decoder, *the boy*, complete the action. Although the meanings of each sentence are related lexically, phonologically and graphologically, the subtle differences in meaning are largely a consequence of different sequential arrangements: the realm of *syntax*.

Syntax refers to the meaning that is encoded in the arrangement or sequence of words in a sentence. The study of syntax is *descriptive*, not prescriptive: it describes the way people organize their words, rather than endorsing one syntactic style over another. English has not always relied so heavily on sequence to determine meaning. Old English was a **synthetic** language, where the arrangement of words mattered less than their meaningful morphological inflections. However, as inflections have disappeared over the last millennium, English has become an **analytic** language, where sequence carries the meaning that inflections once did.

Sentences as mini-narrative: nuclear and peripheral

Sentence as a mini-narrative is a pedagogical approach to the study of English syntax that assumes semantic participants usually come first in a statement, events second, goals third and other circumstantial information fourth, fifth and so on. It also assumes that participants, events and goals are more essential, *nuclear*, than *peripheral* circumstances. The notions of nuclear and peripheral are influenced by Pike and Pike's *nucleus* and *margin*. By **nucleus**, they refer to what has a more central semantic role in the sentence, and by **margin**, they refer to what is more peripheral to the meaning of the sentence (1982, p. 13). Peripheral circumstances add extra information to the sentence. A sentence nucleus is necessary; peripheral elements are not.

While **sentence** is most obviously a graphological unit delineated by a capital letter and terminating mark of punctuation, it is also a unit of the syntax. The syntactic hierarchy or **rank scale** from non-inclusive to most-inclusive unit is *morpheme, word, group, clause, sentence, turn*. Word *sequence* is described by elements of **structure**. The *first **nuclear*** element of *clause* structure, often a semantic participant, is the syntactic **Subject**. The second nuclear element of clause structure, encoding the *event*, is the **Predicate**, and the third element of clause structure, encoding a variety of *goals*, is the **Complement**. The fourth *peripheral* element of clause structure, encoding a range of circumstances, is the **Adjunct**. **Clause** is defined as a unit that typically includes: Subject, Predicate, Complement, and sometimes Adjunct (SPCA).

Sentences include one clause or more. The number and type of clause determine the type of sentence. The encoder's choice of sentence type corresponds to his register, purpose and audience / decoder. Children acquiring language start with single word utterances, then simplified simple sentences, and eventually they are able to encode all types of sentences. Some registers like philosophical texts and

adjunct=add

nineteenth century legal documents involve sentences that are a hundred words long. In other registers particularly informal ones like texting, teenage encoders use an abbreviated syntax that their parents won't even recognize. A few years ago, parents thought *sup* was a short form for *supper*, not *what is up?* In this text, such abbreviated syntax is acceptable for taking notes and recording findings. Only Conclusions need to be written in complete sentences.

Sentence types

gvin

Simple sentence

		Nucleus	
Semantic	*Participant*	*Event*	*Goal*
Syntactic	**S**	**P**	**C**
	1. She	made	a chocolate cake.
	2. Ralph	remembered	the book.
	3. The big brown dog	ran	to the park.
	4. The picture	is	beautiful.
	5. Your idea	seems	interesting.

Note: Not all participants are animate or concrete.

Some sentences contain a nucleus only; others contain nuclear and peripheral meaning.

center →*outside*

	Nucleus			Periphery
Semantic	*Participant*	*Event*	*Goal*	*Circumstance*
Syntactic	**S**	**P**	**C**	**A**
	The young man	made	a cake	yesterday.

Compound Sentence

Some graphological sentences contain more than one sentence nucleus.

	Nucleus				Nucleus		
Semantic	*Participant*	*Event*	*Goal*		*Participant*	*Event*	*Goal*
Syntactic	**S**	**P**	**C**		**S**	**P**	**C**
	The picture	is	beautiful, / and /		your idea	seems	interesting.

cordinating conjuction   *·equally important*

Complex sentence

Some graphological sentences contain a nucleus *embedded* in another nucleus.

		Nucleus		
Semantic	*Participant*		*Event*	*Goal*
	[Event Goal]			
Syntactic	**S**		**P**	**C**
	[P C]			

The child [wearing the raincoat with a yellow collar] remembered the book.

clause

predicate + complement

Sentence Fragments and Abbreviated Syntax

Some graphological sentences do not include a complete syntactic clause or nucleus because of artful prose, expediency or informality.

>   ***Abbreviated Syntax*** "first paragraph following conventions for most part"
>   ***Artful Fragment***   Green.

*Exercise: SPC

[handwritten: The year 2001 (fragment)]
[handwritten: The dog ate (not a fragment)]

Clause structure

Subject

Subjects often encode the *participant* in the mini-narrative of the sentence. It can be realized by a single word, *Ralph,* or a group of words *The child wearing the raincoat with a yellow.* However, Complements can also be realized by the same word(s), for example, She <u>gave</u> *Ralph* the salt. To describe a Subject more precisely, then, it needs to be described in terms of **function** and **form**, or **structure** and **class**. **Function** or **structure** describes the impermanent sequential arrangement of words. If Ralph occurs *before* the event, in the *first* position of a statement, it is a Subject; if it occurs *after* the event, in the *third* position of a statement, it is a Complement. Subject and Complement are elements of clause ***structure***. Whether the arrangement is before or after, first or third position, *Ralph* is always a ***noun*** in terms of **form** or **class**. A **noun** is a *class* category, or *part of speech*. Parts of speech reflect their more permanent, inherent, characteristics, as will become apparent in the lengthy definitions that follow. From the perspective of syntax, each word is described in terms of both its impermanent position in the clause (structure): SPCA and its permanent qualities (class): nouns, verbs, etc.

Parts of speech (Class)
Nouns (n)

- In terms of *lexical* meaning, nouns identify people, places, things, feelings etc. **Concrete** nouns describe real tangible people, places, or things like *Jay, Toronto, car.* **Abstract** nouns describe qualities, feelings, etc. like *name, weather, courage.*
- Nouns may be classified *graphologically* as **proper** *Monday* (upper case) or **common** *day* (lower case).
- *Morphologically*, many nouns are formed by **derivational** suffixes (endings): *-ness, -sion, -tion, -hood, -ship, -tude, -dom* in words like *kindness, admission, description, neighbourhood, friendship, solitude, freedom.*

Inflectional affixes (suffixes or infixes) indicate *plurality* (**number**): *-s* or *-es* as in *girl / girls, box / boxes, child / children, goose / geese.* **Count** nouns encode number in regular or irregular ways. **Non-count** nouns do not designate discrete countable units and have no distinct plural form, for example, *sheep, advice, equipment.* **Collective** nouns refer to an individual or group, for example, *crew, team, family.*

- *Phonologically*, the choice of plural **number** is marked by the /s/, /z/, or /iz/ *inflectional* suffix. The particular suffix depends on the preceding phoneme.
- *Syntactically*, nouns function as Subjects, Complements, or Adjuncts.
  There are two **cases** left in contemporary English: the *subjective* / nominative case *girl* and the *possessive* / genitive case *girl's*.
  All nouns are considered third **person**.

Pronouns (pn)

- *Lexically,* pronouns 'substitute' for nouns or noun groups (if they are not used as deictics), for example, *The old woman made tea.* *She took hours.* This means they occur anywhere noun groups do; however, pronouns seldom form groups (exceptions: *only **he** . . ., the **both** of them, the correct **one*** etc).
- *Syntactically,* **personal pronouns** are distinguished by **person** (*1st-* I / we; *2nd-* you; *3rd-* she / he / it / they), **number** (*singular-* I, you, he, she, it; *plural-* we, you, they) and *case*. There are currently three pronoun **cases**: (1) when the pronoun substitutes for the Subject, the **subjective** / nominative case *She left home,* (2) when the pronoun functions as Complement (or when it follows a preposition, e.g. *to **him***) the **objective** / accusative case *The child loves **her**,* and (3) **possessive** case *The book is* **hers**.
- *Morphologically*, there are still remnants of case endings of earlier forms of English in contemporary personal pronouns: 's' in possessive *his, hers, theirs, ours;* 'm' in objective *him, them.*
- There are several types of pronouns other than *personal* pronouns:
  - **Demonstrative pronouns** (this / that / these / those) carry **number** (singular- *this, that;* plural- *these, those*) and **proximity** (close- *this, these;* distant- *that, those*). They can act as nominal substitutes *That is the point.* or deictics *that book. Now, then, here* and *there* are called **demonstrative *adverbial* pronouns**.
  - **Interrogative pronouns** are used in questions: ***Where** are you going?* ***What?*** ***Why** do you ask?* (also *which, who, whose, whom, what, how, when, where?*). Only *who* shows **case** *who, whose, whom* (subjective, possessive, objective).
  - **Relative pronouns** 'connect' dependent clauses to main clauses, for example, *which, who, whom, whose, what, that, than* for example, *The umbrella [**which** was broken] was lost.*
  - **Indefinite pronouns** like *other, some, such,* are used as nominal substitutes *He finished **all** of his work* and deictics ***both** books.* However, some like *everything, no one* are used when the specific nominal antecedent is unknown ***Somebody** left this book.* ***Anyone** know him?* ***Nothing** is ready.*

o **Reflexive pronouns** like *myself*, *themselves* following certain verbs are not common in Canadian English, for example, *She washed / wounded / burned / hurt herself*, but add emphasis *The car* **itself** *was* fine. or *He worked by* **himself**.

o **Reciprocal pronouns** like *each other* and *one another* are rare *We were taught to help* **one another**.

Deictics (d)

- *Lexically*, deictics are *function* words that precede, introduce, *point to* nouns, e.g. **the** books.

- The most common deictics are the definite and indefinite article. *The*, denoting specificity, is the **definite article**; while the more general *a* and *an* are **indefinite** articles. *The* is used with singular and plural nouns, *a / an* with singular nouns only.

- *Morphologically*, deictics do not take inflectional or derivational affixes except possession, e.g. *someone's* book.

- *Syntactically*, deictics precede, and modify, common nouns in *noun groups* (see following).

  Possessive personal pronouns (*my*, *its, their*), demonstrative pronouns (*this, that, this, those*), and some indefinite pronouns (*each, both, some, . . .*) also function as deictics when they precede nouns, e.g. *her* book, *this* book, *all* books.

- Deictics are called determiners by some.

Adjectives (aj)

- *Lexically*, adjectives describe nouns.

- *Morphologically*, some adjectives are formed by **derivational** suffixes like *-ible, -ive, -al, -ous, -ly, -able, -ate, -ful, -y, -less, -like* in *gullible, descriptive, lexical, famous, friendly, predictable, fortunate, tactful, gloomy, careless, childlike*.

- Many adjectives show comparison by adding certain **inflectional** affixes:
  adding *-er* forms the *comparative*, and indicates a comparison between two things.
  adding *-est* forms the *superlative*, and indicates a comparison between more than two things. Some adjectives, however, form comparative and superlative forms phrasally, rather than morphologically *taller, tallest; more intelligent / most intelligent*. And some comparisons are irregular *good, better, best*.

- *Syntactically*, adjectives typically follow deictics, but precede, and modify, nouns in noun groups (see below) functioning as Subjects, Complements or Adjuncts. They also follow certain Predicates (copula verbs) as Complements *She is **nice***. Multiple adjectives have their own internal sequence, but that lies beyond the scope of this book Eg. not *green old truck*, but *old green truck*.

The *Noun* group (ng)

While single nouns or pronouns occur as Subject, Complement or Adjunct, sometimes groups of words realize these clause structural elements: *last night, the cold weather.* Basic noun groups consist of at least one noun or pronoun with deictics and adjectives that describe it.

class: *noun group*

a. *he* b. *Cyndy* c. every *dog* d. that *old* *gray* *cat* e. *a stone wall*
ng   ng   ng   ng   ng
pronoun noun   deictic noun   deictic adjective adjective noun   deictic noun noun

Noun group structure: Noun groups exhibit a specific internal sequence or syntax. The *structure* of the noun group is determined by the position of the main noun, which is called the **Head**. Everything that precedes the Head in the noun group is called a **Modifier** (see following example), and everything that follows it is called a **Qualifier** (examples to follow after additional parts of speech are introduced). Although there is usually a single Head noun or pronoun, there can be *compound* Heads too, where two nouns are joined by *and*, *or* (see f).

structure: *noun group*

a. *she* b. *Cyndy* c. *every* *dog* d. *that old* *gray* *cat* e. *a stone* *wall* f. *Jay* and *Justina*
ng   ng   ng   ng   ng   ng
H/pr   H/n   M/d   H/n   M/d M/aj M/aj H/n   M/d M/n H/n   H/n + H/n

Graphic analysis

Clause (SPCA) and **group** (MHQ) **structural** labels, written to the left of the slash, are capitalized.

Parts of speech, written to the right of the slash, are not: ng, n, pr, d, aj.

Every word is labelled in terms of both **structure / function** and **class / form (parts of speech).**

Abbreviations are used for both.

Predicates are underlined in this chapter.

Connecting words like *and* are symbolized by +.

***Exercise: Noun Group Exercise**

Predicate

Predicates express the *event* in the mini-narrative of the sentence <u>*Come*</u>. She <u>*might not have been going*</u> to the party. Predicates include from one to five verbs in the verb group ('not' is *not* a verb). The Predicate is the structural element that determines the number of clauses in the graphological sentence: there is one Predicate / verb group in each clause.

no other meaning
only linking

Parts of speech (Class)
Verbs (v)

Linking verbs

- ***Lexically*** verbs encode a physical or mental action or a state of being.
- **Copula verbs** are 'functional' rather than lexical, in that they function to 'relate' the Subject which precedes the Predicate to the Complement which follows it: *Kai is ten.* When the Predicate is a form of the verb *to be* (*am, is, are, was, were, be, being, been*), without any other verb, it operates as a copula, as do verbs such as: *feel, seem, appear, live, have, become, get, turn, grow, sound, smell, look.*
- ***Morphologically*** some English verbs are formed from the **derivational** suffixes *-ate, -ify, -ize, -en* in *integrate, unify, specialize* and *broaden*.
- Many English verbs add **inflectional** suffixes that agree with the *number* and *person* of the Subject (see pronouns) as well as verb *tense*:
  Although there was a different verb suffix for each Predicate in Old English depending on **number** (sg. / pl.) and ***person*** (1st, 2nd, 3rd) of the Subject, in the ***regular*** verbs of Contemporary English the only suffix left in the present tense is the **s** on third person singular verbs: *She / he / it loves the cat.; I / you / we / they love the cat.* ***Irregular*** verbs have more forms:

		to be		to have		to do	
		sg.	pl.	sg.	pl.	sg.	pl.
present	1st person (I)	am	(We) are	have	have	do	do
	2nd "	(You) are	(You) are	have	have	do	do
	3rd "	(S / he / it) is	(They) are	has	have	does	do

Tense refers to the time of the verb: *past* or *present*. While *-s* indicates third person singular *present* tense, *-ed* added to regular verbs indicates *past* tense. The past tense of what were Old English strong verbs are irregular: is / was, are / were, do / did, give / gave, lie / laid, take / took, has / had, go / went, sit / sat, speak / spoke.

- **Finite** verbs show tense, number, person, polarity, aspect, voice and modality: *They have not been happy* (see the Verb group for definitions).
- **Non-finite** verbs or **verbals** do *not* show tense, number or person. They include the **infinitive** (to + verb *to be*), **present participle** (verb + ing *running*), **past participle** (verb + ed / en *given*). Past participles are ***regular:*** finished, spoken, or ***irregular:*** told, gone.
  Participles can be used as adjectives: *the **enlarged** gland* and nouns: ***Learning** is fun.* The word 'participle' is not used in graphic analysis: participles are labelled aj, n or v.
- **Monotransitive** verbs *bake, make* take one Complement; **bitransitive** *give, send, fetch*, take two; and **intransitive** verbs *snow, blink, vanish, die, cough* take no Complements.

Irregular Verbs

infinitive	present tense	past tense	past participle
to be	am / is / are	was / were	been
to have	has / have	had	had
to do	does / do	did	done
to begin	begin(s)	began	begun
to blow	blow(s)	blew	blown
to draw	draw(s)	drew	drawn
to know	know(s)	knew	known
to eat	eat(s)	ate	eaten
to speak	speak(s)	spoke	spoken
to sink	sink(s)	sank	sunk
to lie	lie(s)	lay	lain

Particle (pa) *phrasal verb*

- *Lexically* and *morphologically*, particles are 'function' words that do not inflect.
- *Syntactically*, they follow the Head / verb, e.g. He <u>looked into</u> the matter.
- *Semantically*, particles complete the meaning of the action in phrasal and prepositional verbs: *touch on, make for, deal with, care for, call for, see to, look into, broke up, go off, take back, turn on, do away with, look forward to, run up against* (see Downing and Locke, 1992, pp. 334–6).

The *Verb* group (vg)

A verb group includes one to five verbs that describe a single event. The main verb that occurs last in the group carries the lexical information describing the event, for example, *jump, think.* The first verb in each verb group indicates the tense, number and person of the main verb (except modals). Verbs that precede the main lexical verb are function words that add meaning concerning *tense, number, person, polarity, aspect, voice* and *modality.* Verbs such as *to be, to have,* and *to do* can act as main lexical verbs as well as function verbs that carry aspect, voice and more. All words in the verb group are verbs except *not* (see polarity) and *particles.*

Polarity: Verb groups are either *negative or positive* in polarity. <u>Negative</u> <u>polarity is carried by the word *not*</u>, or its contracted form *n't*, e.g. *I <u>was **not** say-ing</u> that.* If a verb group does not include *not* or *n't* it is considered *positive* in polarity automatically. 'Not' is not considered a separate part of speech, but a negation of the main verb in the verb group. Hence, it is described by a nega-tive / minus sign -*P/vg.* 'Not' follows the first verb *was **not** given, must **not** have*

been going. If the Predicate is realized by a single verb, a form of the verb *to do* is added to carry the negation (as the first verb) and the tense, e.g. *He came*. *He didn't come*. *Not* is neither a part of speech, nor a structural element.

Aspect: In English two types of **aspect** refine the notion of time that is carried by *tense*.

1. The **continuous**, or progressive, aspect indicates that the action of the Predicate is *continuing*, e.g. She ***was reading*** her book. The continuous aspect is realized by a form of the verb ***to be*** and an ***ing*** suffix (present participle) on the main lexical verb.

continuous: to be + ____ing

2. The **completed**, or perfective, aspect indicates that the action has been *completed*, e.g. He ***has finished*** his homework. She ***could have gone*** home. The completed aspect is realized by a form of the verb ***to have*** and an ***en/ed*** suffix (past participle) on the main lexical verb.

completed: to have + ____ed/en

Voice: The idea of **voice** concerns the positioning of the *doer* or participant of the action. In the **active** voice, the doer of the action is the Subject *Dad baked the cake*. In the **passive** voice, the *doer* of the action is either omitted or is an Adjunct (preceded by *by*). What was the Complement of the *active* sentence becomes the Subject of the *passive* sentence, e.g. *The cake was baked*. or *The cake was baked by dad*. This means there are no Complements in passives unless there were two Complements (bitransitive) in the active. **Passive** voice is encoded by a form of the verb ***to be*** followed by an ***ed/en*** suffix (past participle) on the main lexical verb. If a verb group is not passive voice, it is **active**.

passive: to be + ___ed/en

Modal Verbs: The meaning of the main lexical verb can be coloured *interpersonally* by the use of **modal verbs** (see Metafunctions). Modal verbs take first position in the verb group, but do not carry person, number, or tense: *may, can, could, might, must, should, would, will, shall, let, going to, gotta, got to, ought to, have to*. In addition to these modal verbs, there are some that function as modals sometimes, and main lexical verbs at others: *to begin / start, to cease / stop, to want, to keep, to continue*. These ***quasi-modals*** do show tense, number and person.

Verb group structure: Sequence is important in the verb group. The final main lexical verb is called the **Head** of the group. If there are no auxiliaries, the Head also carries tense, number, and person information, and it agrees in number with the Head / noun in the Subject. Verbs that precede the Head / verb are called **Auxiliary** verbs (X): forms of *to be* (in continuous aspect and passive voice), *to have* (in completed aspect), *to do* and the *modal* verbs. The first auxiliary which carries tense, number and person (unless a modal) is sometimes called the *operator* of the entire verb group. Modal auxiliaries come first when there are more than one auxiliary verb. Forms of *to do* can:

1. act as Head *He **does** his homework.*
2. carry negative polarity or interrogative mood *He came. He **didn't** come. **Didn't** he come?*
3. add emphasis, e.g. *He **did** do his homework.*
4. act as a verbal substitute, e.g. *He laughed. She **did** too.*

Although most verb groups include verbs only, there are a few phrasal and / or prepositional verbs where the main lexical Head is semantically completed by a ***particle*** that resembles a preposition but functions differently: They *blew up* the train. In terms of verb group structure the particle is called a **Relator.**

Examples

In the following examples, the Head of the verb group is bolded.

a. She ***sat*** on her chair. past tense
  H/v

b. They **laughed** and **cried**. compound Head
  H/v   +   H/v

c. He *was* **sitting** on her chair. + continuous aspect.
  X/v   H/v

d. She *had* been **sitting** on her chair when . . . + completed aspect
  X/v X/v   H/v

e. She had *not* been **sitting** . . . + negative polarity
  X/v   X/v – H/v

f. He had not been *being* **hunted** by the police for three years. + passive voice
  X/v   X/v   X/v – H/v

g. She *could* not have been being **hunted** by the police for three years. + modality
  X/v   X/v X/v X/v – H/v

h. He cared for the baby. She looked at the painting. + particle
  H/v R/pa   H/v R/pa

R = relator
pa = particle

* **Exercise: Verb Group Exercise**

Complement

Often a Subject and Predicate is followed by a single Complement. In the mini-narrative of the sentence Complements encode a range of *goals*. Like the Subject, they are often realized by noun groups: *My sister loves **her cat**.*

However, they are realized by additional groups including new parts of speech as well: *That song is* **very beautiful**. *The dog ran* **through the yard**.

Parts of speech

Adverb (av) (see 'Adjunct: part of speech' for *lexical* adverbs)

- *Syntactically* and **semantically**, **intensifying adverbs** *very, rather, quite, more, most, really, too* modify and precede adjectives: **very** *beautiful*.
- *Lexically* and **morphologically**, they are function words that take no inflections.
- **Limiting adverbs** *only, just, quite, right* precede, modify and form groups with parts of speech like deictics, pronouns and more, that do not usually form groups: **only** *the,* **only** *he . . . .*

The *Adjective* group (ajg)

In *That song is* **very beautiful** the most important word in the Complement, the **Head** of the group, is the adjective *beautiful*. Hence, the group is called an **adjective group**. In *adjective group structure* only intensifying adverbs like *very* can **Modify** the Head. Words that follow the Head but refer to it are called **Qualifiers**. Qualifiers of adjective groups may be adverbs, prepositional groups or dependent clauses.

Preposition (pr)

- *Syntactically*, prepositions are primarily *function* words that introduce noun groups; although sometimes they carry directional meaning **lexically** *up, over*.
- *Morphologically*, prepositions are usually short monosyllabic words without inflections, e.g. *in, at, with, for, of, through;* however, there are also **phrasal prepositions**, e.g. I *sat* (**next to** the door). (See following list for more.)
- If words that are usually used as prepositions do not introduce a noun group, they are not considered prepositions He *cared for* her (*for* R/pa). She *ran* out (*out* C/av). [Before he *ate*] he *read* (*before* A/cs).

More Prepositions

against, around, between, despite, for, into, of, outside, toward, along, as, beyond, down, from, like, on, under, upon, within, across, at, beneath, during, near, onto, throughout, underneath, versus, without, among, beside, except, inside, out, since, until, via, as a result of, aside from, by means of, in addition to, in defence of, in reference to, instead of, on behalf of, along with, as for, because of, contrary to, in connection with, in front of, in regard to, in support of, together with, apart from, as well as, by way of, due to, in contrast to, in place of, in spite of, on account of, with regard to.

The *Preposition* group (pg)

In the Complement *He walked* (***through the yard***), the **Head** / preposition usually comes first, and is followed by a noun group or equivalent: pn, rc, nfc. In terms of ***preposition group structure***, this noun group is called the **Completive**. Both Head and Completive are necessary or obligatory. **Modifiers** of Head / prepositions are rare, but possible, for example *She arrived* (***just after her birthday***). The Modifiers are realized by limiting adverbs.

Five types of complements

1. ***Objective* Complement (Co)** e.g. *He wanted **a postcard**. She wondered [what to do].*
   - typically realized by a ng or equivalent: pn, rc, nfc.
   - answers the question ***what*** in *She did **what**?*
   - traditionally called *direct* object
   - ***Projected*** clauses, in direct speech, are described as Co/ε. *She said, **Yeah, what do you want**?*

2. **Dative Complement (Cd)** e.g. *She gave **him** the drink. She gave the drink (**to him**).*
   - does not occur alone, but occurs with a Co that follows bitransitive verbs of transfer: *to give, to send* etc.
   - acts as recipient with transfer verbs (see Chapter 6)
   - typically realized by pn or n (if precedes Co); pg with H/pr *to* (if follows Co)
   - answers the question *She sent **who** what?*
   - traditionally called *indirect* object

3. **Subjective Complement (Cs)** e.g. *The man is **very old**. She lives (**in Toronto**).*
   - follows a *copula* verb, which is a function word, carrying no lexical meaning.
   - complements the Subject
   - typically realized by ajg, ng or equivalents, and occasionally pg
   - verbs that take Cs seldom take Adjuncts.
   - traditionally called *predicate adjective* or *subjective completion*

4. **Predicative Complement (Cp)** e.g. *He walked **home**. She ran (**to the store**).*
   - typically realized by a ng or equivalent, pg or sc
   - usually encodes *time* or *place* semologically, but as nuclear, not peripheral, information
   - answers questions: *arrive **when**? walk **where**?*
   - with bitransitive verbs, required with Co: *He put / placed his fork (**on the table**).*
   - follows what some consider intransitive verbs

5. **Appositional Complement (Ca)** e.g. *It made the show **worthwhile**.*
   - complements the Complement, like the Cs does the Subject
   - typically realized by n or equivalent, aj or ajg, pg
   - each Complement answers a different question *He likes his coffee **black**. (**what, how?**)*

Examples

a. He <u>was</u> the man *[I <u>told</u> you about]*.
    Cs/ng

b. The postal worker <u>passed</u> *Jay the mail.*
       Cd/n Co/ng

c. He <u>ran</u> *(to the forest)*. She <u>arrived</u> *(right after supper)*.
    Cp/pg   Cp/pg

d. The man <u>is / seems / feels / appears</u> *very old and very frail.*
          Cs/ajg + Cs/ajg

e. He said / thought *"//And / unfortunately / I <u>can do</u> nothing about it //"*.
         Co/ε

f. He <u>appointed</u> *Dr. James Director.* He <u>found</u> *her very tiresome.*
    Co/n Ca/n   Co/pn Ca/ajg

g. He <u>directed</u> *it (towards her).* He <u>knocked</u> *me (off the bike).* She <u>placed</u> *the blame (on John).*
 Co/pn Cp/pg   Co/pn Cp/pg   Co/ng Cp/pg

Graphic analysis

In this chapter, preposition groups are enclosed by parenthesis. Group structure is analysed under the particular clause structural element where appropriate.

Notes:

- Monotransitive verbs in the passive voice do not include Complements (the active Complement has become the Subject of the passive); however, bitransitive verbs in the passive, still have a single Complement, e.g. *She <u>was found</u> very tiresome.*
- To determine whether *tired* is a H/v in a vg or Cs/aj (participle) in *She is tired*, place an intensifying adverb like *very* between the *is* and *tired* to see whether the *very* Modifies the H/aj, e.g. *He is **very** tired*, in which case describe *tired* as a Cs/aj. If it does not make sense, e.g. *She has **very** finished*, leave *finished* as H/v in the vg.

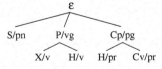

Example

1) He <u>has gone</u> (to Toronto).
    ε
   / | \
S/pn P/vg Cp/pg
   / \ / \
  X/v H/v H/pr Cv/pr

*Exercise: *Complement* Exercise

Adjunct

Thus far in the chapter, every example has included a sentence **nucleus:** Subject, Predicate and Complement, for example, *They ate spaghetti.* However, many sentences include additional **peripheral** pieces of information that add circumstantial or *setting* information to the mini-narrative of the sentence, for example *They ate spaghetti (with a fork) quickly (on Monday)* pertaining to instrument, manner, time respectively. In terms of sentence structure, these circumstantial pieces of information are called **Adjuncts** and usually occur in final position in the sentence, but occasionally *before* and even in the *midst* of the sentence nucleus (SPC). They are typically realized by n, pn (demonstrative adverbial pronouns: *now, then, here, there*), ng, av, avg, pg, sc and nfc (see clauses). A sentence may have a single Adjunct or several.

E.g. She <u>drove</u> *(to the store)* **yesterday**. or **On Saturday**, she <u>drove</u> *(to the store)*.
　　S/pn P/v　　　Cp/pg　　　　A/n　　　　A/pg　　S/pn P/v　　Cp/pg

In addition, there is another type of Adjunct that is *functional*, not carrying circumstantial lexical information at all, called the initial Adjunct. **That** is a relative conjunction that is described as an **initial Adjunct (Ai)** when the relative clause already has an S and C.

E.g. She <u>decided</u> *[***that** she <u>would give</u> him a book*]*.
　　S/pn P/v　　　　　　　　Co/rc
　　　　　　Ai /cr S/pn　P/vg　　Cd/pn Co/ng

Parts of speech

Adverbs (av) (see Complement: part of speech for *function* adverb)

- *Lexically*, Adjunct / adverbs that are *lexical* items pertaining to time, place, manner, reason, instrument etc. are part of *clause* structure (SPCA). **Intensifying** and **limiting** adverbs that are *functional* are part of *group* structure (MHQ).
- *Syntactically*, Adjunct / adverbs occur finally, initially or medially in the clause eg. He **soon** <u>forgot</u> the reason.
- *Morphologically*, some adverbs (like adjectives) form **comparatives** or **superlatives** by adding the inflections *er / est* or the words *more / most* in phrasal examples eg. *quicker, most happily.*
- Many adverbs can be identified by an *-ly* suffix He <u>went</u> home **quickly / carefully / quietly**.

The *Adverb* group (avg)

In terms of *group structure*, the *lexical* item in the adverb group is the **Head /** adverb, for example *very **soon**. Functional* adverbs may precede the Head /

adverb as **Modifiers,** for example *quite quickly*. Occasionally the Head / adverb may be followed by an adverb, prepositional group or dependent clause acting as **Qualifier,** for example *Soon **enough** <u>he will be leaving</u>* home.

Examples
    a. *Last night* he <u>ran</u> home *just quickly enough.*
      A/ng   S/pn P/v Cp/n   A/avg
      M/aj H/n   M/av H/av Q/av

    b. *Now* she <u>left</u> Toronto (*for a job*).
      A/pn S/pn P/v Cp/n   A/pg

    c. She <u>would</u> *soon* <u>be leaving</u> Canada.
      S/pn   A/av   P/vg   Cp/n
           X/v   X/v H/v

Graphic analysis: Clause and group structure
Preparation: *Underline* the P/vg, and surround any pg with *parenthesis*. Each tree starts with the Greek Epsilon sign at the top ε.

    1. a. Identify **clause** structure: SPCA.
       b. Determine the *part of speech* or *group* that realizes each element of clause structure, e.g. S/ng.
    2. a. Identify **group** structure: MHQ (ng, ajg, avg), XHR (vg) or HCv (pg).
       b. Determine the *part of speech* or *group* that realizes each element of group structure,
          e.g. M/av H/pr Cv/ng.
       c. If there are groups within groups, continue 2.a. and b. until every word has *two* labels: *structure* and *part of speech*. Then, the analysis is complete.

Notes:
- Arrange all these two-part labels in a hierarchically arranged **tree** with the most inclusive labels at the top (the entire sentence) and the least, the individual words, at the bottom.
- Make sure that the lines always join the group structural elements to the appropriate clause structural element which they realize.
- Because all clause structural elements occur at the same **level**, they are written on the same horizontal line, in the same sequence as the words in the sentence. As much as possible, try to place the label in the tree under the corresponding word in the sentence written above.
- As sentences become increasingly complex, the ideas of nucleus (SPC) and periphery will help you decipher sentence structure.

Example

The wall (of very old stone) <u>is</u> (in Scotland)

```
                            ε
          _____|_____
         |                   |           |
       S/ng                 P/v        Cs/pg
      ___|___                        ___|___
     |   |   |                      |       |
    M/d H/n Q/pg                   H/pr    Cv/n
          ___|___
         |       |
        H/pr   Cv/ng
              ___|___
             |       |
           M/ajg    H/n
          ___|___
         |       |
        M/av    H/aj
```

*Exercise: **Adjunct** Exercise*

The clause

Knowing *five groups*: *ng, ajg, vg, avg, pg*, and *eight parts of speech*: *n, d, aj, pn, v, pa, av, pr* enable the analyst to describe all simple sentences. However, the last part of speech, in a way, changes everything. **Conjunctions (+)** *connect* things: words, groups and clauses:

e.g. *Cyndy **and** Jay <u>drove</u> (through the woods **and** the town), **and** I <u>followed</u> them.*

Sentence	ic			**+**	ic		
Clause	S/ng	P/v	Cp/pg		S/pn	P/v	Co/pn
Group	H/n + H/n		H/pr Cv/ng + Cv/ng				

Although the idea of connecting one clause to another was exemplified in the compound and complex sentence types mentioned earlier in the chapter, there has been no way of analysing the connections operating between clauses. To do so, requires the syntactic rank of **sentence**, and a further distinction between types of conjunctions and types of clauses. There are **independent clauses (ic)**, which are complete in themselves, and **dependent clauses**, which are not. Each clause must include a *finite* **verb group** (shows person, number, tense, aspect, voice and polarity) or a *non-finite* **verbal group** (does *not* show tense, person, or number). Hence, the number of clauses equals the number of P/vg.

In some independent clauses both dependent (*secondary clause*) and main clause (*primary clause*) are complete (see *a*); in others the main clause is incomplete without the dependent clause (see *b*).

a. [After she <u>completed</u> her studies] she <u>travelled</u> (to Flensburg).
b. She <u>wondered</u> [what <u>to do</u>].

(The dependent clause in 'a' realizes an optional peripheral Adjunct; while the dependent clause in 'b' the nuclear Complement.)

Parts of speech
Conjunctions (c)
- *Lexically*, conjunctions are *function* words.
- *Syntactically*, conjunctions *connect* words, groups and clauses to others that are the same class, e.g. n + n, pg + pg, ic + ic.
- Some conjunctions connect **independent clauses** that are equal: coordinate conjunctions.

  Others *introduce* **dependent clauses** connecting them to the main clause in the ic: relative and subordinate conjunctions.

  Others connect **interdependent clauses**: betas to alphas in alpha-beta clause complexes

  And some conjunctions connect **turns / adjacency pairs**, e.g. questions & responses.
- Six types of conjunctions: *coordinate, correlative, relative, subordinate, beta* and *polar*.

Six types of conjunctions
    Coordinate and **correlative** conjunctions join things words, groups and clauses that are *equal*.

    Relative and **subordinate** conjunctions introduce clauses that are *not* equal

    Beta conjunctions join clauses that are mutually dependent or interdependent (alpha-betas).

    Polar conjunctions join questions to answers in spoken turns.

Coordinate Conjunctions (cc)
- Coordinate conjunctions join things that are *equal*: words, groups or clauses.
- *And, but* and *or* are common coordinate conjunctions.

  e.g. over the bridge **and** through the woods (pg + pg); I <u>like</u> yoga, **and** he <u>likes</u> biking (ic + ic)

Correlative Conjunctions (cl)
- Correlative conjunctions also connect things that are *equal*.
- They involve a *pair* of conjunctions, which surround or frame the words, groups or clauses that are connected.

  e.g. *Neither* Susan **nor** John . . . He <u>went</u> **not only** (to school) **but also** (to work).
      Either / she <u>gets</u> a good night's sleep / **or** / she <u>feels</u> dreadful /.
- With correlative conjunctions, the first conjunction in the correlative pair is ignored in graphic analysis, the second is marked by + .

Relative Conjunctions (cr)
- Relative conjunctions join clauses that are *not* equal.

- They introduce *relative dependent clauses* and connect them to the main clause of the ic.
- Relative conjunctions are the relative pronouns: *who, whom, what, whose, which, that, than*. e.g. The woman [**who** lives there] is my mom.
- All, but *that* and *than* form compounds by adding *ever*, e.g. *whichever*.
- Sometimes, the cr is *implicit*, not *explicit*, e.g. She gave me the one [* I like].
- On occasion, *where* and *when* act as cr: the room [*where* I sat], the time [*when* I arrived].

Subordinate Conjunctions (cs)
- Subordinate conjunctions join clauses that are *not* equal.
- They introduce *subordinate dependent clauses* and connect them to the main clause of the independent clause.
- Subordinate conjunctions usually refer to time or place: after, before, when, where, why,
  e.g. He ate supper [*after / before* he washed his hands].

Note: cs are followed by dependent clauses including a P/vg; pr are followed by ng only. Eg. [**Before** he ate] he called us. He ate (before the movie).

                  cs   pr

Beta Conjunctions (cb)
- Beta conjunctions introduce clauses that are *interdependent*.
- Beta conjunctions such as *if, although, unless, since, while, because, for* begin the **beta** clause in alpha-beta clause complexes: e.g. / **If** it rains = I will return /.
  / He made the decision = **because** time was passing. /
- An alpha-beta clause complex, including a beta clause and an alpha clause, comprises a single independent clause.

Polar Conjunctions (cp)
- Polar conjunctions link *two turns*: a question with its answer.
  E.g. Speaker 1- Do you want this one? Speaker 2 – **Yes** *
- Polar Links are positive *yes* or negative *no*.
- The turn / response which includes the cp, often involves clausal *ellipsis* (see Textual Metafunction p. 142).

Types of clause

Independent clause /ic/
- **Semantically**, independent clauses are complete in themselves.
- **Syntactically**, each ic includes possible clause structural elements: SPCA, with the Predicate realized by a **finite verb**.
- On occasion some clause elements are missing in an ic, but are understood *elliptically* from prior discourse E.g. / He ate dinner /, and then / * went home. /

Dependent clause

- **Semantically**, dependent clauses are *not* complete alone, they depend on the main clause.
- **Syntactically**, dependent clauses may include SPCA, or only PCA depending on the type.
- Three types of dependent clause: **relative clause** (rc), **subordinate clause** (sc), **non-finite clause** (nfc).

Note: When a coordinate conjunction joins two independent clauses it adds *cohesion*; When a coordinate conjunction joins words, groups or dependent clauses within an ic, it is called **compounding**, which is non-cohesive, and is marked by a '+' (see Textual Metafunction p. 142).

Types of dependent clause

Relative clause [rc]

- Relative clauses are dependent clauses that include a **finite verb**.
- They begin with **relative conjunctions**: *who, whose, whom, which, that, what, than* (unless the conjunction is implied only).

    E.g. He <u>decided</u> [**that** he <u>would eat</u> early].

    He <u>decided</u> [* he <u>would eat</u> early].

- Relative clauses are **nominally** inclined: they substitute for, modify or qualify a H/n
- Relative clauses are equivalent to ng when they realize S or C in clauses; Cv in pg.

    E.g. *[**That** he <u>is</u> kind]* <u>is</u> important. I <u>know</u> *[**what** you <u>want</u>]*.

    You <u>will be</u> happy (with [**whatever** you <u>choose</u>]).

    The man [(with **whom**) she <u>danced</u>]) <u>was wearing</u> a military uniform.

- Relative clauses also qualify H/n in ng.

    E.g. She <u>wanted</u> the dress *[**that** <u>had</u> the gold buttons]*.

    The ball <u>bounced</u> (down the driveway [**that** <u>had</u> just <u>been</u> tarred]).

Subordinate clause *[sc]*

- Subordinate clauses are dependent clauses that include a **finite verb**.
- They begin with **subordinate conjunctions** like *before, after, when* and more.
- Subordinate clauses are **verbally** inclined: they add circumstances / setting to the event P/vg.
- Subordinate clauses realize A and Cp.

    E.g. *[**After** I <u>win</u> the award]*, I <u>will celebrate</u> my good fortune.

    The train <u>left</u> the station [**when** the last person <u>boarded</u>].

    The dog <u>wandered</u> [**wherever** it <u>wanted</u>].

Non-finite clause *[nfc]*

- Non-finite clauses are dependent clauses which include a **non-finite verb (verbal)** in the infinitive, past or present participle form, none of which show tense, person or number.
- They do *not* begin with a *conjunction*.
- They may show aspect and voice.

  E.g. [*Having learned* math] I <u>will</u> now <u>study</u> physics.   M/nfc in S/ng is completed.

  He <u>wanted</u> [*to be finished* his work].   Co/nfc is passive

- In order to be called a non-finite clause, the P/verbal must be followed by a Complement or Adjunct. (Alone, verbals act as adjectives or nouns (gerunds)).

  E.g. [<u>Learning</u> *linguistics last year*] <u>was</u> challenging.   S/nfc

      P/vb   Co/n   A/ng   Cs/aj

- Although they usually begin with verbals, they may start with Subjects, but Subjects that are not in the subjective case.

  E.g. He <u>wanted</u> [*her* <u>to leave</u> home].   Co/nfc

      She <u>thought</u> [that [*his* <u>learning</u> math] <u>was</u> great]   S/nfc in Co/rc

- They may function anywhere a relative or subordinate clause does.

  E.g. (*By [<u>rolling</u> her eyes]*) she <u>hoped</u> [*to catch his attention*]. Cv/nfc in A/pg Co/nfc

      [*Having spent* his grief] he <u>moved</u> quickly.   M/nfc in S/ng

      The woman [<u>filled</u> with anticipation] <u>ran</u> to the post office   Q/nfc in S/ng

Note: The *to* that signals an infinitive form is considered part of the Head / verbal, not a separate word in itself. It is not a preposition (prepositions precede noun groups, not verbs).

Alpha Beta clause complexes

- **Semantically**, different beta conjunctions signal different types of logical relationships between the two clauses (see Chapter 6, p. 177).
- **Syntactically**, alpha and beta clauses are mutually **interdependent** clauses that comprise a single independent clause (cf. Gregory, 1995, p. 218).
- *beta* clauses begin with a beta conjunction like *because, if, although, since, unless*, and the other clause involved is the *alpha* clause.
- *beta* clauses may come first or second in the clause complex.

  e.g. / **If** *it rains* = our picnic will be cancelled. /

      / He left = **because** *he was tired*. /

      / He left = **so** *he would make the train on time*. /

      / **Although** *she is tired* = she could have helped. /

Note: The single pair of slashes indicates that the clause complex is considered a single independent clause. The equals sign indicates that both clauses are interdependent.

Graphic analysis: Sentence, clause and group structure

Preparation: *Underline* the P/vg, and surround any pg with *parentheses*. *Bracket* all dependent clauses. Alpha-beta clause complexes are separated by =. *Surround* all sentence elements with slashes, and *write* ε at the top of the tree.

- **1.a.** Identify the number of *ic* in the sentence.
  - **b.** After reading the section on sentence structure, identify all elements of **sentence** structure. At this point identify the class of Proposition only, as ic. Identify the class of the Proposition only, as *ic*.

- **2.a.** Identify **clause** structure in each *ic* then *dc*: SPCA.
  - **b.** Determine the *clause*, *group* or *part of speech* that realizes each element of clause structure.

- **3.a.** Identify **group** structure: MHQ (ng, ajg, avg), XHR (vg) or HCv (pg).
  - **b.** Determine the *part of speech, group* or *dependent clause* that realizes each element of group structure
    E.g. M/av H/pr Cv/ng.

- **4.** Check that in clauses you have clause structural labels only: SPCA, and in groups, group structure only: MHQ, XHR or MHCv. If you see SPH on one level, it's wrong. Levels consider clause structure only, not group structure.

Notes:

- When a unit such as *clause* operates in a less inclusive unit such as *group*, it is called **rankshifting**, e.g. Q/rc in S/ng.
- Every time there is another clause in the tree, with its clause structural elements (SPCA), there is a new **level** of syntax. The top SPCA (the main clause in the ic) below the epsilon is level 1, and SPCA in any dc is level 2, and so on.

Examples
Independent clauses

1) /Sometimes he <u>eats</u> tortillas/, and /at other times he <u>eats</u> pizza/.

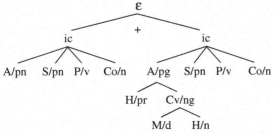

Relative clauses

2) She <u>thinks</u> [that he <u>will want</u> his breakfast really soon].

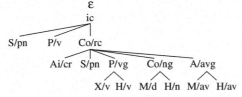

3) I <u>thought</u> [he <u>might try</u> this].

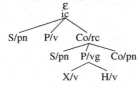

4) The book [which <u>was left</u> (in the rain)] <u>is</u> dry

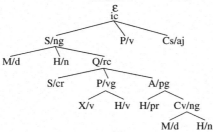

Subordinate clauses

5) She <u>came</u> home [before she <u>went</u> (to the airport)].

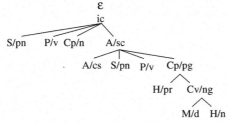

Verbals = infinitive ed ing

Non-finite clauses

not a prep

6) Jay <u>has decided</u> [<u>to leave</u> Toronto next week].

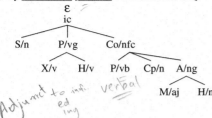

```
              ε
              ic
      ┌───────┼────────┐
     S/n    P/vg     Co/nfc
          ┌───┴──┐  ┌──┬────┬────┐
         X/v    H/v P/vb Cp/n A/ng
                              ┌──┴──┐
                             M/aj  H/n
```

Not Adjunct to infi. verbal
ed ing =

modifier of the noun

7) [<u>Broken</u> (in spirit)], Paul <u>lost</u> hope (for his survival).

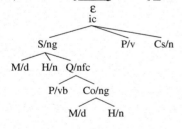

```
                     ε
                     ic
        ┌────────────┼──────────┐
       S/ng         P/v        Co/ng
     ┌──┴───┐              ┌────┴────┐
   M/nfc   H/n            H/n       Q/pg
   ┌──┴──┐                       ┌──┴───┐
  P/vb  A/pg                    H/pr   Cv/ng
       ┌──┴──┐                        ┌──┴──┐
      H/pr  Cv/n                     M/d   H/n
```

8) The woman [<u>wearing</u> the coat] <u>is</u> Linda.

```
                   ε
                   ic
        ┌──────────┼──────┐
       S/ng       P/v    Cs/n
   ┌────┼────┐
  M/d  H/n  Q/nfc
          ┌──┴───┐
         P/vb   Co/ng
              ┌──┴──┐
             M/d   H/n
```

9) (By [<u>rolling</u> her eyes]) she <u>hoped</u> [<u>to catch</u> his attention].

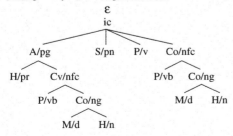

```
                       ε
                       ic
        ┌──────┬───────┬──────┐
       A/pg   S/pn    P/v   Co/nfc
     ┌──┴───┐               ┌──┴───┐
   H/pr   Cv/nfc          P/vb   Co/ng
        ┌──┴───┐               ┌──┴──┐
       P/vb   Co/ng           M/d   H/n
            ┌──┴──┐
           M/d   H/n
```

10) She <u>is</u> quite intelligent but personable enough.

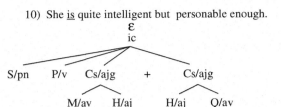

*Exercises: Relative, Subordinate and Non-finite Clause**

Sentence

Traditionally, the *independent clause* was considered the most inclusive unit of discourse. However, as soon as linguists began to analyse authentic spoken discourse, it became apparent that some words, phrases and even dependent clauses operated *outside* the independent clause: commenting on it, introducing its topic, connecting it to surrounding discourse, adjusting its mood and so on. In the sentence *when I was uh / I want to be a teacher [when like I grow up]* there are several previously indescribable phenomena. The speaker begins by making a false start *when I was*, then she shows hesitation with *uh* and later *like*. And some speakers use sounds that cannot be described by traditional parts of speech, for example, *uh, mm, oh, hey, hi.*

Creating new structural labels for such phenomenon is one thing, deciding what to call the unit of analysis itself is even more challenging. *Independent clauses* are only one feature of this larger structure. Calling it *sentence* is not entirely satisfactory because sentence has typically been defined graphologically (capital and period) in a way that is inappropriate for spoken discourse, where phonological choices do not correspond to graphological conventions. And dictionary definitions of sentence such as 'a set of words containing a verb, which is complete in itself and conveys a statement, question, exclamation, or command'. are more appropriate as definitions of independent clause (The Oxford Dictionary). Definitions of the units of spoken discourse: *utterance* and *turn* are often indistinguishable. Both are described as any stretch of talk by one person, before and after which there is silence on the part of that person, despite their different focus. *Utterance* focuses on what is being said; *turn* focuses on the succession of speakers in conversation. Such a definition does not differentiate between units that include a single Proposition/ic with its attending structural elements, and a lengthy turn which includes several of these units. Although the demands of analysing the syntax of spoken discourse illustrate the limitations of traditional grammar's ideas of clause and sentence, the written facsimile of spoken discourse in prose and dramatic dialogue also shows the need for a more sophisticated grammar to describe certain registers and strategies of written discourse.

For the purposes of Communication Linguistics, **sentence** will be redefined as not only a graphological unit, but a syntactic one which includes minimally one sentence level structural element like *mmm* (F) and maximally several *sentence level structural* elements that surround a Proposition / independent clause: Link, Speaker's Attitude, Topic, Vocative, Tag Question, False Start, Feedback, Discourse Marker. These elements of sentence structure are realized by clauses *which is unfortunate*; groups *for example*; words *and, unfortunately*; and sometimes just sounds *mm*. However, the 'class' of sentence level structural elements need not be specified, other than that for the Proposition which is an independent clause Pp/ic. Some add experiential or interpersonal meaning; however, many fulfil a textual function only. **Turn**, as the stretch of talk of a single speaker (in monologue or multi-party talk), is considered the most inclusive unit of the syntactic rank scale in that it may encode one or several syntactic *sentences*.

Sentence *structure*

Proposition /Pp/

- **Semantically** describes some state of affairs: participant, event, goal and optional circumstance / setting.
- **Syntactically**, the sentence level structural element realized by independent clause (class).
- a simple or complex sentence includes one Pp/ic;
  a compound or compound-complex sentence includes more than one Pp/ic
  e.g. / She <u>is going</u> [<u>to try</u> sailing] /, and / tomorrow she <u>might try</u> sail boarding /.
  Pp/ic Pp/ic

Link /L/

- **Semantically**, carries different logical meanings (see list below).
- **Syntactically**, connects one Proposition to another
- realized by coordinate (cc) and polar conjunctions (cp), a few adverbs (av), and prepositional groups (pg)

  logical Links /Ll/ elaboration a. *Apposition*: in other words, for example
  b. *Clarification*: rather, by the way

extension	a. *Addition*: and, also, in addition	
	b. *Adversative*: but, yet, however	
	c. *Variation*: on the contrary, instead, or	
enhancement	a. *Spatio-temporal*: there, then, and then, now, first	
	b. *Manner*: thus, likewise, so, as, similarly, like	
	c. *Causal-conditional*: therefore, consequently	
	d. *Matter*: in that respect, as to that, elsewhere	

e.g. / She <u>ate</u> supper /; then, / he <u>ate</u> /.

Pp/ic Ll/cc Pp/ic

dialogic Links /Ld/	**assent**	/ 'Do you want tea?' / '**Yes**, / I do /'
	dissent	/ 'Do you want tea?' / '**No**, / thanks /'

Note: Links signal 'conjunction': a type of *intersentential cohesion* (see pp. 142, 176–7).

In written discourse, punctuation devices like the colon and semi-colon operate between Prop/ic as a graphological Link. Periods end *ic*; they do not separate *ic* in a compound sentence.

Speaker's Attitude /Sa/

- **Semantically** evaluates or comments on the entire Pp/ic in a subjective evaluative way.
- **Syntactically** may precede, interrupt or follow the Proposition
  In final position is realized by a relative clause beginning with *which*.
  Otherwise, it is realized by adverbs.
  e.g. Unfortunately, / the child *probably* <u>doesn't understand</u> /, *which <u>is</u> a pity.* /
  Sa/av   Pp/ic   Sa/av   Sa/rc

Topic /T/

- **Semantically** introduces the topic that is developed in the Pp/ic.
- **Syntactically** precedes the Pp/ic, and is typically realized by a pg.
  E.g. *As for Susan* / she <u>has decided</u> to stay /.
  T/pg   Pp/ic

Vocative /V/

- **Semantically** names someone in a conversation or literary dialogue.
- **Syntactically** precedes / follows the Pp/ic, and is typically realized by a noun.
  E.g. *Eku*, / <u>come</u> for dinner. /
  V/n   Pp/ic

Tag question /Q/

- **Semantically**, *experiential* tags (Qe) function to supplement the speaker's knowledge; *interpersonal* tags (Qi) soften a command, *textual* tags (Qt) show a desire to continue talking. (The different types of Q are not specified in graphic analysis).

- *Syntactically* follows the Pp/ic.
  Realized by an elliptical P/vg (X/v only) + S/pn, with positive or negative polarity, or more informally, by mood particles *right? eh? OK?*
  e.g. She <u>arrived</u> yesterday. *didn't she?* <u>Open</u> the door. would you / *OK?* It'<u>s</u> green. *right / eh?*
       Pp/ic   Qe   Pp/ic   Qi   Pp/ic   Qt

False Start /F/

- *Semantically*, empty: lexical content ignored with correction in Pp/ic
- *Syntactically*, precedes Pp/ic
- Enables the speaker to hold the floor or fill the silence in spontaneous speech while she thinks what she wants to say, which she then abandons once the message is encoded in the Pp/ic.
  E.g. *I wonder.* / do you <u>think</u> [she'<u>ll come</u>]? /
     F   Pp/ic

Hesitation Filler /H/

- *Semantically*, empty
- *Syntactically*, precedes or interrupts Pp/ic
- Enables the speaker to hold the floor or fill the silence in spontaneous speech while she thinks what she wants to say; marks interpersonal uncertainty; excessive use marks teenage social dialect of contemporary North America.
  E.g./ *Well.*/ *um.* / *like.* / *ya know* / I kinda / *well* / *uh* / I <u>believe</u> you /
     H   H   H   H   F   H   H   Pp/ic

Feedback /D/

- *Semantically*, empty
- *Syntactically*, interrupts or follows prior speaker's turn
  realized by *mm, mhmm, OK, yeah, right* (with falling intonation; rising changes to Q)
- Signals that the decoder is listening to the speaker.
  E.g. / She <u>went</u> to Toronto /. / *mhmm* /

Note: If the encoder of the feedback responded with *great*, showing evidence of appraisal, the analyst would describe it as a Sa.

Discourse Marker /M/

- *Semantically*, fulfils ritualistic speech acts like greetings *hi*, closings *bye*, attention seekers *hey,* discourse boundary markers *so . . . ,* exclamations *oh*, certain dated words that signal irony *not, whatever, duh, hello* (each with marked intonation contour as a separate tone group).
- *Syntactically*, often occurs as an entire turn, occurs at opening and / or closing boundaries of entire discourse.

Note: Generally, each element of sentence structure takes its own tone group, phonologically speaking. Graphologically, in a transcription of spoken discourse, there are often tiny moments of silence between each sentence level element which are marked by a pause (.). In written discourse, commas are often used to capture these fragments of separation and silence between elements of sentence level structure.

Graphic analysis

The 'class' of sentence level structural elements need not be specified, other than Pp/ic. In the written transcriptions of spoken discourse, the conventions of written discourse do not apply: dots mean moments of silence, not periods, and question marks describe the rising intonation of questions.

When graphically analysing spoken discourse, each *sentence* (including all sentence level structural elements) is described in its own tree diagram that is topped with an epsilon. However, only the Pp/ic is analysed in terms of clause and group structure.

Parentheses are used to indicate a structural element that is missing, but elliptically understood from prior discourse eg. (S)- missing Subject.

Examples

Mmm . Uh. I <u>didn't.</u>

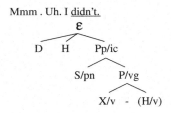

well . unfortunately . he has . /you <u>can't come</u> = because mom <u>is</u> (in Toronto)/ . ok?

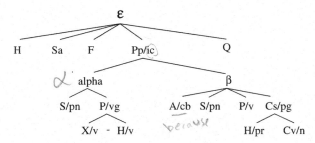

*Exercise: Sentence Level Syntax A & B

Summary of sentence, clause and group

Sentence structure

Proposition (Pp) – the structural name for the independent clause.

Link – logical (Ll) – a coordinate or correlative conjunction etc. that connects two *ic*.

    dialogic (Ld) – a polar conjunction that serves as, or begins, a response to a question.

Speaker's Attitude (Sa) – an adverb or relative clause that comments on the independent clause.

Topic (T) – a prepositional group that anticipates the Subject of the independent clause.

Vocative (V) – a noun that calls, or addresses, the Subject of the independent clause.

Tag Question (Q) – X/v + S/pn, or informal marker, that changes the speech function of the *ic*.

False Start (F) – an incomplete Proposition prior to the Pp/ic.

Hesitation Filler (H) – a verbalized hesitation before, or during, a Pp/ic.

Feedback (D) – a word or sound, without semantic content, that indicates the decoder is listening.

Discourse Marker (M) – a formulaic word that carries a boundary marking speech act etc.

Clause class

Independent clause (ic) – complete in itself as Pp/ic, includes a finite P/v.

Relative clause (rc) – begins with a relative conjunction, and includes a finite P/v.

Subordinate clause (sc) – begins with a subordinate conjunction, and includes a finite P/v.

Non-finite clause (nfc) – includes, and often begins with, a *non-finite* P/vb.

Alpha-beta clause complexes (αβ) – two interdependent clauses; the beta begins with a beta conjunction

Clause structure

Subject (S) – the first *participant* in the nucleus realized by *n, pn, ng* (including *ajg*), *rc*, or *nfc*.

Predicate (P) – the second *event* in the nucleus realized by *v, vb, vg* in *ic, rc, sc, nfc*

Complement (Co/d/s/p/a) – the third positioned *goal* in nucleus realized by *n, pn, aj, ajg, ng, pg, rc, nfc*.

Adjunct (A) – peripheral *circumstances* in statements realized by *n, pn, av, avg, pg, sc, nfc*.

    (Ai) – function word that introduces an rc, when S and C are already present in the *rc*.

Group structure in group class: ng, ajg, avg, vg, pg

<u>noun / pn group</u> – structure: Modifier, Head, Qualifier (M)H(Q).

Head H – a noun, gerund (participle), or its pronominal substitute.

Modifier (M) – Modifiers of H/n preceding the Head realized by d, aj, n, nfc.

Qualifier (Q) – Qualifiers of H/n following the Head realized by n, av, ng, pg, rc, nfc.

<u>adjective group</u> – structure: Modifier, Head, Qualifier (M)H(Q).

Head H – an adjective or participle, e.g. *nice.*

Modifier (M) – Modifiers of H/aj preceding the Head must be function adverbs, e.g. *quite.*

Qualifier (Q) – Qualifiers of H/aj following the Head are usually av, pg, rc, nfc.

<u>adverb group</u> – structure: Modifier, Head, Qualifier (M)H(Q).

Head H – a lexical adverb (p. 122) e.g. *fast.*

Modifier (M) – Modifiers of H/av are function adverbs (p. 119) e.g. *very.*

Qualifier (Q) – Qualifiers of H/av are usually av, nfc, e.g. *enough.*

<u>verb group</u> – structure: Auxiliary, Head, Relator (X)H(R).

Head H – the last verb in the verb group that carries the lexical meaning.

Auxiliary (X) – verbs that *precede* the H/v, the first X/v usually carries tense etc.

Relator (R) – the small particle required by phrasal verbs, e.g. *care **for**, look **at**.*

<u>prepositional group</u> – structure: Modifier, Head, Completive (M)HCv.

Head H – the preposition that usually begins the prepositional group. (Occasionally, two or three words act as a single preposition, e.g. She <u>walked</u> (*out of* the house)).

Modifier (M) – a limiting function adverb that *precedes* the H/pr, e.g. *just.*

Completives Cv – noun groups, or their equivalents, that *follow* the H/pr.

Note: parentheses mark optional elements In terms of *sequence*, Modifiers and Auxiliaries come before Heads; Qualifiers, Relators and Completives come after.

Word class

noun (n) – a lexical person, place, thing or quality, takes an s / es to show plurality.

pronoun (pn) – substitutes for a noun; signals dc, cohesion / coherence.

deictic (d) – a function word: articles, demonstratives, indefinite and possessive pronouns.

adjective (aj) – a lexical item, shows comparison by adding -er / est or more / most.

adverb (av) – a lexical item, shows comparison -er / est or more / most; suffix -ly.

verb (v) – describes a lexical event, shows tense, person, number, aspect, voice, polarity.

particle (pa) – a small function word that *completes* the meaning of the *verb*.

preposition (pr) – a small function word that *introduces a noun group*.

conjunction (cj) – a function word that *connects* words, groups or clauses (equal or not).

Syntax and the metafunctions

Experiential systems: *language as representation*

The following systems encode information pertaining to the participant, event, goal and / or circumstance.

A. Person – *first* I / we, *second* you, or *third* he / she / it / they; all nouns are third person

B. Number – *singular* one: *I, you, he, she, it; this, that,* all nouns without plural inflection

   plural more than one: *we, you, they, these, those,* nouns with plural inflection s / es

C. Case- *Subjective* / nominative *he,* **Objective** / accusative *him,* **Possessive** / genitive *his*

D. Comparison – *Comparative*: **-er / more** *nicer;* **Superlative: -est / most** *cutest*

E. Tense – *present* e.g. *Today she begins / is / has / walks*

   past   *Yesterday he began / was / had / walked*

F. Aspect – *continuous* 'to be' auxiliary + ___ing *He is running*

   completed 'to have' auxiliary + ___en / ed *She has finished / gone*

G. Voice – *passive*   'to be' auxiliary + ___ en / ed *The cake was made/done by Ruth*

   active   not passive *Ruth made / did the cake.*

H. Polarity – *negative* not / n't follows the first verb (operator) in vg e.g. *did not, didn't*

   positive no negative in vg

I. Transitivity – *monotransitive*: Predicate takes one Complement *He baked a cake.*

   bitransitive: Predicate takes two Complements *She gave him the ball.*

   intransitive: Predicates takes no Complement   *He vanished.*

J. Theme – **Experiential / topical theme** describes the clause structural element (SPCA) that comes first in the Pp/ic. At sentence level, **Topics** also encode experiential theme.

In the following sentences, the themes are italicized, and the boundary between theme and rheme is *marked* by #.

In **declarative** clauses, the ***unmarked*** theme is the Subject.

    a. *That she learns math at an early age* # <u>is</u> important.   S/rc unmarked theme

Marked themes are Adjuncts or Complements that precede the Subject:

    b. *You,* # I <u>love</u>.   C/pn marked theme

In **WH interrogatives** the first element, the WH word itself, is theme:

    c. *How many / which oranges / what* # <u>are / is</u> there in the frig? WH unmarked theme

In **polar interrogatives**, the first X/v (+negative polarity) is the ***unmarked*** theme together with the S/ng that follows. ***Marked*** themes are rare in interrogatives:

    d. <u>*Wouldn't*</u> *you* # <u>like</u> me to visit?   X/v + neg. + S/pn unmarked theme

In **optative imperatives**, the Predicate (+ negative) is the ***unmarked*** Theme. The ***marked*** theme occurs with an explicit *you* (see *f*) or an Adjunct in first position:

    e. <u>*Don't give*</u> # her the book.   P/v unmarked theme
    f. *You,* # <u>keep</u> quiet!   *you* as marked theme

In ***jussive imperatives***, '*let's*' (+ negative) is the ***unmarked*** theme:

    g. <u>*Don't let's*</u> # <u>give up</u> just yet.   neg. + let's unmarked theme

Interpersonal systems: *language as interaction, language as exchange*

The following systems encode the relationship between the interlocutors.

A. Mood

    declarative mood – Subject comes before Predicate. *She <u>ate</u> lunch.*
    interrogative mood – X/v of P/vg precedes Subject. <u>*Did*</u> *she eat lunch?*
        polar interrogative begins with X/v and demands *yes / no response.*
        WH interrogative begins with an interrogative pronoun: *who, which, where*
    imperative mood – often begins with P/v (Subject *you* is implied)
        optative imperative   e.g. <u>*Eat*</u> *your apple.*
        jussive imperative   + *let us*   <u>*Let*</u> *us <u>eat</u> the apple.*

Note: Initial definitions of clause and sentence presuppose declarative mood sequence SPCA. *Subjunctive* mood follows Ab *if* and P/v *wish* e.g. *If he were . . . ; She wished she were . . .*

B. Modality – modal X/v: *might, will, may, could, should, can, ought to, would, let, have to, got to,* temper meaning of H/v in P/vg; do not encode tense, person or number.

C. Sentence Structural Elements – V, Sa, F, D, M, Q, H encode interpersonal meaning e.g. ***Sir / Sweetie***, I would like *some too.;* ***Stupidly / Unfortunately***, *he* forgot *his briefcase.*

D. Theme – When V, Sa, F, D, M, H precede the Pp/ic, they encode ***interpersonal theme***.

E. Links / conjunction – Choices of L/cj reflect ***formal***: *moreover, in addition to, nevertheless* or ***informal*** interpersonal relationships: *but, and.*

Textual Systems: *language as enabler*

Cohesion and theme encode *textual* meaning. **Cohesive devices** connect one sentence / ic to another; **theme** indicates what is of thematic significance in the sentence / ic to the encoder (cf. experiential and interpersonal theme).

Thematic structure

Halliday defines **theme** as the first element of clause structure, the clause's point of departure; the rest of the clause he calls the **rheme** (Halliday, 1994, pp. 299–302). There is a close semantic relationship between phonological *information* structure and syntactic *thematic* structure. The ***Given-New*** of information structure is *listener*-oriented in that the listener already knows what has been Given; whereas, the ***Theme-Rheme*** of thematic structure is *speaker*-oriented in that it is what the speaker chooses to highlight as her point of departure. When the Given coincides with the Theme, the New with the Rheme the order is called ***unmarked***. There are, however, ***marked*** situations where the Theme coincides with the New, and the Rheme with the Given.

Experiential theme is the first element of clause structure in every Pp/ic, as well as any Topic in the sentence. **Interpersonal theme** occurs when one of the sentence level structures that encodes interpersonal meaning: V, Sa, F, D, M, H precedes the Pp/ic. **Textual theme** occurs when logical or polar Links precede the Pp/ic. **Multiple themes** may occur in a single sentence.

e.g. / *However* / *sadly* / *[when she left]* # he suddenly became interested. /
　　　　Ll　　　Sa　　　　　　　　　Pp/ic
　　　　　　　　　　　A/sc　　　　　　S/pn　A/av　P/v　　Cs/aj

Textual theme: *However*; **Interpersonal theme:** sadly; **Experiential** *marked* **theme:** *[when she left]*.

*Exercise: **Theme***

Cohesion

Cohesion is the **endophoric** (within the text), *intersentential* (between sentence / ic) binding power connecting two sentences or independent clauses. **Exophoric** signals, joining the text to its immediate *situation* or *gnostology* (memory), are non-cohesive, but add **coherence** (Malcolm, 1984, pp. 274–82). *Written* discourse is known for its cohesion; *spoken* for its coherence.

Cohesive devices

1. **Pronouns** (personal and demonstrative primarily) create cohesive ties with nominal antecedents operating in previous (or subsequent) independent clauses (see 'Reference' in Chapter 6, p. 175).
2. **Link / conjunctions** add cohesion to a text by connecting two *ic* (cf. Coordinate, Correlative and Polar Conjunctions). Syntactic *compounding* (non-cohesive) between words, groups and dependent clauses contributes to a *paratactic* style that adds *coherence* to a text e.g. *Ted and Sue*.
3. **Substitution** adds cohesion to a text by forming a tie between a particular class of words in one *ic*, and its substitute in another *ic*. There are nominal (Sn) *one, none;* verbal (Sv) *do,* and clausal substitutes (Sc) *so, not, neither, nor.*
   (presupposing signals bolded, presupposed antecedents italicized only).
   a. Which *textbook* <u>is</u> better? The **one** for math <u>is</u> excellent.   Sn
   b. Too bad, the bookstore <u>has</u> **none** left.   Sn
   c. She *walks* that path in half an hour. I **do** it in twenty minutes.   Sv
   d. *I decided to leave at five.* **So** did I.   Sc
   e. *Do you want to go home* yet? **Not** if I can help it. **Neither** do I.   Sc
4. **Ellipsis** forms cohesive ties between an omission and what it refers to. The class of the missing word or clause determines the type of ellipsis, i.e. nominal, verbal or clausal ellipsis.
   a. The *man* <u>walked</u> to the store. And then * <u>continued</u> to the park.   En
   b. Here <u>are</u> the ten *glasses*. Where <u>are</u> the three * that I <u>borrowed</u>?   En
   c. <u>Have</u> you *<u>been</u> <u>skiing</u>*? Yes, I <u>have</u> * . (X/v & H/v omitted)   Ev
   d. <u>Is</u> he *<u>leaving</u>*? He <u>may be</u> * . (H/v missing)   Ev
   g. What <u>are</u> *they* <u>doing</u>? * <u>Washing</u> dishes. (S/pn & X/v missing)   Ec
   h. Who <u>is *going to wash*</u> the *dishes*? I <u>am</u> * . (H/v & C/ng missing)   Ec
   i. When <u>did</u> *she* <u>arrive</u>? * Yesterday. (S/pn, P/v missing)   Ec

Note: When the Ai/cr, introducing a relative clause, is missing, it is *not* considered ellipsis.

*Exercise: **Cohesive Devices***

The syntactic analysis of verbal communication

Preparation

Before beginning the analysis, take a few moments to reflect on the register of which the text is an example, and the way syntactic patterns might contribute to its meaning. Once you have taken note of your **expectations**, reread the text and record your *first impressions* of it, in terms of syntax. Does the syntactic style appear to meet your expectations or deviate from them? Does it look quite ordinary or unusual? Think about the text, its cultural and linguistic context, and how it compares to other examples of the same register, strategy, communicative purpose that you have experienced. If it looks different than your expectations, be as specific as possible, without doing the analysis, about the differences you perceive. At this point you may be able to formulate a **preliminary hypothesis**, for example *Because this text was written by an eight-year-old, the syntactic style is fairly simplistic and limited in range. Moreover, because it is a description of his pet, it includes expanded noun groups.*

First impressions and preliminary hypotheses are just a place to start. Perhaps, the analysis will substantiate them; or alternatively, it may reveal a much more complicated story that illumines how the young encoder described his pet in a more complex style than predictable. Uncovering unpredictable syntactic styles, however, is not the goal. Discovering the unique character of each communicative event is. The number of variables at risk may be limited, but the range of possible combinations is limitless.

Analysis

You might treat the analysis as merely another exercise. Start by numbering the graphological sentences if it is a written text. If it is a spoken text, number the turns (1,2,3) and letter the sentences (a,b,c) in each turn. Then, prepare your sentences by underlining and bracketing, and continue with the trees: a structural and class label for each word. Remember to keep a page nearby to record your comments / insights. This will prove invaluable when you write your conclusions. Once the trees are complete, describe other syntactic features where applicable (see systems in 'Syntax and the Metafunctions').

Contextualization

You contextualize your data by thinking of it in terms of its situation and register. Many of the features you have noted in your syntactic description encode experiential, interpersonal and textual meaning; others encode communicative purpose and strategy. Some features are a consequence of the encoder's cultural context (CCC: temporal, geographical and social provenance). Some are interpreted differently than intended, perhaps, because the actual decoder lives one hundred years after the original communicative event and intended decoder. Linguistic context refers to two things: A. where the *analysed* text fits into a larger document (beginning of a section, middle, final argument etc.), and B. how other linguistic findings (lexical, semological etc.) relate to your syntactic ones.

Results

Once you have noted contextually relevant information to your analysis, it is time to table the data retrieved from the analysis itself. The results to your syntactical analysis involve listing and counting. However, counting each item from thirty trees is not as straightforward as counting items in a lexical set. There are different ways of organizing your data in order to *count* it. The following table offers one possibility, or you might devise your own table.

Labelling clause levels

Keep in mind, it is important to keep track of what is happening at each *level* of analysis separately. At sentence level, you need to count the number of each sentence level element. When it comes to the Proposition / independent clause, you can count the different types of sentences: simple, compound, complex, compound-complex, fragment. And then, within the independent clause, you count the clause structural elements (SPCA) within the main clause (level 1: *primary* level). If one of these elements is realized by another clause, its clause structural elements (SPCA) are level 2 (*secondary* level). If one of the structural elements in level 2 is realized by a clause, its structural elements (SPCA) are level 3 (*tertiary* level), and so on. *Group* structure does *not* determine *level*; however, it is recorded on the same chart as its clause structure (see next page).

L.2 L.3 L.1
E.g. / *The woman [wearing the red dress [which she bought in Toronto]] is my mom.* /
Pp/ic

Level 1   **S**/ng   **P**/v   **Cs**/ng
         M/d   H/n   Q/nfc   M/d   H/n
Level 2   **P**/vb   **Co**/ng
                   M/d   M/aj   H/n   Q/rc
Level 3   **Co**/cr   **S**/pn   **P**/v   **A**/pg
                                      H/pr   Cv/n

Numbering levels 'vertically' in the tree is not enough to identify each clause, because some clauses occur on the same 'horizontal' level as others. To deal with this, the analyst resorts to letters (upper or lower case) to describe which comes *first* (A) in the clause at a given level, which comes *second* (B), *third* (C) and so on. What is important is that each clause is identified uniquely. In the following sentence, once the description is completed, each clause is labelled individually (above its P/v).

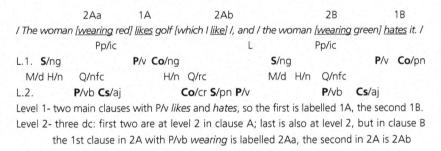

2Aa   1A   2Ab   2B   1B
/ *The woman [wearing red] likes golf [which I like] /, and / the woman [wearing green] hates it.* /
Pp/ic   L   Pp/ic

L.1.   **S**/ng   **P**/v   **Co**/ng   **S**/ng   **P**/v   **Co**/pn
      M/d   H/n   Q/nfc   H/n   Q/rc   M/d   H/n   Q/nfc
L.2.   **P**/vb   **Cs**/aj   **Co**/cr   **S**/pn   **P**/v   **P**/vb   **Cs**/aj
Level 1- two main clauses with P/v *likes* and *hates*, so the first is labelled 1A, the second 1B.
Level 2- three dc: first two are at level 2 in clause A; last is also at level 2, but in clause B
           the 1st clause in 2A with P/vb *wearing* is labelled 2Aa, the second in 2A is 2Ab

Counting

Colour-coding each *level* on the syntactic tree before counting can be helpful (e.g. L.1- yellow highlight, L.2- green, L.3- pink). Some analysts use a separate counting sheet for each level; others keep track of different levels on one counting sheet by bracketing the count for each level as follows: L.1 no brackets; [L.2]; (L.3); {L.4}. Although it is important to keep the results from each *level* distinct; the analyst can combine results from different clauses at the same level (e.g. 2Aa, 2Ab & 2B in the previous example).

You start the counting sheet by filling in the top sections concerning sentence structure. When that is complete, start counting the various realizations of Subject (involving groups and / or clauses) on level 1. After this, count the

Predicate, Complement and Adjuncts on level 1. Once the clause structure of level 1 has been noted, proceed to level 2, marking everything in square brackets. See below for a count of *The woman [wearing red] likes golf [which I like], and the woman [wearing green] hates it.* All level 1 clause structural elements: S/ng, P/v, Co/ng; S/ng, P/v, Co/pn (see earlier analysis) were counted without brackets. All level 2 clause structural elements: P/vb, Cs/aj; Co/cr, S/pn, P/v; P/vb, Cs/aj, were tallied inside the square brackets [ ].

Counting Sheet

Number of graphological sentences / or turns in your text: 1
Sentence Elements: Props 2, Alpha-betas , Ll 1 , Ld , F , V ,T , Sa, H , Q , D.
Types of sentences: Simple, Compound, Complex, Compound-complex 1, Fragment.
Clause Elements: Level 1 no brackets; [L.2]; {alpha & beta}

Note: In L2–4 keep bracket open until you complete all instances.

		S	P	Co	Cd	Cs	Cp	Af	Ai/Ab
ng	M/d	11							
	M								
	H	11		1					
	Q								
png	M								
	H	[1]		1[1]					
	Q								
ajg	M								
	H					[11]			
	Q								
vg	X								
	H		11[111]						
	R								
avg	M								
	H								
	Q								
pg	M								
	H								
	Cv								
rc				1					
nfc		11							
sc									

Note: if a Qualifier, mark in group where appropriate and then mark as pg/dc below; do *not* count the Cv/ng structure in pg; *do* count SPCA in all dependent clauses

Syntactic style totals

Once each feature of the syntactic description has been tallied on the counting sheet, the counts are added up to give totals of each feature. If the passage that has been described is very brief, writing a brief summary of the frequency totals as follows (for the previous example) might suffice:

S/ng: Md2 H/n2 Q/nfc 2   **P**/v 2 [3]   **Co**/ng: H/n1 Q/rc1   **Cs**/aj [2]
S/pn [1]   **Co**/pn 1 [1]

However, for longer passages such as the Example (p. 151) that follows, more complete totals are necessary. One of the most straightforward ways of doing this is to copy the counting sheet a second time, but this time, count the totals of each feature and record that. Any features that were not encoded can be removed from the totals summary (see Example p. 158).

Most discourse does not include syntax *below* the third level: dependent clauses within tertiary clauses. However, some encoders do resort to such complex, hypotactic syntax, particularly in registers known for their lengthy and complex sentences, for example, philosophical discourse. The point is that the syntactic tendencies of level three clauses might be very different from the 'superficial' syntactic style of main / primary clauses. In a sense, the syntax of the primary clause is more 'overt', than the more 'hidden or covert' style of deeply embedded clauses below level two. Each may represent a very different linguistic agenda of the encoder. That is why it is so important that the tallies are made for each different level separately.

Conclusions

The question is, once you have a final tally of the encoder's syntactic choices, how do you (a) use these syntactic abstractions to *describe / summarize the syntactic style* of the text, and (b) *interpret* it in a way that is meaningful and revealing. There are three ways of organizing your results that have proven useful when summarizing the encoder's syntactic style: making distinctions between a *paratactic* or *hypotactic* style, a *nominal* or *verbal* style, and a *right-hand* or *left-hand embedded* style.

When describing the ***syntactic style*** of the writer or speaker, it is useful to mention the types of sentences he relies on, and to decide if the words *paratactic* or *hypotactic* apply. A **paratactic** style (/ic/ + /ic/) may include not only compound sentences, but also examples of compounding between words, groups or dependent clauses. A **hypotactic** (/ic[dc]/) style includes complex sentences involving dependent clauses. A complex hypotactic style would include clauses within clauses at level three or more.

It is also useful to describe the encoder's style as *nominal, verbal* or *mixed*. **Nominal** styles emphasize the noun in a variety of ways. Some by expanding the noun group with Modifiers or Qualifiers; others by adding extra nouns or adjectives, where you do not always see them. This means that encoders who write or speak in a nominal style may use lots of Head / nouns; adjectives or adjective groups as Modifiers, relative and possibly non-finite clauses as Qualifiers. If the participant is the focus, this nominal expansion will likely occur in the Subject; if the goal / result is the focus, in the Complement. In some versions of nominal styles, encoders find another 'outlet' for adjective or nominal groups at Subjective Complement. In nominal styles Predicate / verbs are often copula verbs: action is lacking, as are Adjuncts giving circumstances of time and place. Strategically, nominal styles are employed more to describe people and things than narrate events. In literary works, nominal styles are often used to develop characters or describe settings.

Verbal styles, on the other hand, emphasize the Predicate / verb, the semantic event. They do so by increasing the number of Predicate / verbs, and hence clauses, in the independent clause, and by focussing on the Adjunct circumstances relevant to these actions. In texts exhibiting verbal styles, Subjects and Complements are often minimal: pronouns, proper nouns, or noun groups including a deictic and noun only. Encoders use verbal styles to narrate events (tell stories), to advance the plot in literary works, to lead decoders through a series of steps and processes in instructional manuals.

There are several syntactic factors, though, which can effectively *negate* the effects of a verbal style, and which must be considered. *Voice* is one. If the text encodes an action-oriented verbal style, but many of the Predicate / verbs are in the passive, the dynamic reality of the event is diminished, for example *The award is given for excellence in community service.* When the completed *aspect* is used, for example *She has run the race*, the immediacy of the action seems lessened. And negative choices in *polarity*, and certain *modals*, in effect, *negate* the whole action by making it hypothetical, for example She <u>might / would / could win</u> the race. Similarly, if the encoder has used a verbal style in her work, but the Subject agents of the action are inanimate, the concrete reality of the action disappears, for example *The wind <u>ran</u> through her hair.* When it is the *wind* that is doing the running there is no visible, tangible evidence of action. It is important, then, not only to classify a style as verbal, but also to ensure that all the other relevant syntactic details are included to give the complete syntactic picture.

An additional way of describing syntactic style considers the positioning of dependent clauses. If dependent clauses occur to the left of the Predicate, in other words *before* the verb group, the style is called **left-hand embedding**. If the secondary clauses occur after the Predicate / verb, to the right, it is called **right-hand embedding**.

Style is not a black or white matter, you may analyse texts that are not completely paratactic or hypotactic, nominal or verbal, right-hand embedded or left-hand. Perhaps the encoder's syntactic choices show evidence of both, or perhaps they start one way, but then, somewhere within the text, change. If syntactic choices change dramatically at some point in the text, it might be a good idea to tabulate the Results for each section separately, to avoid potentially 'neutralizing' or misrepresenting the depiction of either section. It is important to describe the encoder's syntactic choices as accurately as possible, and then as you prepare to interpret your findings, ask yourself how these choices serve the encoder in achieving her communicative purpose.

By itself, a summary of your data says little; it needs **interpretation** which is done by contextualizing the data in terms of register, metafunctions, purpose, strategy, linguistic and cultural context.

As you summarized your syntactic findings, you may have wondered *what effect these choices had on the decoder's response to the text*? In casual spontaneous speech, people often speak in quite simple, short sentences and turns. When telling stories, however, they may resort to a more cumulative rambling *paratactic* style of speaking using compound sentences. Such complexity is encoded at the end of the sentence in a *right-hand embedded* style. Literary authors create a facsimile of this conversational style by doing exactly the same: joining successive clauses together with the coordinate conjunction *and*. Encoders who wish to approximate the speech or early writing attempts of a youthful encoder may resort to a similar syntactic style.

On the other hand, the discourse, particularly written discourse geared to a highly educated audience, may be very complex (*hypotactic*). And one of the ways syntactic complexity is emphasized is when it interrupts the Subject and Predicate (a *left-hand embedded* style). This style of sentence is so important to classical authors, it has been given its own rhetorical label: the ***periodic sentence***. By effectively delaying the P/v or action of the sentence, contemporary authors also use this style to create suspense. Formally written legal and philosophical discourse also makes use of this syntactic style. Decoding such choices takes effort: time and a level of understanding that not all readers can, or are willing, to make.

The choice of nominal or verbal style often relates to the strategy the encoder has selected in order to achieve her purpose in that particular register. *Nominal* styles describe; *verbal* styles narrate a series of events. Many registers require a mixture of both. In science fiction, authors narrate their story while they describe the new worlds their characters inhabit. This may lead to lengthy Subject / nominal groups next to Predicates surrounded by lots of Adjuncts. A mixture of nominal and verbal styles can make a description more dynamic. Some authors, like Virginia Woolf, use a nominal style at one level of the syntax and a verbal one lower in syntax (cf. Malcolm 1987). Such combinations can also affect the pacing of a passage: while a descriptive passage slows reading and narration speeds it up, a mixture leads to a middle pace.

A syntactic analysis tells the analyst a great deal about the writer / speaker and the intended reader / hearer, not just the strategy, purpose and register. It tells about the temporal, geographical and social provenance of both interlocutors, and more specifically, about the experiential, interactive, purposeful and medium relationships involved. To the North American reader the sentence *I amn't coming* sounds incorrect, since there is no contraction for the first person singular form of the present tense *to be* in common usage. However, it is acceptable in certain British dialects. Shakespeare's plays are full of *thee* and *thou* as the predominant second person singular pronoun, identifying them as temporally distinct from contemporary texts. And spoken utterances like *I love um like ya know peanuts, not!* identify not only the encoder's temporal and geographical provenance as North American in the 1990s, but also her social provenance as a teenager. Other syntactic features are more common in other social dialects (cf. Bonvillain Chapters 6, 7, 11).

The subtleties and nuances of sentence arrangement may not be consciously contrived by the encoder, nor obvious to the analyst initially. Nevertheless, they are effective in creating meaning and influencing the decoder's interpretation of a text and her response to it.

Thus far you have learned about syntax from *artificial* examples, examples which may or may not have been manifested by real speakers or writers. Naturally occurring discourse is often so complex that it is difficult to control one language variable long enough to teach it, and then focus on something else. However, it is important that once you learn the descriptive apparatus suggested that you take it to *real* discourse, both spoken and written, in order to discover how real discourse compares to the isolated and artificial examples used thus far. In the following example, you will have an opportunity to review an application of this descriptive framework to real discourse.

In spoken discourse, there is no punctuation to distinguish sentence boundaries. As a consequence, the first job of the analyst is to decide on Pp/ic boundaries and the other sentence level structural elements that accompany it. In spoken discourse, each speaker's **turn** is considered the primary descriptive unit. When a turn is quite lengthy, it may include several syntactic sentences: Pp/ic, each with their sentence level structural elements. In spoken discourse, the epsilon symbol which tops each tree, denotes not the graphological *sentence*, but the phonological *turn*.

Example
Text

R – did you get a lot of harassment?

C – no. I didn't have any problems there . another place I worked I had problems

R – there's always something to think about even in the office . you see it . like a couple of secretaries that worked in the office where I worked had to do extra things like get a coffee or

C – mmm

R – or you know get the boss' clothes from the cleaners or

C – oh yeah

R – you know

C – certainly wouldn't want to do that . guess if you want to keep your job .. you know. it's fine I suppose if I was a secretary or whatever and if my boss asked me to do something like that . if he's a nice guy and I knew he wasn't taking advantage of me

R – right

C – I wouldn't mind doing it

R – and it depends on how many years you've been with him and

C – like if you're sort of friends with the guy you don't mind doing favours for him. like not . I don't mean favours (laughs)

Analysis

Preparation

Expectations – spontaneous spoken discourse so abbreviated syntax, errors, sentence level syntax

Hypothesis – informal syntax indicative of casual talk between friends, adults

In turns 3, 8 and 12, which follow, the turns included so many Pp/ic I could not analyse them on a single line; hence I called them 3a, 3b, and 3c for example. Each was divided along Pp/ic boundaries.

Text

1. R – <u>did</u> you <u>get</u> a lot (of harassment)?
2. C – no . I <u>didn't</u> <u>have</u> any problems there /. another place [I <u>worked</u>] I <u>had</u> problems
3a. R – there<u>'s</u> always [something <u>to</u> <u>think</u> <u>about</u> (even in the office)] /. you <u>see</u> it .
   b.   like a couple (of secretaries [that <u>worked</u> (in the office [where I <u>worked</u>]) <u>had to do</u> extra things / like <u>get</u> a coffee / or
4. C – mmm
5. R – or you <u>know</u> / <u>get</u> the boss' clothes (from the cleaners) / or
6. C – oh yeah
7. R – you know
8a. C – certainly <u>wouldn't</u> <u>want</u> [<u>to</u> <u>do</u> that] /. <u>guess</u> if you <u>want</u> [<u>to</u> <u>keep</u> your job] .. you know. it<u>'s</u> fine
   b.   I <u>suppose</u> if I <u>was</u> a secretary or whatever / and / if my boss <u>asked</u> [me <u>to do</u> something (like that)] .
   c.   if he<u>'s</u> a nice guy / and / I <u>knew</u> [he <u>wasn't taking</u> advantage of me]
9. R – right
10. C – I <u>wouldn't mind</u> [<u>doing</u> it]
11. R – and it <u>depends</u> <u>on</u>[how many years you<u>'ve been</u> (with him) and
12a. C – like if you<u>'re</u> sort of friends (with the guy) = you <u>don't mind</u> [<u>doing</u> favours (for him)] .
   b.   like not . I <u>don't mean</u> favours (laughs)

Syntactic description

1) <u>did</u> you <u>get</u> a lot (of harassment)?

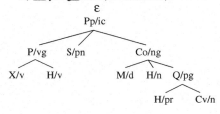

2) /no . I <u>didn't</u> <u>have</u> any problems there/ . /another place [I <u>worked</u>] I <u>had</u> problems/

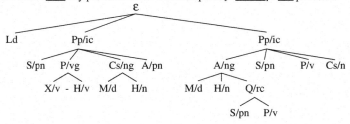

3a) /there's always [something <u>to think about</u> (even in the office)] /. /you <u>see</u> it /

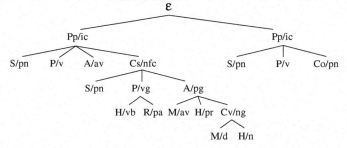

3b) /like a couple (of secretaries) [that <u>worked</u>
(in the office [where I worked]) <u>had to get</u> extra things /like <u>get</u> a coffee or/

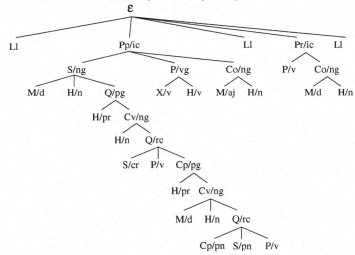

4) mmm

ε
|
D

5) or you <u>know</u> the boss' clothes (from the cleaners) or

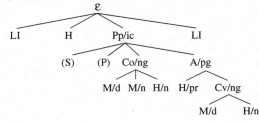

6) oh yeah

7) you know

ε
|
F

8a) - / certainly <u>wouldn't want</u> [<u>to do</u> that] /. / guess if you <u>want</u> [<u>to keep</u> your job] = you know . it'<u>s</u> fine /

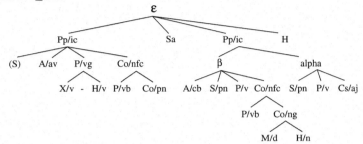

8b) /I suppose if I <u>was</u> a secretary or whatever and if my boss <u>asked</u> [me <u>to do</u> something like that] . if /

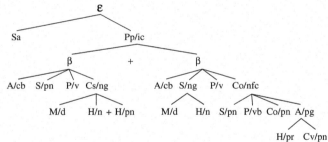

8c)/ he'<u>s</u> a nice guy / and / I <u>knew</u> [he <u>wasn't taking</u> advantage (of me)]

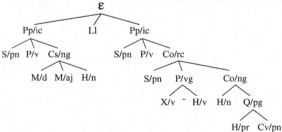

9) right

ε
|
D

10) I <u>wouldn't mind</u> [<u>doing</u> it]

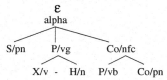

11) and it <u>depends on</u> how many years you'<u>ve been</u> with him and

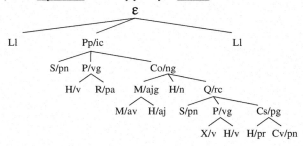

12a) like if you'<u>re</u> sort of friends (with the guy) = you <u>don't mind</u> [<u>doing</u> favours (for him)] ./

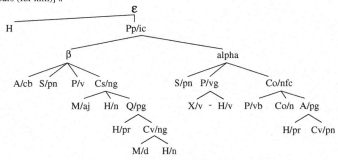

12b) like not . I <u>don't mean</u> favours (laughs)

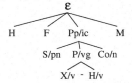

Comments – sentence 8 b, c, and 10 are really one alpha-beta clause complex (8a and 8b with explicit beta conjunction, 8c with implied beta conjunction and 10 as alpha); ordinary casual talk full of very simple turns (T. 6,7,9) and very complex ones (T. 2,3,8,12)

Contextualization

Situation (represented) – two women (in their twenties) talking to one another in a room

(hypothetical) – male boss and female employee in job situation

(interactive) – the student, reading this example of syntactic analysis; the author having written it

Register – casual conversation

Purpose – to give information that answers question (Turn 1), and in so doing to exchange ideas about sexual harassment in the workplace

Strategy – dialogue explicitly, with elements of interior monologue within, which carry the speculative aspect of the discourse

Metafunctions

Experiential – impersonal *you*, and *I*; present tense mostly, some completive and continuous aspect; active, some of negative polarity (6x); monotransitive Predicates; experiential theme Subject

Interpersonal – after opening interrogative, declarative mood, hypothetical modality (with negative polarity 2x), and necessity (1x); sentence level syntactic elements indicative of informal discourse (F,D,H); interpersonal theme (1x)

Textual – Cohesion – endophoric conjunction (5x) creating textual theme (3x) personal pronouns coherent to situation

Linguistic context

This passage is taken from the middle of a longer exchange between the young women. Phonologically marked *favours*. Semologically mixed process types. Lexical appraisal.

Cultural context and dialect

encoders – two women in their twenties from Toronto, Ontario in the early 1980s

intended decoder – each other

actual decoders – twenty-first century discourse analysis students

Results

Counting Sheet

Number of graphological turns in text: 12

Sentence Elements: Props 17, Alpha-betas 3, Ll 8, Ld 2, F 2, V 0,T 0, Sa 2, H 5, Q 0, D 2.

Types of sentences: Simple 2, Compound 0, Complex 2, Compound-complex 4, Fragment 4.

Clause Elements: L.1 no brackets; [L.2]; (L.3); {alpha & beta}.

Note: In L2–4 keep bracket open until you complete all instances.

		S	P	Co	Cs	Cp	A	Ai/Ab
ng	M/d	1{1}		111 [1]	11{1}		1	{1111}
	M			111	1{1}			
	H	1{1}		1111111 [1] {[1]]	11{11}		1	
	Q	1[11]		11 [1]	{1}		1	
png	M							
	H	1111111111[11111]{111111[11}		1[1]{[1]}	{1}	[1]	1[1]	
	Q							
ajg	M							
	H				{1}			
	Q							
vg	X		11111 [11] {1}					
	H		1111111111111[11111111]{11111[11]}					
	R		1 [1]					
avg	M							
	H						11	
	Q							
pg	M						[1]	
	H	1		1[1]	[1]{1}	[1]	11[1]{[11]}	
	Cv	1		1[1]	[1]{1}	[1]	1[1]{[11]}	
rc		1[1]		11			1	
nfc				11111	1			

Comments – Cd and sc were removed from the chart because there were none

All the vg counts belong in the Predicate

Because there are so many S/ng counts, the Co counts are slightly to the right

If there are square brackets inside double brackets {[3]}, the number inside refers to the number of dc inside the alpha or the beta clause. Both alpha clauses and beta clause elements were counted inside { }.

Syntactic Style Totals

Frequency totals of each feature.

Number of graphological sentences / or turns in your text: 12

Sentence Elements: Props 17, Alpha-betas 3, Ll 8, Ld 2, F 2, V 0, T 0, Sa 2, H 5, Q 0, D 2.

Types of sentences: Simple 2, Compound 0, Complex 2, Compound-complex 4, Fragment 4

		S	P	Co	Cs	Cp	A	Ai/Ab
				Clauses				
ng	M/d	1{1}		3 [1]	2{1}		1	{4}
	M			3	1{1}			
	H	1{1}		7 [1] {[1]]	2{2}		1	
	Q	1[2]		2 [1]	{1}		1	
png	H	10[5]{6[2}		1[1]{[1]} {1}	[1]	1[1]		
ajg	H				{1}			
	Q							
vg	X		5 [2] {1}					
	H		13[8]{5[2]}					
	R		1 [1]					
avg	H						11	
pg	M						[1]	
	H	1		1[1]	[1]{1}	[1]	2[1]{[2]}	
	Cv	1		1[1]	[1]{1}	[1]	1[1]{[2]}	
rc		1[1]		2			1	
nfc				5	1			

Conclusions

Summary

There are a dozen turns in this brief passage of casual conversation between two female university students. Since four of these turns are sentence fragments, more specifically examples of feedback like *mmm* or *right*, false starts or hesitation fillers, the seventeen Proposition / independent clauses are encoded in the eight remaining turns. Although Links, mostly logical Links, are the dominant other sentence level element, there are a few examples of many of the other sentence elements. The types of sentences are quite varied from brief fragments to several complex and compound complex sentence turns. Interestingly, while turn eight includes two explicit betas *if I was a secretary* and *if my boss asked me . . .* , and two more implicit ones *he's a nice guy* and *I knew he wasn't taking advantage of me,* the alpha *I wouldn't mind doing it* does not occur until turn ten, after the decoder's feedback (turn 9).

Within the Proposition / independent clauses the Subjects are usually the first and second personal personal pronoun, exophorically coherent to the communicative situation. The *you* that is encoded several times, though, is used more impersonally than referentially while discussing a hypothetical event. Both because of the pronominal emphasis of the Subject, and the little modification other than definite articles in noun groups, the syntactic style seems more right hand embedded than left.

Yet the right hand embedding is not really associated with a plethora of Adjuncts and the verbal style that they would denote. Complements are important, particularly objective, but also subjective. And these are usually realized by noun groups, with some modification and some qualification. The dependent clauses are usually in the objective Complement: five non-finite clauses and two relative clauses.

Adjuncts, comparatively, are less important. There are no subordinate clauses; the few Adjuncts that are used are more likely prepositional groups. Although there are many Predicate / verbs (28), over half of which are at primary level, as a consequence of the compound sentences and the alpha beta clause complexes, the style is more nominal than verbal.

In summary, what is most significant of the syntactic style of the interlocutors in this passage is the range of sentence types and sentence elements. Within independent clauses, the style is more nominal than verbal, mostly as a consequence of the Complements. Hence, the experiential weight is to the right, the end of the turn. The style is neither particularly paratactic nor hypotactic, although both are important. Some of the logical Links (T.3,5,11) do not really add cohesion to the text, so much as they enable the dominant encoder to hold the floor while she thinks up what to say next *like get a coffee or* (T.3), *or you know the boss's clothes from the cleaners or* (T.5), *you know* (T.7). The discourse is not equal: many of the turns comprise the response of one woman to the other's introductory question *did you get a lot of harassment?* Three of the four fragment turns act as feedback to the interlocutor in power as knower of the experience.

Interpretation

This passage is an unmarked version of the register known as casual conversation. Although it is dominated by one encoder, the interlocutors are peers and likely shift back and forth in terms of who holds the power, depending on whose story and whose opinion is being exchanged. The dominant strategy is dialogue, revealed graphologically by the alternation of R C R C indicating the interlocutors' turntaking. However, in a spoken transcription of casual conversation such as this, there is no need for the syntactic style of projected speech: *She said, "…",* nor the semological style of mental processes of verbalization *said*. Secondary strategies are embedded within the dialogue. There is description *she's confused, I was a secretary*, but there are also elements of interior monologue *I know, I think*, and narration *I worked*. The mixed embedded strategy is not surprising when the purpose of the discourse is considered. In responding to the other's question, the dominant encoder is sharing both her story and opinion.

The way she does so is interesting. Rather than answer the question with a mere dialogic negative Link, she continues *no, I didn't have any problems.* Because she has no experience of harassment to convey, she invents the possibility which accounts for the examples of negative polarity and hypothetical modality. But the possibility is not one of being harassed, but the possibility of being 'exploited' in an acceptable way *[if] he's a nice guy and I knew he wasn't taking advantage of me I wouldn't mind doing it* and the other adds *it depends on how many year's you've been with him* before the first continues *like if you are sort of friends with the guys you don't mind doing favours for him,* then laughingly she corrects the possible sexual entendre *I don't mean favours* (phonologically highlighting *favours*).

Such mutual speculation, while politically incorrect from contemporary standards, is not so surprising given the social provenance of the interlocutors. The two women are twenty-year-old university students, potentially disempowered by their gender, age, institutional role and lack of career, financial stability.

Still, they are equals with some prior friendship. Hence their discourse has all the syntactic marks of informal spoken discourse between friends: speaker's attitudes, false starts, hesitation fillers, contractions encoding negative polarity, sentence fragments, modals, extended reference (T.8,10). The range in complexity of turns shows their gnostological comfort with a variety of styles as adult interlocutors.

The most marked feature of the discourse is the dominant encoder's choice of hypothetical situation as a response to her friend's question. This hypothetical situation accounts for the syntactic complexity of the seriated explicit and implicit beta clauses to a single alpha (T.8,10). Although the decoder could have argued with her, she does not. The two, in this communicative event, at least, seem to share the values that one might expect of two young women talking in a particular geographical, temporal and social provenance (York University, Toronto, Canada; 1980s; female, twenty-year-old students).

Review of syntactic analysis

Analysis

Preparation

1. Describe your **expectations** of the syntactic character of the text based on your experience with similar texts in your culture.

2. Note your **first impressions** of the syntactic style, and record your **preliminary hypotheses**.

3. Number each sentence in your text, and write each sentence across the long side of a page in a single line if possible.

4.a. Underline the verbs, b. identify the /ic/, c. bracket the dc: [rc / sc / nfc] and d. draw parentheses around any (pg), and if it Qualifies a H/noun, draw a line from the Q/pg to the H/n.

Description

1. Under each graphological sentence (from written texts) or transcribed phonological turn (from spoken texts) write an ε to begin the syntactic tree.

2. Describe the **sentence** in terms of **sentence structure**: T, Sa, V, H, Pr, Q, D, M.

3.a. Describe the Pp / **independent clause** in terms of **clause structure:** SPCA.

b. Classify the *parts of speech* (dependent clauses, groups or word) that realize each element of clause structure.

4.a. Describe the **clause structure** SPCA of each **dependent clause**.

b. Classify the *parts of speech* (dependent clauses, groups or word) that realize each element of clause structure.

5.a. Describe the **group structure** of each **group** in the sentence.

b. Classify the *parts of speech* (dependent clauses, groups or word) that realize each element of group structure.

6. Continue the process of labelling each clause, group and word until each individual word has been described in terms of *structure* and *part of speech*, e.g. *H/n*.

7. Highlight and label each *level* of clause (main clause, then dc) to facilitate the frequency counts of the results. (Each level will include (S)P(C)(A).

8. Once your graphic analysis is complete, note experiential, interpersonal and textual choices.

9. Note insights and patterns you become aware of on a **comments sheet** throughout description.

Notes:

- As much as possible, keep the labels under the actual words of the sentence they describe.
- Check that in groups, you have only *group* structural labels; in clauses, *clause* structural labels, and try to keep all clause structural labels, or alternatively, all group structural labels, on the same horizontal line. (This will make finding and highlighting specific levels within the clause easy, when it comes to compiling your *Results*.)
- Remember that whatever is *inside* something else, should have a line drawn to connect it to the more inclusive unit in the tree above it. For example, there will be a line drawn from the ng and vg that realize S and P to the Pp/ic above; a line from the M/d, H/n, Q/rc to the S/ng above etc. This means that the higher you are in the *tree,* the larger (more inclusive) the patterns become, groups, then clauses, and finally the sentence.

Contextualization

Situation – Label the situation (*interactive-* yours and *represented-* in the text) and make a few notes concerning its field, mode, personal and functional tenor, for example *renting apartment: property, money, time, written, formal, contract.*

Register – Identify the **register** of the text: e.g. *rental agreement.*
What aspects of the register explain the syntactic features of the text, e.g. *formality?*
What syntactic nuances make your text unique in terms of its register, e.g. *time?*

Purpose – Identify the purpose of this text, e.g. *to legalize* rental agreement.
How does syntactic information develop this purpose, e.g. *Legal lexis and syntax?*
Strategies: Does the syntactic style have any relationship to the strategies chosen e.g. *description of property, legal form and signatures?*

Metafunctions

Describe how the syntactic choices encode particular **metafunctions.**

i. Experiential – *participants*: person, number, case, (theme); *events*: tense, aspect, voice, polarity; *goal*: transitivity, (theme); **circumstances**: A, (theme)
What elements of the experience do the encoder's syntactic style feature and / or highlight (nominal / verbal / mixed)?

ii. Interpersonal – How do choices in *mood, modality, polarity*, **sentence elements** affect or 'colour' the experience?

iii. Textual – *coherence –* What pronouns, conjunctions, substitutions and ellipsis add to the text's **cohesion?**
What syntactic patterns contribute to the text's coherence, for example grammatical parallelism, adjacency pairs?
theme – Describe multiple themes: experiential, interpersonal, textual.

Linguistic context

a. From where in the book / article is the text taken?
b. Describe the ways other linguistic information relates, reinforces and challenges the syntactic choices of this text, e.g. *lexical, semological, graphological, phonological.*

Cultural context and dialect

a. Who is the **encoder**? How do her syntactic choices reflect her situation, culture, beliefs and values. How does her syntactic style contribute to constructing her social identity and reality?
b. Who is the *intended* **decoder** (the expected / target audience)?

c. Who is the *actual* **decoder**? How might her situation, culture, and experience of the register affect her interpretation of the encoder's syntactic choices?

Results

a. **Label** clause levels.

b. **Count** each instance of structural element and part of speech.

Counting Sheet

Number of graphological sentences / or turns in your text:

Sentence Elements: Props , Alpha-betas , Ll , Ld , F , V , T , Sa , H , Q , D .

Types of sentences: Simple , Compound , Complex , Compound-complex , Fragment .

Clause Elements: Level 1 no brackets; [L.2]; (L.3); {alpha & beta}.

Note: Keep brackets open until all instances are counted.

		S	P	Co	Cd	Cs	Cp	Af	Ai/Ab
ng	M/d								
	M								
	H								
	Q								
png	M								
	H								
	Q								
ajg	M								
	H								
	Q								
vg	X								
	H								
	R								
avg	M								
	H								
	Q								
pg	M								
	H								
	Cv								
rc									
nfc									
sc									

Note: if a Qualifier, mark in group where appropriate and then mark as pg/dc below; do *not* count the Cv/ng structure in pg; do count SPCA in all dependent clauses.

c. Total each feature of encoder's syntactic style.
Number of graphological sentences / or turns in your text:
Sentence Elements: Props , Alpha-betas , Ll , Ld , F , V , T , Sa , H , Q , D .
Types of sentences: Simple , Compound , Complex , Compound-complex , Fragment .

Note: As suggested earlier, frequency totals may be recorded on a revised copy of the counting sheet, where totals replace individual counts, and where unused features are omitted.

Conclusions

1. **Summary** – Describe the encoder's **syntactic style**, in prose, in terms of the syntactic level, then combine findings to make statements concerning syntactic style: (**a**) *nominal, verbal* or *mixed*, (**b**) *paratactic* or *hypotactic*, (**c**) *right-hand* or *left-hand embedded*.
   Is this style consistent throughout, or does it change at certain points in the text?
2. **Interpretation** – How does the encoder's syntactic style relate to her semological, phonological style etc.?
   How do you explain the encoder's choices in terms of situation, purpose, strategy, register; the encoder's and decoders' geographical, temporal and social provenance?

Further reading

Bache, Carl (1997), *The Study of Aspect, Tense and Action*. 2nd edn. Berlin: Peter Lang.

Eggins, S. (1994), *An Introduction to Systemic Functional Linguistics*. London: Pinter Publishers.

Eggins, S. and Slade, D. (1997), *Analyzing Casual Conversation*. London: Cassell.

Schiffrin, D. (1987), *Discourse Markers*. Cambridge: Cambridge University Press.

Stenstrom, A. (1994), *An Introduction to Spoken Interaction*. London: Longman.

Thompson, Geoff. (1997), *Introducing Functional Grammar*. London: Arnold.

Semology 6

Each form of analysis introduced thus far describes a different type of meaning. *Graphological* meaning is encoded in the visual selection and arrangement of graphs and images. *Phonological* meaning is encoded in the choices and relationships between sounds and silence. *Lexical* meaning is encoded in the choice and juxtaposition of conceptually related words and sets, and *syntactic* meaning is encoded in the sequence of, and relationship between, words, groups, clauses, sentences and turns.

Semology, like syntax, is concerned with the arrangement of meaning. However, not the abstract relationships between class / parts of speech and elements of structure, but the more semantically inclined relationships between actors / participants, processes / events, goals / participants, and circumstances / setting. In the sentences *Jyota <u>threw</u> the ball*, *Eku <u>learns / loves</u> math*, and *Yoga is fun* the syntactic Subject describes the **participant** (*Jyota, Eku, yoga*) involved; the syntactic Predicate describes the event or **process** (*threw, learns / loves, is*) and the syntactic Complement describes the **goal** (*the ball, physics, fun*). Semological **circumstances** are realized syntactically by syntactic Adjuncts: ***Yesterday, in Killarney****, Jyota <u>threw</u> the ball*.

Semological roles are given to all elements of clause structure (SPCA), not sentence or group structure. In *semology*, the independent clause is called a **proposition** (which is a different usage than the syntactic sentence level structural element for the *ic*). Each syntactic clause, both dependent and independent, comprises a semological **predication**. In a proposition that is a simple sentence, there is one predication with its participant, process and goal roles. In a complex sentences the single semological proposition includes at least two predications (ic + dc).

There are three types of semological processes: *action, relational* and *mental*. **Action processes** express some kind of action, for example *Jyota <u>threw</u> the ball*. **Mental processes** describe some sort of cerebral activity, with the occasional emotional overtone, for example *Eku <u>learns / loves</u> math*. And **relational processes** are functional rather than lexical in that they 'relate' the goal role to the participant role, for example *Yoga is fun*. In the next section, these processes are further classified, and the nuclear semological roles that co-occur with each as *participants* and *goals* are introduced.

In the *descriptive methodology* associated with semology, the first three or four letters are used to abbreviate (bolded) the various kinds of semological roles operating as *participant* or *goal*. And the processes themselves are labelled *ap*, *mp*, *rp*, followed by a colon and a letter that represents the specific classification, for example *mp*:c. In this book, when **semological predications** are analysed, a plus sign (+) is written between each *semological role*.

*Exercise: Three Semological Processes

Mental Processes

With mental processes the *participant* (Subject) is called the **processor**, and the *goal* (Complement) is the **phenomenon** (in unmarked active statements).

Participant Role

> **proc**essor – the one who does the processing; assumed to be human, and, if not, is personified and marked by an asterisk e.g. *She* thought about it for hours.
> **The air* whispered . . .

Goal Role

> **phen**omenon – what is processed, not necessarily a thing, e.g. He wants *a drink*.
> She wondered *[what she would do]*.
> He said *["I understand you"]*.

Note:
- The particular role is italicized in the example.
- Usually, the processor precedes the phenomenon. proc + mp:r + phen. However, at times this order is reversed:
  E.g. *"Are you* kidding?*" she* yelled. *The news* reached *us*.
  phen + proc + mp:v   phen + mp:p + proc

Mental Process classifications

Mental Process		Example
Cognition	**mp:c**	She *learned / knew / understood / forgot* math.
Perception	**mp:p**	He *touched / saw / heard / tasted* the fish.
Reaction	**mp:r**	They *liked / hated / wanted* the book. (Processor first)

The joke _amused / horrified_ them. (Phenomenon first)
Creation **mp:e** Handel _composed_ the Messiah.
Verbalization **mp:v** She _said / told / mumbled / ordered / replied / wrote_ "Go home."

Note:

- A mental process can seldom be substituted for by 'do'.
- The present tense of a mental process is typically realized by the simple present, e.g. She <u>knows</u> her work.

*Exercise: Mental Processes

Action Processes

The _participant_ associated with action processes is usually the actor in active statements, although there are a few other possibilities, as the following list indicates. _Goal_ roles vary. A _participant_ begins an active sentence; a _goal_, a passive.

Participant Roles

act*or* – the animate 'doer' of the action, who carries out the action,
    e.g. _John_ <u>opened</u> the door.
    If the actor is _not_ animate, use an asterisk to indicate that it is marked.
    e.g. *_Her words_ <u>parted</u> the waves, like a knife.
for*ce* – an inanimate force that carries out the action
    e.g. _The wind_ <u>opened</u> the door.
ins*trument* – the entity used by an actor to carry out a process
    e.g. _The key_ <u>opened</u> the door.
    An instrument that _follows_ the Predicate is likely a 'circumstance' (Adjunct).
ini*tiator* – the being / thing that initiates a process carried out
    e.g. _The general_ <u>marched</u> his men.
    When an _initiator_ is the participant, the Actor is usually a 'goal'.
pat*ient* – the entity that is affected / undergoes a change of state   e.g. _He_ <u>shaved</u>.
    _he_ is actor and patient unless the two roles are differentiated by adding the reflexive pronoun _He <u>shaved</u> himself_ in which case the participant role is 'actor'.
rec*ipient* – the entity to whom the process is directed
    e.g. _She_ <u>received</u> a gift. _He_ <u>has been nominated</u>.

Goal Roles

pat*ient* – the entity that is affected, or undergoes a change of state
        e.g. She <u>washed</u> _the clothes_.
res*ultant* – the entity that results from the action
        e.g. They <u>made</u> _a cake_. He <u>built</u> _a house_.

*med*ium – the entity that is moved or involved in a transfer

    e.g. She <u>gave</u> him *a book*.

    The wind <u>dislodged</u> the kite.

*rec*ipient – the entity to whom the process is directed

    e.g. She <u>gave</u> *him* a book. <u>Give</u> it *to him*.

*con*tinuant – spatial (cont:p) or temporal (cont:t) etc. nuclear roles 'required by' the process e.g. She <u>walked</u> *to the store*. He <u>arrived</u> *at eight*.

*ran*ge – the role which specifies or de-limits the process

    e.g. She <u>ran</u> *the marathon / hundred yard dash*. He <u>climbed</u> *the mountain*.

*act*or – the doer of the action

    e.g. He <u>drilled</u> *the soldiers*. The explosion <u>dispersed</u> *the crowd*.

Note: Syntactic function helps determine 'goal' roles, e.g. *recipients* are usually Cd's with action processes, *continuants* are Cp's, and the rest are Co's. To identify a *range*, the process of elimination helps: a range is *not* one of the other goal roles.

Action **Process** classifications

With action processes, the ***goal*** role determines the sub-classification of the process. If the goal is not explicitly realized, classify the process in terms of the goal it would take normally. For example, in *She <u>left</u>* the action process *leave* typically takes a continuant; hence, it is an ap:e.

Goal	Action Process		Example
patient	Affected	**ap:a**	She <u>*washed*</u> the wall.
resultant	Resulting	**ap:r**	He <u>*made*</u> a cake.
medium	Motion	**ap:m**	The wind <u>*dislodged*</u> the kite.
"	Transfer	**ap:t**	They <u>*sent*</u> flowers.
recipient	Personal	**ap:p**	The flowers <u>*were sent*</u> to her.
actor	Personal	**ap:p**	The mother <u>*burped*</u> the baby.
continuant	Extended	**ap:e**	He <u>*started*</u> this afternoon.
range	Designative	**ap:d**	She <u>*sang*</u> a song.
----	Behavioural	**ap:b**	He <u>*watched*</u> from the sidelines. He <u>*blushed*</u>.
----	Ambient	**ap:am**	It<u>*'s raining / snowing / hailing.*</u>

Note:

- The present tense of an action process is typically realized by the present continuous as in <u>*She is building*</u>.
- Action processes can be substituted for by a form of 'do'.
- **ap:d** Not all action processes are concrete, physical events; they may be abstract: e.g. *The politician <u>resigned</u> her office*. They still answer the question 'What did the actor do?'.

- **ap:b** There are two types of ap which do not take a 'goal' role:
  - a. True intransitive verbs which express involuntary behaviour, manifested in the past tense e.g. *He died / cried / blushed / slept / materialized / disappeared*.
  - b. When 'mental-sounding' processes like *learned (mp:c), watched (mp:p)* are surrounded by circumstantial information rather than a goal / phenomenon. e.g. *She learns effortlessly*.
- **ap:am** Ambient processes do not take either a goal or a participant role (only the 'dummy' *it*). Encodes continuous aspect and weather lexis. e.g. *It's snowing / hailing*.
- **Bitransitive** Predicate / verbs (including verbs of transfer) take two semological goal roles: e.g. *Give* the book to her. She *put* the log on the fire.

                    ap:tp   med   rec   ap:te   med   cont:p

*Exercise: Action Processes

Relational Processes

The semological **goal** role of relational processes determines both the classification of the *relational process* and the semological role of the *participant* (see below).

Goal roles

attribute – realized syntactically by aj/ajg. E.g. She *is / seems / appears* tall/ *tired / smart*.

classifier – realized syntactically by a ng which suggests a general or group affiliation, often introduced by an indefinite article. E.g. He *was* a *coach / father / skier*.

identifier – realized by a ng identifying a specific, unique designation, often introduced by a definite article or possessive pronoun. E.g. She *is* the / *her doctor*.

possessed – realized by a ng, that is owned / possessed by another. E.g. He *has / owns four cats*.

circumstance – these nuclear 'goals' may follow such rps as: *weighs, cost, lasts, concerns, follows, crosses, accompanies, resembles, takes up*. They take the same roles as Adjunct circumstances, and are often signalled by a preposition. E.g. They *are / live (in Toronto)*.

existent – realized by a ng that follows the 'dummy' *there* as Subject. E.g. There *was a child*.

Participant roles and **Relational** Process classifications

Participant	Relational Process	Goal	Example
item	+ Attributive	**rp:a** + **att**ribute	She *is* kind / generous / funny
classified	+ Classificatory	**rp:c** + **cl**assifier	He *is* **a** boy. / The house *is* stone.

*id*entified	+ Identificatory	**rp:i** + **id**entifier	He *is* **the** boy that I mentioned.
			Love *is* the best cure.
***pos**sessor*	+ Possessive	**rp:p** + **pos**sessed	She *has* / *owns* a horse.
carrier	+ Circumstantial	**rp:r** + **cir**cumstance	He *is* in London. (cir:p)
--	Existential	**rp:e** + **exis**tent	There *was* an old horse.

Notes:

- To determine whether participle is the H/v in a P/vg, or a Cs/aj, place *very* before the participle, e.g. *I* *am* **very** *scared* / *tired* / *pleased* / *worried*. If it makes sense, the participle is a Cs/aj; if is does not, it is part of the P/vg, for example *The flowers* *were* **very** *given* to me.

- Relational processes are frequently realized *implicitly* by nominal groups, for example good dog (attributive); stone house (classificatory); this house (identificatory); country house (circumstantial); my book (possessive). However, most analyses deal with *explicit* predications only.

- Some processes are **relational** in some contexts and action or mental in others: *seem, appear, look, feel, remain, keep, equal, represent, form, show, reflect, suggest, feature, indicate*, for example It *sounds* silly. (rp:a) She *turned* professional. (rp:a) She *became* a dancer. (rp:c) (cf. Halliday, 1994, pp. 120–3).

- Relational processes in the completed or continuous aspect seem more **mental** than relational, for example He *had been scared* all day.

- **rp:r** *Circumstantial relational processes* are sub-classified by the type of circumstance:
  e.g. She *is* early. She *is* here. She *is* with a child. She *is* like a child. She is in mourning.
      cir:t   cir:p   cir:ass   cir:comp   cir:man

*Exercises: Relational Processes

Circumstantial Roles (Peripheral)

Peripheral circumstantial roles (none or many in a single clause), syntactic Adjuncts, usually occur with action processes. In passive sentences even participant roles become peripheral circumstances, for example He *was appreciated by his colleagues*. Particular prepositions are often key in identifying the type of circumstance (labels are bolded ; examples of circumstances are italicized).

manner: He *washed* the dishes *quickly*.
time: She *knew* it *at once*.
place: The child *was* very noisy *in his playroom*.
associated actor: She *went* to the store *with* / *as well as* / *without* / *instead of Sally*.
beneficiary: He *built* a house *for his dad*.
recipient: He said 'Leave me alone' *to his brother*.

material: He <u>made</u> the salad *with spinach.*

reason: He <u>read</u> the book *for fun.*

purpose: I might call her *to arrange child care.* He <u>read</u> the book *to learn math.*

cause: The woman ruined the shirt *by bleaching it.*

contingency: *In case of fire*, <u>find</u> the exit. *Despite the rain*, the picnic <u>was</u> a success.

comparison: She <u>wished for</u> a toy train *like his.*

perspective: The deal <u>is</u> good *according to Jay* . They're guilty *in her eyes.*

issue: *I advised him of / about the circumstances.* Who <u>remembers</u> his position *on this matter?*

actor: She <u>was given</u> a gift *by her teacher.*

force: The door <u>was opened</u> *by the wind.*

initiator: The soldiers <u>were drilled</u> *by the sergeant.*

instrument: She <u>opened</u> the door *with a key.*

Note: In rp:r circumstantial information is *nuclear,* not peripheral.

*Exercises: Processes and Circumstances

Summary of nuclear semological roles

Actor (**force**, **init**iator, **inst**rument, **pat**ient, **med**ium) + **ACTION PROCESS** + *Goal role*

Goal	PROCESS		Example
patient	Affected	**ap:a**	She <u>washed</u> the wall.
resultant	Resulting	**ap:r**	He <u>made</u> a cake.
medium	Motion	**ap:m**	The wind <u>dislodged</u> the kite.
"	Transfer	**ap:t**	They <u>sent</u> flowers.
recipient	Personal	**ap:p**	The flowers <u>were sent</u> to her.
actor	Personal	**ap:p**	The mother <u>burped</u> the baby.
continuant	Extended	**ap:e**	He <u>started</u> this afternoon.
range	Designative	**ap:d**	She <u>sang</u> a song.
----	Behavioural	**ap:b**	He <u>watched</u> from the sidelines. He <u>blushed</u>.
----	Ambient	**ap:am**	It<u>'s hailing</u>.

PROCESSOR + **MENTAL PROCESS** + **PHEN**OMENON

	PROCESS	Example
Cognition	**mp:c**	She <u>learned / knew / understood / forgot</u> math.
Perception	**mp:p**	He <u>touched / saw / heard / tasted</u> the fish.
Reaction	**mp:r**	They <u>liked / hated / wanted</u> the book. (Processor first)
		The joke <u>amused / horrified</u> them. (Phenomenon first)
Creation	**mp:e**	Handel <u>composed</u> the Messiah
Verbalization	**mp:v**	She <u>said / told / replied / wrote</u> "Go home."

Participant Role + **RELATIONAL PROCESS** + *Goal Role*

Participant		PROCESS		Goal	Example
item	+	Attributive	**rp:a** +	**att**ribute	She <u>is</u> kind / tall / generous / funny
classified	+	Classificatory	**rp:c** +	**class**ifier	He <u>is</u> **a** boy. / The house <u>is</u> stone.
identified	+	Identificatory	**rp:i** +	**id**entifier	He <u>is</u> **the** boy I mentioned.
possessor	+	Possessive	**rp:p** +	**pos**sessed	She <u>has / owns</u> a horse.
carrier	+	Circumstantial	**rp:r** +	**cir**cumstance	He <u>is / lives</u> here / London.
---		Existential	**rp:e** +	**exist**ent	There <u>was</u> a woman / country.

Peripheral semological roles: circumstances

manner, **time**, **place**, **ass**ociated actor, **ben**eficiary, **recip**ient, **mat**erial, **reas**on, **pur**pose, **cause**, **cont**ingency, **comp**arison, **persp**ective, **issue**, **act**or, **force**, **init**iator, **instrument**

Identifying and describing multiple predications in single propositions

Until now, all examples of semological Propositions have included a single predication. When there are multiple predications, they are labelled in much the same way as the *syntactic **levels*** of Chapter 5 with numbers describing 'vertical' depth of clause structure and letters describing 'horizontal' sequence: first, second etc. at that level (p. 144). Each predication is labelled as a semological predication (SP1, SP2, SP3), below or above the predication's *process*, and is then described.

When a full predication realizes a single semological role in the 'level' above it, that predication is noted in the description (see b. phen(SP2)). The sequence of the roles follows the sequence of the syntax. The semological choices reflect the syntactic ones.

Examples

    a. *She <u>knows</u> her music.* 1 syntactic level; 1 semological predication.

        SP1

    SP1 proc + mp:c + phen

    b. *She <u>knows</u> [what she <u>wants</u>]* 2 syntactic levels; 2 semological predications.

        SP1   SP2

    SP1 proc + mp:c + phen (SP2)

    SP2 phen + proc + mp:r

c. *Jyota likes Lego / and / Eku likes playmobile.*   1 syntactic level; 2 predications
       SP1A   SP1B
SP1A proc + mp:r + phen
SP1B proc + mp:r + phen

d. *Jyota likes [reading books] /, and / Eku likes [coaching volleyball].*   2 levels; 4 predications
      SP1A SP2A   SP2A SP2B
SP1A proc + mp:r + phen (SP2A)
SP1B proc + mp:r + phen (SP2B)
SP2A mp:c + phen
SP2B ap:d + range

e. *I realize [that she knows [what she wants]] / and / [that she will find it].*   3 syntactic levels;
   SP1   SP2A   SP3A   SP2B   4 predications.
SP1   proc + mp:c + phen (SP2A) + phen (SP2B)
SP2A proc + mp:c + phen (SP3A)
SP2B act + ap:d + ran + fut int
SP3A phen + proc + mp:r

f. *The woman [who brought the CD] loves [hearing Bach], / but / the man [who is new] hates Bach.*
                           SP1A   SP1B (hates)
            SP2Aa   SP2Ab   SP2B
SP1A proc (SP2Aa) + mp:r + phen (SP2Ab)
SP1B proc (SP2B) + mp:r + phen
SP2Aa act + ap:m + med
SP2Ab mp:p + phen
SP2B item + rp:a + att

g. *Eat.*
SP1 ap:a

Note: When the syntax is complex (see f), draw the tree to help you label the SPs.

*Examples & Exercise: Multiple Semological Predications

Semology and the metafunctions

Experiential Systems *clause as representation*

    A. Transitivity – All the semological roles belong to the system of transitivity. They reflect and encode the participants, events, and things of our world of experience in nuclear and peripheral semological roles.

    B. Polarity – A choice of negative polarity (*not*) *negates* the semological action / event of the following process (Predicate / verb group).

Interpersonal systems *clause as exchange*

Speech function

Semological **statements** are typically realized syntactically by declarative mood choices; **questions** by interrogative mood choices, and **commands** by imperative mood choices. However, syntactic mood choices are not the only way to encode semological speech function. Questions are also realized phonologically by a rising tone even though they might be in the declarative mood syntactically. Commands can be encoded using a marked phonological tone and a variety of syntactic mood choices depending on the degree of politeness used between interactants. For example *open the window* (imperative), *could you open the window?* (interrogative), or *I'm too hot* (declarative, indirection), all encode a semological command.

Event mediation

Modal verbs are used to mediate the event semologically in the following ways typically:

can	– ability	must / have to / gotta	– necessity
could	– probability	should / ought to	– obligation
might/get to	– possibility	would	– hypothesis
may	– permission	will / shall / going to	– future intention
let	– allow		

Note: Modals do not always mediate the process in the same way: *may* tempers the process with permission in 'You *may* go', but possibility in 'She *may* come'.

In addition, the following processes mediate events when used as X/v in P/vg. Although their temporal aspect might suggest more of an experiential meaning, they also temper the H/v interpersonally by adding a dimension of uncertainty. Marked phonological stress can reinforce such interpersonal meanings.

begin / start	– inception	E.g. He <u>begins to understand</u> my dilemma.
stop / cease	– closure	<u>Stop worrying</u> every time the going gets tough!
keep / continued	– duration	He <u>keeps giving</u> me presents.
try	– attempt	She <u>tried to remember</u> her mantra.
like / want	– desire	She <u>wants to tell</u> her son a story.

Interlocutors related *asymmetrically* (e.g. parents / children) are more likely to use modalities of necessity, obligation, permission and future intention; while interlocutors related *symmetrically* (peers) are more likely to use modalities of ability, possibility, probability and hypothesis. The *formality* of the communicative situation also determines event mediation. In *formal* situations, interlocutors who temper the meaning of their processes with necessity would be more likely to use *must* than those who resort to *got to* or *gotta* in **informal** situations.

Polarity

If negative polarity is selected frequently, the cumulative effect may cast a subjective interpersonal veil of negativity or uncertainty over the text.

Textual systems *clause as enabler*

Focus and prominence

Semological *focus* and *prominence* capture the *communicative dynamism* of a sentence, the effect of sequence on the interpretation of information encoded in the message. Prague linguists suggest that what comes first in a sentence makes the greatest impact on the decoder, what comes last receives less attention, and what is in the middle receives the least attention (Firbas, 1972). The *syntactic* system of theme and rheme, the *phonological* system of new and given and the *semological* system of focus and prominence describe this phenomenon.

Semologically speaking, the **focus** is the *starting point* or *point of departure* of the message, and the **prominence** is the message *highlight*. When responding to the question *What does Eku like?*, in the sentence *Eku likes hotdogs,* the focus is on the phonological given element which precedes the new information: *Eku likes* and the prominence is on the *new* element (the tonic prominence and often the last element in clause structure): *hotdogs.* This is **unmarked**. If, however, the encoder gave *Eku* the tonic prominence in response to the question *Who likes hotdogs?* making it phonological *new* and semological focus, with the semological prominence on the phonological *given*, the textual meaning would be considered **marked**.

Cohesion and coherence

Cohesive devices

1. **Reference** adds cohesion to a text by forming a semantic tie between a pronoun and its nominal antecedent (cf. Syntax p. 142 #1).
   - Reference is **anaphoric** if the pronominal signal *follows* the nominal antecedent, and **cataphoric** (**+c**) if it *precedes* the antecedent. Anaphora is the **unmarked** version of reference.
   - Reference can be **endophoric** (adding *cohesion* within the text) or **exophoric** (**+x**) (adding *coherence* between the text and its situation or gnostology (Malcolm, 1984)). First and second person personal pronouns often signal situational exophora, as do the demonstratives *this, that, now, there, here.*

- There are three types of reference depending on the type of pronominal signal used to signal the cohesive tie: **personal (Rp)** *she, he, it, they, hers, his, its, theirs* etc., **demonstrative (Rd)** *this, that, these, those* as well as demonstrative adverbials *here, there, then, now* and **comparative (Rc)** *more, fewer, less, further, additional, so many, better, same* etc.

  (presupposing signal is bolded, antecedent is italicized):

  a. *Cyndy* is great. **She** started a company last year. **Her** company is doing well.
             Rp   Rp

  b. **She** loves *cute little puppies.* **Those** are **my** favourites too.
    Rp   Rd   Rpx

  c. **She** snorkels down by the *reef*. **I** went swimming **there** yesterday.
    Rp   Rpx   Rd

  d. The *tea* tastes great. Please give **me** some **more**. **I** will give **you** the **same** amount.
                                Rpx   Rc Rpx   Rpx   Rc

  e. **I** had a great *breakfast* today. However, **I** want a **different** selection tomorrow.
    Rpx   Rpx   Rc

  f. **Her** *child* is very big for ten months. However, **my** sister's son is **bigger**.
    Rp   Rpx   Rc

- **Extended Reference:** In some cases the referential signal refers to more discourse than a single nominal referent. The pronominal signals *it, this* and *that* signal **extended reference (+e)** more often than other possible referential signals.

  E.g. *They threw a party for her last week at the beach. There was piles of food, and lots to drink. And the weather was perfect.* **It** *was a great time.*
                                                          Rpe

- **Referential and participant chains:** The series of cohesive ties between the first instance of a noun and all the pronominal signals that refer to it form a **chain of reference** that may operate throughout a text (especially in narratives). In some texts several chains of reference interweave throughout the text at the same time (usually involving third person endophoric Rp in written discourse; first or second person exophora Rpx in spoken discourse).

- **Participant chains** include these *referential chains* as well as the *chains* of *identity* from your analysis of lexical relations (see p. 104). Nominal substitutes and ellipses relevant to a particular participant / character / thing also contribute to such participant chains. They show how various cohesive devices work together when developing a character.

2. **Logical Conjunctions** *between* certain predications and propositions, also contribute to textual meaning (cf. Syntax p. 142 #2). The semological connections that relate one proposition to another by *expansion* add **inter-sentential coherence**, also known as **cohesion** (see *A*). The semological relationships that operate within a single proposition either between a main clause and its *projections* (see *B*), or between the *alpha and beta* clauses in an alpha-beta clause complex (see *C*) add **intra-sentential coherence** to the text.

A. The three types of conjunction that signal **inter-sentential expansion** are *cohesive* (cf. Halliday for sub-classifications, 1994, pp. 221–37):

1. **elaboration** – one clause elaborates the meaning of the other by specifying or describing it E.g. *in other words, for example, to be precise* . . .
2. **enhancement** – one clause enhances the meaning of the other by qualifying it in terms of *cause, condition, temporal, spatial, manner* E.g. *and so, still, now, first, then, to his left*
3. **extension** – one clause extends the meaning of the other by adding something new. E.g. *Additive*: and, but yet, nor; *Variation*: instead, but, only, or; *Alternation*: or

B. **Projection**: After *mental processes of verbalization and cognition*, the phenomenon may be expressed as a complete proposition involving numerous predications and sentence level structural elements. e.g. *She <u>said</u>, 'As for Tom, well, he <u>drives</u> me nuts, which <u>is</u> a pity'*. Processes of verbalization and cognition **project** a phenomenon that is either a *locution* or an *idea* respectively.

E.g. **Locution** – // *She said,* // "**Don't forget me**"//

   Idea – // *He thinks* // **he will come**. //

C. **Alpha-beta clause complexes** also involve various logical semological relationships operating between the interdependent alpha clause and beta clause (cf. Gregory, 1995, pp. 223). Beta Conjunctions are bolded, and beta clauses are italicized; alphas are not.

Reason	/ *Because /since/as / for he made many mistakes* = he was fired. /
Concession	/ *Although, while he made many mistakes* = he was still promoted. /
Condition – **positive**	/ *If she makes one more mistake,* = I will fire her. /
negative	/ *Unless she goes,* = I will not be able to finish this. /
Insurance	/ *In case you finish,* = here is some more work. /
Result	/ He made many mistakes = *so he was fired*. /
Purpose	/ She worked hard = *so / in order that she would finish first*. /
Comparison	/ She treated him = *as / like she treated everyone*. /

*Exercise: Cohesive Devices

The semological analysis of verbal communication

Preparation

Before beginning your semological analysis, think about the communicative situation in which the text occurred. Of which register of language is your text an example? From your past experience with this register, what *expectations* do you bring to your interpretation of this text? Once you have acknowledged your gnostological awareness of the register, reread the text and note your *first impressions* of it, in terms of the author's semological choices. From your expectations and first impressions, suggest *preliminary hypotheses* concerning the role of the encoder's *semological style* in determining the decoder's interpretation of the text.

Prepare for the semological analysis by considering the **syntax**: underline the verbs, note conjunctions, draw slashes around independent clauses, square brackets around dependent clauses, and parentheses around preposition groups. E.g. / The woman [called Roxanne] is my mother's friend /.

Analysis

Using the syntax as a guide, **label** the predications in each proposition under each process, for example SP1, SP2. Once the labelling is complete, describe the **semological roles** in each predication. Remember that each element of *clause* structure (not group or sentence), syntactically speaking, is given a semological role (except Ai). When a semological role is realized by, or includes, a new predication (SPCA at a lower level in the syntax), the label of that new predication is written beside the role, for example *phen (SP2)*. The analyst assumes that if a role is developed by an entire semological predication, it is significant to the encoder.

By correlating the semological predication with the level of syntactic embedding, the analyst discovers what is most important to the author. In *unmarked* texts, the semological roles within the *primary* predications are considered most important. In *marked* texts, what is, in a way syntactically *hidden* or *covert* (in secondary and tertiary predications) may be of greater consequence in the final interpretation of the text, than what is obvious at primary predication.

For instance, in several memorable *descriptive* passages, where static relational processes predictably dominated the primary predications, more dynamic action processes were more deeply, and covertly, embedded in SP2, SP3, SP4 (Malcolm, 1987). In addition, participial Modifier / adjectives, and gerund Head / nouns increased the *semological dynamism* of the passage, even though they were not accorded the status of predication (ibid.).

E.g. The old house <u>was</u> quiet (with [shadows <u>dancing</u> on the ceiling].
                           SP1   SP2

SP1 item + rp:a + att + man (SP2)

SP2A *act + ap:e + cont:p

Note: *Marked* roles, for instance, *inanimate* actors are marked with an asterisk *.

In **narrative** passages, authors *advance* the *plot* in the action of the primary predication, but may *develop* their *characters* through relational processes, mental processes, or both, in secondary predications.

> E.g. She ran (through the forest) (with [eyes screaming 'No')].
>   SP1   SP2
> SP1 act + ap:e + cont:p + manner (SP2)
> SP2 * proc + mp:v + phen

Shadows do not really *dance*, nor *eyes*, *scream*. In such personified examples, the role of the process should be assigned as usual, although the marked actor / processor, in effect, *negates* the action / mental process because with an inanimate participant nothing really happens. There is no action in the external world. Not only do *personified actors* / processors effectively *negate* the semological process, so do choices of *negative polarity* and *event mediation*. As a consequence, it is important to note such choices in the analysis and account for them in the conclusions.

> E.g. She might give me a present.   SP1 act + ap:tp + rec + med + possibility
>   She didn't give me a present.   SP1 act + ap:tp + rec + med + neg
>   The air gave me a present.   SP1 act* + ap:tp + rec + med

Often, it seems that the semological character of the embedded predications is different than that of the primary predication in significant, thematically or strategically, relevant ways. That is why precise labelling of semological predications is important.

Contextualization

Once your analysis is complete, *contextualize* your text in terms of its culture, situation, register, purpose, and strategy in preparation for *interpreting* it. You might consider what features of the **communicative situation** and **setting** are encoded in this specific instance of the non-instantial register. For instance, in a casino, the register of talk used by people as they operate slot machines is partially dependent on the physical context of the machine they are using, the proximity of other potential interlocutors nearby, the noise level and so on. In addition, the **cultural context** of the interlocutors: their temporal, geographical and social provenance, and the ideology, beliefs, assumptions and values associated with each, affect the way people encode and decode this register. For instance, slot machine talk in a cruise ship casino in the Mediterranean will likely differ from slot machine talk in a Las Vegas Casino, not to mention slot machine talk at a VLT (video lottery terminal) in a small bar in Northern Manitoba. Still, the **register** will likely remain much the same in terms of experiential, interpersonal and textual choices with lexical sets pertaining to money, winning and losing, and slang and expletives colouring the discourse typical of the informality of the spoken medium.

As well as considering how communicative situation, cultural context of the encoder and decoder, registerial expectations, purpose and strategy contextualize the semological choices made in the text, it is useful to consider how syntactic, phonological, graphological and lexical meanings reinforce or challenge semological ones (linguistic context). Once you have taken a few notes about relevant contextual matters in preparation for interpreting your analysis, you are ready to record your results.

Results

The first part of recording your results is to **count** the number of each role in the text and record these numbers on your results counting sheet (see following bracketing suggestions).

A. Frequency counts of different semological roles:
no brackets = primary predication, [ ] = secondary, ( ) = tertiary, { } = 4th predication

Sentence #	Action processes	Mental processes	Relational processes	Circumstances
S.1	Ap:a 1 [ap:e 1]			[time]
S.2			Rp:a 1	

Once you have tabled your results, sentence by sentence add the instances of each role and come up with a final frequency for each role at the particular SP. Keep your totals in the context of their number of predication (level / depth of syntax), in order to appreciate which roles are primary, secondary and so on. The results sheet is a record of all your semological findings. In a **comments** section, keep notes concerning the semological style.

B. Total semological roles (different columns for different process types + circumstances; different participant or goal roles in italics if marked)

	ap		mp	rp		circumstances
ap: e	[1]	mp:c	rp:a	1	place	
ap:a	1	mp:r	rp:r		time [1]	
total ap	**1[1]**	**total mp**	**total rp**	**1**	**total circumstances [1]**	

*Comments – What is the **semological style** of the encoder?*
　　　　　E.g. 2 ap, 1 rp, 1 circumstance
　　　　　How does this style serve her in encoding this text?
　　　　　E.g. narration with description of character.

Conclusions

There should be two parts to your *prose* **conclusions**: the first, ***summarizing*** the semological features of the encoder's style including results and examples, and second, ***interpreting*** these findings by contextualizing them.

Look at the number of action processes, compared to the number of mental and relational ones. Are there some of each, or are there predominately action processes, or maybe a split between action and relational? Are there more of one or two sub-categories of action and / or relational process than a full range of process sub-categories? Can you see any particular patterning to the processes? For instance, do the action processes *frame* the relational (before and after)? Or are they interspersed with no apparent sequence? Are there chunks of consistency of process types that shift at certain points? What is happening at *primary* predication as opposed to *secondary* and *tertiary* predication? Does the *same* process predominate? And how many and what kind of processes have been *negated* or tempered by modals, and at what level? In other words, what processes do not really happen?

With regard to the participant and goal roles, only those roles that are unpredictable given the sub-category of process warrant recording and comment. Inanimate participants require discussion as does negative polarity. Peripheral circumstances should be mentioned, as should interpersonal matters pertaining to event mediation and / or speech function.

Once you have described the ***semological style*** of the encoder in the text, it is time to reflect on, to interpret your findings: *What do they mean? How have they served the encoder in achieving her purpose?* To answer these questions, begin by reviewing the details of your contextualization. What are the elements of the **communicative situation** that you identified? What are the **cultural** beliefs, assumptions and values that contributed to the *encoder's* linguistic choices? And what cultural knowledge, experience and expectations would the *decoder* bring to his / her interpretation of, and response to, the text?

How did you classify your text in terms of **register**? What linguistic choices did the encoder make **experientially, interpersonally** and **textually** in how she encoded her semological meaning? What semological style typifies the register of your text? In what ways does the semological style of your text reinforce certain registerial tendencies, while challenging others? Many registers are quite predictable semologically in order to fulfill their **purpose** most effectively and efficiently. After all, predictability facilitates interpretation, and interpretation is essential in order to educate. Similarly, in the business world where reports, memoranda and instructional manuals must be clear and concise, semological innovation would be inappropriate. Even in the more formulaic of literary genres predictability is important to readers who want a *relaxed* read, not a challenging one.

One way of creating linguistic predictability is by following the semological characteristics of particular **rhetorical strategies** used to accomplish certain purposes (see Chapter 7). Relational processes dominate character and setting *descriptions*. Mental processes dominate *interior monologues* and *dialogue* where a character's thoughts, feelings or words are expressed. Action processes dominate *narrative story telling* where the plot is moving forward and circumstances of time and place add a sequence and spatial orientation to the process. Action processes also dominate 'as it happens' sports comentaries, 'how to' instructions, and 'where to' directions. However, in registers like advertising, if the text does not take creative leaps beyond non-instantial registerial expectations, receivers might never be attracted to, or remember, the product advertised in the text, so it would not fulfill the producer's purpose of persuading and selling. Deliberate, market-researched, innovations continuously recreate a demand and market for products and services.

In the complex texts involving persuasion and potentially manipulation, analysts might find it useful to distinguish between the producer / encoder's *overt* (what is happening at the primary predication) and *covert* (what is happening at a deeper level) semological agendas. What happens covertly could be more interesting than what happens more superficially and obviously. Communicative purpose accounts for such matters.

In semological analysis, as with the other forms of analyses, it is important to remember not only what is semologically manifested, but what isn't. What could have been, and usually is, in that particular situation: register, audiences, purpose, might not be manifested in the instantial version of the text. In other words, how are the expectations you bring to the passage from past experience thwarted, as well as reinforced? A car advertisement full of mental rather than action processes says more about a subtle communicative agenda with the receivers than actions appropriate to cars.

Deciding what is, and is not, significant can be tricky for a beginning analyst without comparative experience of similar texts. Until you have such experience, let your *first impressions* and *initial hypotheses* guide you. They represent your preliminary responses to the choices the encoder made in the text. As a decoder you are not a blank slate; you come with a wealth of linguistic experience and expectations of the culture and of the register. If you respond in a particular way to a text, there must have been something within that text that triggered those responses. Your analysis shows you how these reactions were caused by patterns of similarities and differences encoded in the text. Your preliminary hypotheses may also draw your attention to features you forgot to mention. Let your first responses guide your interpretations. Your reactions tell you *what* the author achieved; your analysis shows you *how* she did it, and your contextualization suggests *why*.

Example

Analysis

Preparation
Because the following spontaneous monologue is so elliptical, and so coherent to its situation, I have 'filled in' possible words in italics in order to facilitate a description of the commentator's semological tendencies. Capitalized letters refer to the proper names of various hockey players. In the transcription I have numbered stretches of discourse that were separated by pauses.

Text
1. Leafs <u>have</u> just <u>been pounding</u> at Montreal in waves the entire period
2. here<u>'s</u> X
3. *he* <u>tries to feather</u> it in only / that <u>doesn't work</u>
4. now X *<u>skates</u>* off the boards and back up to centre
5. *he* <u>can't get</u> it past centre though again / and / the Leafs just <u>dump</u> it back in along the boards
6. S <u>tries to centre</u> it for M
7. M his shot *<u>is blocked</u>* by C
8. B *<u>is</u>* in the centre
9. puck <u>is</u> clear / but / *it <u>doesn't go</u>* not out again
10. there<u>'s</u> a shot by L [that <u>goes</u> wide]

11. S <u>dumps</u> it in
12. he <u>takes</u> a sturdy shot from K in the process
13. now T <u>slides</u> it ahead to M
14. *he* <u>dumps</u> it in
15. and the Leafs <u>will change</u> all 5
16. B <u>*is*</u> in the middle
17. Y <u>fires</u> it in
18. J <u>*skates*</u> out of the net [<u>to play</u>]
19. *he* <u>tips</u> it back along the board
20. G <u>knocks</u> it down

Hypothesis – Action processes will dominate in a transcript of a live hockey broadcast.
Description (conjunctions are bolded)

1. Leafs <u>have</u> just <u>been pounding at</u> Montreal in waves the entire period
   SP1 act + ap:a + pat + man + tim
2. here'<u>s</u> X   SP1 cir:p + rp:r + car
3. *he* <u>tries to feather</u> it in / **only** / that <u>doesn't work</u>
   SP1A *act* + ap:t + med + place + attempt
   SP1B*act + ap:b + neg
4. now X *<u>bounces</u>* off the boards and back up to centre
   SP1 time + act + *ap:e* + con:p + con:p
5. *he* <u>can't get</u> it past centre though / **and** / the Leafs just <u>dump</u> it back in along the boards
   SP1A *act* + ap:t + med + place + abil + neg   SP1B *act* + ap:t + med + place
6. S <u>tries to centre</u> it for M   SP1 act + ap:t + med + ben + attempt
7. M his shot *<u>is blocked</u>* by C   SP1 ran + ap:d + act + pass
8. B <u>*is*</u> in the centre   SP1 car + *rp:r* + cir:p
9. puck <u>is</u> clear / **but** / *it <u>doesn't go</u>* out again
   SP1A item + rp:a + att SP1B med + *ap:t* + place + neg
10. there'<u>s</u> a shot by L [that <u>goes</u> wide]
    SP1 rp:e + exist (SP2) + act   SP2 *act* +ap:e + con:m
11. S <u>dumps</u> it in   SP1 act + ap:t + med + place
12. he <u>takes</u> a sturdy shot from K in the process   SP1 act + ap:t + med + man
13. now T <u>slides</u> it ahead to M   SP1 time + act + ap:t + med + place
14. He <u>finds</u> B   SP1 act + ap:d + ran (not mp:c here)
15. B <u>does</u> a nice job   SP1 act + ap:d + ran (not rp:c here)
16. B <u>*is*</u> in the middle   SP1 car + *rp:r* + cir:p
17. Y <u>fires</u> it in   SP1 act + ap:t + med + place
18. J *<u>skates</u>* out of the net [<u>to play</u>]   SP1 act + *ap:e* + con:p + pur (SP2)   SP2 ap:d
19. *he* <u>tips</u> it back along the board   SP1 *act* + ap:t + med + place
20. G <u>knocks</u> it down   SP1 act + ap:d + ran + place

Contextualization

Situation (*represented*) – commentator describes hockey game on television Feb. 9, 2002.

Register – spontaneous hockey commentary that accompanies live video recording

Purpose – Primarily to describe what is happening in the hockey game, play by play.

Also to comment on plays, teams and players from time to time.

To contextualize current situation with relevant statistics from time to time.

To build viewer / fan's excitement.

strategies primarily narrative

Metafunctions

Experiential – see results of semological analysis concerning participants, processes, goals and circumstances

Interpersonal – 2 attempt modality, 1 ability, 2 negative polarity, 1 passive voice

speech function consistently statement

Textual – time gets focus 2x, place 1x

spoken spontaneous monologue that follows action of video of hockey

logical relations of extension between propositions: 2 variation, 1 addition

Cultural context

encoder – Canadian Broadcasting Corporation announcer

intended decoders – hockey fans

actual decoder – analyst a week after original broadcast

Results

Total predications 22 [3] = 25 *[secondary predications]

Note: Because the predications are so simple, I have counted and totalled the various semological roles from the description in the *summary* table, rather than completing a separate *results* table.

action processes

ap:t 1111111111 = 10   1attempt, 1 neg

ap:d 1111 [1] = 4[1], 1 pass

ap:b 1,   1 neg

ap:a 1

ap:e 11 [1] = 2[1]   1 abil, 1 neg

con:p 111 = 3

con:m [1]

total ap

      21 [3] = 24 = 80%

Note: both ap:e 'filled in' (verbal ellipsis)

     1 ap:t 'filled in'

     3 act 'filled in'

relational processes
rp:a 1
rp:e 1
rp:r 111 = 3
cir:p 111 = 3

total rp
5 = 20%
2 rp:r 'filled in'

circumstances
time 111   = 3 = 20%
place11111111 = 8 = 53%
man 11   = 2 = 13%
ben 1   = 7%
purp 1   = 7%
total circumstances 15

Conclusions

In this short text 80% of the processes are action, and 20% are relational. There are no mental processes; even the process *finds* (S.14) is more action than mental in this text. Over 90% of the processes occur in the primary predications; both secondary processes are action. Two of the action processes are negated, two are tempered by an *attempt* modality, another by *ability*, and one is passive, rather than active voice. Although half of the action processes involve an item being transferred, in this case the *puck*, the other half are divided between action processes that are designative, extended, affected or behavioural. Both designative and extended action processes refer to the way the 'shot' is continued or situated. Relational processes are usually circumstantial, involving more place circumstances. Attributive and existential relational processes are rare, and other types of relational processes are lacking altogether. Place is the peripheral circumstance added to the predication over 50% of the time, with time, usually used as focus, 20% of the time. Manner is manifested twice; purpose and beneficiary once each.

This text is quite a predictable version of this register the analyst suspects. The original hypothesis suggested that action processes dominate, and indeed they do. The importance of action processes of transfer is quite predictable given the focus of this particular sport: the transfer of the puck from one position and one player to another. Designative processes refine the type of shot required to do so, and extended action processes take into account the nuclear importance of place to the action. Occasional relational processes, particularly spatial circumstantial ones, reinforce the significance of spatial positioning in the game of hockey, both of player and puck. The omission of mental processes is not surprising given the situation: no one's thoughts are being recorded, and the spontaneity and monologic character of the narration do not require mental processes of verbalization in order to facilitate decoding (as in conversations or prose dialogues).

What did surprise the analyst somewhat, was the extent to which circumstances dominate the predications: in a few predications only the actor and circumstance are explicitly realized (T. 8,18), in SP1B of T.9 *out again* only the circumstance is manifested. This is predictable, if one thinks about it, in that a hockey commentator has to be as brief as possible in his description of the action, since the action continues, and if he keeps on about one action, he will miss the next. What is crucial to the game of hockey, what decides who will win and who will lose, is the position of the puck. If it ends up in the net, someone scores, the most shots in the net, and that team wins. Small wonder, place is so important, both in a peripheral sense by the number of place circumstances manifested in over half the propositions, but also in a nuclear sense in the circumstantial relational and extended action processes.

All in all, a very dynamic text: verbal style in the syntax, action and place-oriented in the semology. This text is a typical instance of this register with its purpose to describe the action as it happens in a sport, and using a narrative strategy to do so. And so, the sports commentator, the encoder of the text, fulfils the decoder's expectations. The text is quite typical and predictable as an instance of the register of sports, specifically hockey, broadcasting. In twentieth-first century North America, this register is recognized and appreciated by millions of fans.

Review of semological analysis

Analysis

Preparation

1. In a few words describe your **expectations** of the semological character of your text based on your gnostological experience of similar texts.
2. Note your **first impressions** of the semological character of your text specifically.
3. Record any **preliminary hypotheses**; then put them away until your analysis is complete.

4. Consider the **syntax** by underlining and bracketing minimally or by drawing tree diagrams.

Description

1. Label the predications using numbers and / or letters etc. as required. *Numbers* indicate *depth:* the syntactic level at which the predication is embedded (a tertiary predication will be in a secondary, which will be in a primary predication). Letters indicate *sequence* at the same syntactic level: A comes 1st, B comes 2nd. These predications are often joined by a coordinate conjunction; however at times, the 'A' predication might be Qualifier / rc in the Subject / ng, while the 'B' predication might be an Adjunct / sc after the Predicate.

2. List each predication, and **identify** the **roles** included in each. Only *clause* structural elements (SPCA) are given a semological role. Note which roles are developed in predications (bolded below).

E.g. The child <u>hated</u> the tarts [that grandma <u>made</u>]
            SP1   SP2
SP1 proc + mp:r + **phen (SP2)**
SP2 res+ act + ap:r

Note: Mark personified roles with an asterisk, and add unpredictable information regarding polarity, event mediation and speech function (and possibly concerning tense, aspect and voice).

Contextualization

Situation – Label the situation (interactive and represented) and make a few notes concerning its field, mode, personal and functional tenor, for example bank talk: *money, spoken, informal, ritualized, to exchange service.*

Register – Identify the **register** of the text: e.g. bank deposit talk
What aspects of the register explain the semological features of the text, e.g. *informality*?
What semological nuances make your instantial text unique in terms of its register, e.g. *ritualized*?

Purpose – Identify the purpose of this text, e.g. *to exchange* bank deposit *service.*
How does the semology further this purpose, e.g. *ap:tp*?

Strategies: What strategy do the semological processes suggest, e.g. *narration*?

Metafunctions

Describe how the semological choices highlight particular **metafunctions**.

i. Experiential

What ***semological processes*** communicate the experience that is developed in this text?

Do choices in **polarity, voice, animate / inanimate** participants *negate* any of these roles?

ii. Interpersonal

Describe choices in **speech function** and **event mediation** that contribute to the interpersonal relationship. Do choices in event mediation affect the encoding of the experience?

iii. Textual

Distinguish between **focus** (starting point) and **prominence** (highlight) in each sentence.

Is the focus on the phonological *given* (unmarked) or the phonological *new* (marked)?

What **logical relationships** *within* and *between* propositions add cohesion or coherence to the text?

What **referential** and **participant chains** develop the characters in the text?

Linguistic context

a. Does the placement of the text in its larger linguistic context affect the semological expectations and realizations in the text (e.g. first page, last, middle etc.)?

b. Describe the way other linguistic information relates, reinforces and challenges the semological style of this text, e.g. *phonological, syntactic, graphological.*

Cultural context

a. Who is the **encoder**? How do her semological choices reflect her situation, culture, beliefs and values? How do her semological choices encode her social identity and reality?

b. Who is the **intended decoder** (the expected / target audience)? How might her situation and culture, and experience of the register affect her interpretation of the encoder's semological choices?

Who is the **actual decoder**? How might her situation and culture, and experience of the register affect her interpretation of the encoder's semological choices?

Results

a. Frequency counts of different semological roles.

no brackets = primary predication, [ ] = secondary, ( ) = tertiary, { } = 4th predication

Sentence #	Action processes	Mental processes	Relational processes	Circumstances
S.1				
S.2				

b. Total semological roles:

ap	mp	rp	circumstances
ap: e	mp:c	rp:a	place
ap:a	mp:r	rp:r	time
total ap	**total mp**	**total rp**	**total circumstances**

Comments – What is the semological style of the encoder?
How does this style serve her in encoding this text?

Conclusions

A. **Summarize** your findings. Describe the encoder's *semological style*: Is there a single semological focus or several? Is it consistent throughout, or does it change? Are the semological choices affected by negative polarity, personification, passive voice, event mediation?

B. **Interpretation** and even some *speculation*. Use the following questions to consider *why* the encoder's semological style is appropriate to her situation, register, purpose, strategy etc.

a. How do considerations of register, strategy etc. explain and justify the encoder's semological choices?

How does the non-instantial register compare to the instantial register of this particular text?

b. Which results are *predictable* or *unmarked* given the situation, register, strategy, purpose, audience and which are atypical of the register, and hence, potentially significant?

c. Review your *first impressions* and *initial hypotheses* and make sure that your conclusions have addressed them in light of the greater understanding you have gained from your analysis and contextualization.

d. Why do you think the writer made these selections and not others?

How has the encoder's situation and culture affected her intended message?

How do these selections affect the actual readers?

How might the decoder's situation and culture have affected her interpretation?

How do the encoder's graphological, phonological, syntactic etc. meanings reinforce or contradict her semological choices.

Rhetorical Strategies

Over the years, analyses have shown that register is not the only non-instantial configuration of tri-functional (cf. Metafunctions p. 19) and tri-stratal (cf. Strata p. 23) choices known and remembered by language users. In many registers, people, places and things are *described* in very predictable ways stylistically despite different registerial affiliations. In registers of literary discourse, the **rhetorical strategies** of *description, narration, dialogue* and *interior monologue* account for many of the predictable features of the text (Malcolm, 2005). Non-literary discourse employs a broader range of rhetorical strategies each with its predictable gnostological configuration of linguistic resources: *description, definition, lists, narration, process, dialogue, interior monologue* (Becker and Malcolm, 2008). Both encoders and decoders 'know' the linguistic patterns associated with each of these non-instantial rhetorical strategies, and create texts using them in their daily life. This kind of linguistic knowledge can be useful, like register, when describing *instantial* discourse as well. Instantial examples of particular rhetorical strategies are identified as *marked* or *unmarked* depending on how they compare with the non-instantial versions stored in our gnostology.

Some registers of language include one *primary* rhetorical strategy which accounts for most of the linguistic character of the text; other registers include *secondary* rhetorical strategies within a primary strategy, and still others include a mixture of two or more rhetorical strategies. For instance, recipes typically include two well-defined strategies: first the *list* of ingredients, and second the *process* or methodology of mixing the ingredients. Descriptions often include a narrative 'frame', and sometimes description is intermingled throughout a text.

There is also a second type of rhetorical strategy (also influenced by composition's *strategies of development*); however, these strategies are used in more of a logical organizational way than the strategies mentioned so far. There is a tri-functional aspect to **comparison-contrast, argument, classification, problem-solution, *and* cause-effect**, but it is likely that tri-functional and tri-stratal characteristics are more a consequence of the rhetorical strategies embedded within such logical organizational strategies than inherent features of their own. Further research on such rhetorical strategies will continue to illumine non-instantial gnostological resources, which sometimes specify a particular range of tri-functional and tri-stratal options, and at other times, reveal an embedding of such strategies within broader organizational ones. The more analysts explore the ways rhetorical strategies function, the more they will learn how tri-functional registerial configurations relate to, and possibly depend on, these strategies.

Description

Description typically includes a nominal syntactic style with numerous Modifiers and Qualifiers scattered throughout the Subject, Complement and Completive. Adjuncts are rare. Semologically, relational processes figure prominently with few circumstances. Graphologically, description, in written discourse, is characterized by paragraphs and sentences. Lexically, taxonomies of *people, parts of the body, clothes, professions, emotions, colour* and *size* typically describe people; whereas, taxonomies concerning *landscape, nature, buildings, parts of a house* and *furnishings* characterize descriptions of places. Interpersonally, lexical items may be coloured by appraisal if the encoder's perspective is more subjective than objective. Semological statements dominate, and event mediation is virtually non-existent. Textually, lexical relations are the primary means of binding the text together cohesively, with spatially oriented cohesive conjunctions like *above . . ., to the right . . .,* characteristic of some place descriptions. This, then, describes the prototypical tri-functional and tri-stratal characterization of the rhetorical strategy known as **description** stored non-instantially, gnostologically. However, in a specific instance of description not every prototypical feature need be selected: an encoder's descriptive palette may be much more limited.

In literary texts, description is used to develop characters, settings and symbols; in non-literary texts, it is used to describe scientific and geographical phenomena and sell merchandise. In the following text, noun groups are italicized, and relational processes are bolded.

> *Most adult caribou* **have** *dark brown coats with creamy white manes, necks, bellies, and rumps.* The coat colour **can**, however, **be** quite variable, according to the season and even where the caribou <u>are found</u>. *Most Peary caribou, in the High*

Arctic Islands, **have** *an almost white winter coat,* as **do** *some individual caribou* elsewhere in the North during fall and winter.

Adult caribou males, or bulls, **have** *large and massive bodies,* while *the adult females, or cows,* **are** *generally smaller, with a more slender physique.* All *caribou* **have** *relatively short furry ears, a short furry tail, long noses with a keen sense of smell, and well-furred faces.* They **have** *long legs* and **are** *capable of* *running* at *high speeds.*

(Hummel and Ray, 2008, p. 32)

Lists

Lists are another rhetorical strategy that can be defined very precisely stylistically. They too are nominally inclined like description, but in a more minimalist way. Syntactically, they include only nouns. Graphologically, there is usually, one noun per line, with each new word placed below the other in a column; all justified to the left. Officially, because there are no clauses, there is no semology nor cohesion. However, because each word in the list is often from the same lexical set, there is lexical coherence. This accounts for the endophoric texture of the strategy; however, it is the exophoric coherence to the situation that is even more indicative of the items in the list. Each lexical item, *milk* in a shopping list, or a *screw* in an instructional manual, is related to a 'real life' referent. Lists may occur independently as shopping lists, but they also precede process passages in other registers such as recipes and instructional manuals.

Shopping list
milk
eggs
peanut butter
catsup
brown rice
yogurt

Definition

Texts involving ***definition*** can also be nominally inclined syntactically with noun groups extended by seriated Modifers or Qualifiers, or Qualifiers inside Qualifiers e.g. *Kiln – a large oven, brick-built, generating great heat, in which various materials are dried, calcined or hardened* (Websters). Semologically, action processes and circumstances are rare. In their nominal style definitions resemble description and list strategies; however, in other ways they are quite distinct. Graphologically, the word to be defined is thematically foregrounded by coming first, and in some cases, by being bolded, or written in a slightly larger font than the definition that follows. The definition itself is interesting in that it may or may not be written in complete independent clauses. Lexically, it is rich in synonyms, but only those within the narrow semantic range of the word being defined. Some definitions use concrete nouns; others, abstract, depending on the demands of the particular experience and register. Cohesively, lexical relations are the dominant cohesive device that gives the text its texture. However, in registers involving lists of definitions like Glossaries, often syntactic, semological and graphological parallelism between definitions adds coherence.

Because definition strategies are used in textbooks with a didactic purpose to introduce field-restricted metalanguage or jargon (interpersonal lexical involvement), they are often relatively transparent syntactically and lexically. Abbreviated syntax, lexical synonymy and grammatical parallelism often support this goal. However, as the following legal definition demonstrates, transparency is not always achieved, particularly when the definition is full of abstract field-restricted terms that are only understood by experts in the field, and used in formal discourse. In the following text, noun groups are italicized and relational processes are bolded.

> **Conjecture** – *The dividing line between conjecture and inference* **is** often a *difficult one <u>to draw</u>. A conjecture* **may be** plausible but it **is** of *no legal value*, for *its essence* **is** that it **is** *a mere guess. An inference in the legal sense*, on the *other hand* **is** *a deduction from the evidence*, and if it **is** *a reasonable deduction* it **may have** *the validity of legal proof. The attribution of occurrence to a cause* **is** always *a matter of inference. The cogency of a legal inference of causation* <u>may vary</u> in *degree between practical certainty and reasonable probability.* Where *the coincidence of cause and effect* **is** <u>not</u> *a matter of actual observation* there **is** necessarily *a hiatus in the direct evidence*, but this **may be** legitimately <u>bridged</u> by *an inference between the facts actually <u>observed</u>* and <u>*proved*</u>.
>
> (Murray, 1932, p. 806)

Narration

Unlike description, lists and definition, narration involves action and a verbal style. In ***narration*** actions happen, events take place and often in a particular time and place. Authors advance their plot, and people tell a story. For example, *Yesterday I* <u>*went*</u> *to the zoo. At six I* <u>*ate*</u> *supper, and when I finished I* <u>*saw*</u> *a movie.* Narration's verbal syntactic style typically includes numerous clauses with both finite and often non-finite Predicate / verbs and numerous Adjuncts. Several clauses mean several Predicates. In verbal styles, subordinate and non-finite clauses are more common than relative clauses at a secondary level. Sometimes compounded Predicates add more action. Narratives may follow a first person perspective with 'I' as Subject, diminishing social distance between interlocutors of a third person narration with s / he as Subject, increasing social distance. Subjects are often realized by unmodifiable and unqualifiable pronouns or Proper nouns, or are omitted altogether (nominal ellipsis).

Lexically, narration typically features lexical sets pertaining to different kinds of action: *hand* actions, *walking* actions, *violent* actions and so on. Action processes dominate semologically, often surrounded by circumstances of place, time and manner. Interpersonally, speech function is statement, and event mediation is lacking. Textually, cohesion typically results from personal reference, as long as there is a single participant engaging in all the actions of the passage. In addition, additive conjunction, often followed by nominal ellipsis, is also a typical cohesive device which contributes to the texture of narration. In many narratives, time is important semologically in terms of the experience being narrated, and time is sometimes theme-marked textually (not so much in spontaneously-told casual stories where additive conjunctions fulfill this function).

In non-literary discourse, narration is used in the countless registers in which stories are featured, especially in casual conversation. Narration is also a feature of historical documents, police narratives, doctor-patient talk, journals, letters, newspapers, diary writing and more. In the following claimant's narrative (a register of legal discourse), circumstances of place (Adjuncts) are italicized; action processes are bolded. (Relational processes of circumstance: place, as in the first sentence, reinforce the significance of place in such narratives.)

Hugh William Betzner, Jr.

I <u>was standing</u> *on Houston Street near the intersection of Elm Street.* I **took** a picture of President Kennedy's car *as it* <u>*passed*</u> *along Houston Street.* I <u>have</u> an old camera. I **looked** *down real quick* and **rolled** the film to **take** the next picture. I then **ran** *down to the corner of Elm and Houston Streets*, this <u>being</u> the southwest corner. I **took** another picture *just as President Kennedy's car* **rounded** the *corner*. He <u>was</u> just about all the way around the corner. I <u>was standing</u> back from the corner and **had to take** the pictures *through some of the crowd*. I **ran** *on down Elm a little more* and President Kennedy's car **was starting to go** *down the hill to the triple underpass*. I **was running** <u>trying to keep</u> the President's car in my view and **was winding** my film as I **ran**. I **took** another picture *as the President's car* **was going** *down the hill on Elm Street*. I **started to wind** my film *again* and I <u>heard</u> a loud noise.

(Warren Commission Hearings, 1973, p. 467)

Narrative rhetorical strategies are connected to discourse plot. If the narrative is told in a chronological sequence, the discourse plot is **unmarked**. However, if the narrative is told according to a *non-linear, non-chronological,* discourse plot, beginning at the mid-point perhaps, returning occasionally to earlier events through *flashbacks*, and then anticipating future events in dreams, the discourse plot is **marked**.

Process

Process texts resemble narratives in verbal style and their focus on action in a sequence, experientially; however, interpersonal, textual and functional differences lead to a rhetorical strategy that is stylistically quite different. In both strategies the interpersonal relationship is asymmetrical: the encoder is the knower; the decoder, the receiver. However, in process texts, the encoder is an expert in her field on whom the decoder depends to achieve her goal which is often a non-verbal one like making a cake, assembling a piece of furniture, or giving directions. In narratives, hearing the verbal text / story is the goal; in process texts, the text is merely a means to a non-verbal end.

Assembling something requires a carefully defined order of action processes and place and manner circumstances, semologically. The correct sequence is so important to the desired outcome that it is often highlighted graphologically by the use of numerals and / or cohesively by temporal Links *First, mix the shortening with the sugar, then add the egg and the vanilla. . . .* Frequently, pictures and diagrams illustrate steps in the process. While first or third person Subjects in narration are often minimal, in process texts second persons are only implied. Interpersonally, narration is relayed through a series of statements; process texts are encoded through commands. Lexically, field-restricted technical jargon is common in process texts. In the following text, place and manner circumstances are italicized, imperative action processes are bolded and technical jargon is capitalized.

Wooden Handle Wheelbarrow
Assembly Instructions

A. <u>Set</u> the HANDLES *parallel to one another & <u>elevated</u> from the floor <u>using</u> two boxes or SAW HORSES.* **<u>Position</u>** the NOSE GUARD *around and over handle ends.* **<u>Insert</u>** two 5/16″ x 2″ HEX BOLTS with THREADS *<u>facing</u> outward through the NOSE GUARD.* **<u>Apply</u>** WASHERS *to each BOLT* and **<u>thread</u>** a NUT *onto each BOLT, loosely fastened.*

B. <u>Put</u> the WEDGES *on top of each handle* and **<u>align</u>** the BOLT holes *in the WEDGES with corresponding BOLT holes in the handles.*

C. <u>Slot</u> two 5/16″ x 4 ½″ BOLTS *into the holes of the CLIP-ON BRACKET in tray bottom* and *through corresponding holes in front WEDGES, handles, SHORT STAY and LEGS.* **<u>Apply</u>** a WASHER *to BOLT ends* and **<u>thread</u>** a NUT *onto each BOLT, loosely fastened . . .*

Prose dialogue

Dialogue is also quite predictable and consistent, although not to the extent of description and narration. In real life the spoken word gets much of its meaning from its situation, the memories and ideologies the interactants share (their gnostology, and cultural context), and the way it is said (phonologically). **Prose dialogue** does not have the luxury of phonological innuendo or of maximum communication with minimal verbalization as a consequence of shared values and experiences. 'It is not spontaneous, but must appear to be so. It is permanent, but must seem as ephemeral as the speech it imitates. . . . The dilemma of the writer is to create using one medium a facsimile of another (which would be far too wasteful and disorganized to 'reproduce'), to artificially arrange elaborate echoes of the living language in an evocative, suggestive and concentrated way to make us believe that what we hear is a natural utterance'. (Chothia, 1979, pp. 40–1) (cf. Malcolm, 1991).

In prose, dialogue can be written *directly* or *indirectly*. **Direct speech** appears to be quoted exactly as spoken. Some encoders signal direct speech graphologically by surrounding it with quotation marks and capitalizing the first word, others surround it with dashes, and some use no graphological indication. *She said quietly, '**I'll see you later**'.* In certain registers, names of speakers accompany the direct speech of dialogue (in plays, transcriptions of casual conversation, and prose dialogue in novels). Phonological information is lexicalized, for example *quietly*. Graphological and orthographical (spelling) innovations may encode phonological variations approximating various dialects.

Unlike the direct speech of conversation, prose dialogue usually includes at least two predications semologically: the first the formulaic mental process of verbalization *s / he said*; the second predication: the projected speech itself (graphologically distinct) including a variety of processes. The syntax of dialogue is often quite different from the syntax of other strategies. The Complement in the primary clause, which encodes the direct speech, is realized by a full sentence, for example *She said, 'Unfortunately, she's away'*. This secondary clause includes sentence level elements *unfortunately* as well as one or more Proposition / independent clause *she's away* (ibid.). Interpersonally, prose dialogue, like speech, includes a much greater variety of speech function than many strategies. Questions and commands are common. There is a greater likelihood of exophoric coherence in dialogue than endophoric cohesion. And cohesively, ellipsis is more a characteristic of dialogue than most other strategies.

Indirect speech is not marked graphologically by quotations and capitals. It is usually written in the past tense. Mental processes of verbalization are obligatory at primary predication. Although the signal *that* is not required to introduce indirect / reported speech, it often does, for example, *She whispered **that she would see him later**.* This clause is usually described as a Complement / relative clause, not a Complement / full sentence. The Subject of the main clause is the same as that of the indirect speech.

Dialogue is the primary strategy of many registers involving spoken discourse in scientific, medical, classroom, legal discourse and service encounters. It is marked by turn-taking, interruptions, lexical appraisal and involvement, often abbreviated and elliptical syntax replete with numerous hesitation fillers, false starts, grammatical infelicities, varied mood selections, and exophoric coherence (cf. Malcolm, 1984). Multi-party discourse and monologue are rare in written discourse other than televisions scripts and plays; however, multi-party exchanges, like dialogues, are common in 'real-life' situations where several people discuss, debate as they converse. In the following example of a written interview, examples of direct speech are in quotation marks, indirect speech is italicized, and the mp:v indicative of prose dialogue are bolded. In transcriptions of spoken, as opposed to written discourse, exophoric ellipsis and sentence level structural elements like hesitation fillers and false starts are more important than in this written variety.

> So what better thing to ask a professional interviewer about than what makes a interview?
>   "A good interview is basically where you get the interviewee **to say** things {that} they haven't said a million times – especially if it's a high profile person who does

a lot of interviews," he **said**. "An alchemy of a lot of things" <u>produces</u> that result, he **added**, including "a good chemistry between the interviewer and interviewee."

 <u>Researching</u> your subject, and <u>demonstrating</u> that you'<u>ve done</u> that research, <u>is</u> also important. *Ghomeshi **said** [that] it'<u>s</u> not unusual for him <u>to research</u> a person for 10 or 12 hours, or for a few days if it'<u>s</u> a particularly big interview.*

(Epp, 2009)

Interior monologue

While *interior monologue* is a rhetorical strategy used by some twentieth-century literary authors to mirror a character's thinking, it is seldom used in non-literary discourse other than very informal registers such as diary writing. Although one style of interior monologue seems more the prototypical non-instantial version than others, in fact, there are a few varieties. The most predictable version is the one that uses mental processes of cognition as the primary predication semologically *S / he thought / remembered / knew* with a projected secondary predication that includes assorted process types. In this prototypical version, statements dominate, appraisal is minimal. Personal reference adds cohesion, as do lexical relations. Complex forms of elaboration may be featured, with complex syntax involving lengthy sentences, as authors attempt to capture the rambling progression of a character's sometimes unrelated thoughts. The other version of interior monologue recreates thought using an abbreviated style with incomplete clauses, isolated noun groups and ellipsis that explores a wealth of lexical taxonomies in an illogical sequence (cf. Malcolm, 1987). While the primary rhetorical strategy in the following example is direct speech / dialogue, interior monologue with its focus on cognition certainly contributes to the dialogue's style (mp:c are bolded).

> And **I think** we <u>can</u> probably just <u>slow</u> him down to a little over maintenance, since he'<u>s</u> out under the – he'<u>s</u> under the warmer, uh which <u>will increase</u> his uh fluid requirements uh .. ten or twenty percent .but uh as afar as <u>I can tell</u> right now he'<u>s</u> .. you <u>can</u> <u>wean</u> him,
> <u>Can</u> you <u>explain</u> this .. for me?
> Well – **I think** you <u>might</u> <u>explain</u> that it'<u>s</u> just – this really was .. spinal
> Why <u>do</u> **you think** he <u>had</u> such a large urine output?
> Well, he Mannitol, he <u>had</u> Lasix, uh he <u>had</u> Albinum, um .. I <u>had</u> to **believe** he <u>was</u> hypovolemic, and he <u>seemed</u> <u>to correct</u> them awfully quickly, um and I **was wondering** whether . . .

Rhetorical strategies in combination

Although certain registers regularly employ *unmarked* instantial versions of a particular rhetorical strategy, other registers employ combinations of different rhetorical strategies or *marked* versions of single strategies.

"Hot winger, sharp goalie <u>snip</u> Blades": description and narration
(Narrative features bolded; descriptive, italicized)

Rightwinger Alexander Korolyuk <u>was</u> the sniper, the agitator and the motivator **last night** as the Moose **edged** Kansas City Blades 4-2 **at Winnipeg Arena last night in front of a crowd of 7,389**.

The Russian player, **in his 15th game with the Moose, <u>scored</u>** a pair of goals and **<u>threw</u>** his weight **around all night <u>to keep</u>** alive the team's playoff hopes.

Kansas *is* **now** 22-23-12 for 56 points while Manitoba *is* 19-27-9 and *has* 47 points.

It *<u>was</u>* the last action for the Moose **before Tuesday's all-star game in Grand Rapids, Michigan** in which *defence-man Dale De Gray <u>will be</u>* the *lone Manitoba representative*.

(Prest, 2003)

Children's Casual Conversation: *description in dialogue*
(relational processes are bolded)

S: I <u>wanted</u> [Mark **to be** a medicine man]
F: It'**s** not easy
S: You'**re** right
F: That **would be** nice
F: Nobody'**s** out there
S: **Have** you **been** in here before?
F: You **sat** there
S: The teacher **was** right here
F: That'**s** right

Recipe for 'Nutty Burgers': *list and process*
(action processes are bolded)

5 Tbsp soya sauce	1 tsp ground sage
2 Tbsp corn oil	2 Tbsp Brewer's yeast
1 medium onion, chopped	¾ C nuts, chopped
2 cloves garlic, minced	1 handful green lentils
1 ¾ C boiling water	1 handful sunflower seeds
1 C rolled oats	

Add soya sauce, oil, onion, garlic and lentils to boiling water. **Cook** until lentils are chewable.

<u>Mix</u> together oats, sage, yeast, nuts, sunflower seeds; gradually **sprinkle** into boiling broth, while **stirring**. **Let** cool. **Form** into patties and **brown** in oil in frying pan. Great as a substitute for a hamburger, or **serve** with brown or mushroom gravy as 'meat'.

Directions: *process and description*
(action processes are bolded)
<u>Head</u> north on Lagimodiere, until you **go** past the Perimeter.
<u>Turn</u> right on Garvin Rd. a few minutes north of the Perimeter, and **drive** for about 10 minutes.
<u>Turn</u> left (north) on Highway #206, to the right (south) <u>is</u> Oakbank.
My street, Hillside Rd., <u>is</u> just one mile north of Garvin, off #206.
If you **get** to the back end of Bird's Hill Park you **have gone** too far.
Anyway, one mile north of Garvin on Highway # 206, you **will find** Hillside Rd.
<u>Turn</u> right (east) on Hillside Rd. and **drive** 2.3 kilometers.
My house <u>is</u> #2805 Hillside Rd., on the south side of the street (your right).
It's the weathered cedar.

*Exercise: Rhetorical Strategy Combinations
*Exercise: Rhetorical Strategies and Register

Rhetorical strategies and logical organization

Some rhetorical strategies are tri-functional and tri-stratal in consistent ways as part of the non-instantial realizatory code, and can also be used comparatively in examples of instantial rhetorical strategies and registers of discourse. Other rhetorical strategies are used more broadly determining a logical organization that embeds the tri-functional strategies already introduced. Classification, comparison / contrast, cause and effect, problem / solution and argument are such logically motivated, and textually structuring, rhetorical strategies.

Classification

In the following passage taken from Chapter 5, pronouns are *classified* into different types. In classification, neither temporal nor spatial organization is foregrounded, but instead the overall topic, in this case pronouns, is divided into constituent smaller topics, in this case types of pronouns. What is stylistically distinct about this strategy is that the classifications are separated in a regular fashion by bullets or indentation, graphologically. Each classification is often stylistically parallel, or consistent with the others: lexically, syntactically and semologically. In the following example, each sub-classification is bulleted, beginning with the bolded sub-classification of pronoun and ending with an example. Each sub-classification is the Subject of a Predicate in the present tense, syntactically; encoding much the same lexical range, and using semological processes at primary predication whose effect is relational (with inanimate actors, passive voice, at times). Examples of each type of pronoun are italicized, while the one used in a complete sentence is bolded as well. Classification is common in textbooks; however, it is also used in business discourse and more.

> **Pronouns (pn)**
> There are several types of pronouns other than *personal* pronouns:
> o **Interrogative pronouns** are used in questions: ***Where*** are *you* going*? **What?** **Why** do *you* ask*? (also *which, who, whose, whom, what, how, when, where*?). Only *who* shows **case** *who, whose, whom* (subjective, possessive, objective).
> o **Relative pronouns** 'connect' dependent clauses to main clauses, e.g. *which, who, whom, whose, what, that,* e.g. *The umbrella [**which** was broken] was lost.*
> o **Indefinite pronouns** like *other, some, such,* are used as nominal substitutes *I finished **all** of my work.* and deictics **both** *books.* However, some like *everything* and *no one* are used when the specific nominal antecedent is unknown **Somebody** left *this book.* **Anyone** know *him?* **Nothing** is *ready.*
>
> (Malcolm p.112)

Not all texts developed by classification are encoded in exactly the same way. Still, the distinctions and comparisons between classifications are recognizable with analyses. They may involve graphological indentations, syntactic parallelisms and lexical shifts between classifications, with cohesive devices that act as transitions between each. In this chapter, graphologically highlighted sub-titles are the most obvious markers of the classifications of rhetorical strategies. Each strategy is described and exemplified. Classification is a rhetorical strategy mainstay of written academic discourse.

Comparison

In **comparison / contrast** one topic is compared to another. The similarities and differences between the two ideas illumine the idiosyncrasies of each. The section of this chapter entitled *process* was developed by comparing it to narration. In this book comparison and contrast has been used in every chapter several times: how does one advertisement compare to another, how does language encode interpersonal meaning syntactically compared to semologically? Comparisons can be structured in *chunks*, with several sentences / paragraphs being used to develop one topic in stylistically similar ways and then a subsequent chunk of text developing the other topic, or within the same sentence in subsequent clauses (the *slice* method), for example *Although Jay likes tennis; Cyndy does not. Jay likes cake; whereas, Cyndy likes pie.*

The **chunk** method describes topic A entirely, before moving on to topic B. The **slice** method describes one aspect of topic A then B, perhaps its lexical style; then another aspect of A and B, perhaps its semological style, and so on. If the two items being compared share several qualities, although manifested differently, the slice method is preferable: it makes for a *closer* comparison. However, if the information available makes such a detailed comparison impossible, the chunk method is preferable. These two different methods of organizing a comparison require different *syntactic, lexical, graphological* and *cohesive* styles. However, both include a certain amount of parallelism tristratally. Logical signals encoded by particular conjunctions keep the decoder clear about how the comparison is proceeding, be they contrastive or non-contrastive: on the other hand, alternatively, instead of, rather, however, but; like text A, text B is . . .

Often, in lengthy texts, comparison / contrast may operate as a primary strategy in terms of overall organization, while a secondary strategy like description accounts for the codal consistency within each chunk. Some comparisons, such as the following, use a mixture of chunk and slice methods within the same comparison. Experiential and textual choices that typify this strategy are italicized and bolded, respectively.

> **Process** texts, used in registers such as technical manuals and recipes, **resemble** **narratives** in their focus on action in a sequence, experientially; **however**, interpersonal, textual and functional differences lead to a rhetorical strategy that is stylistically quite different. **In both narratives** and **process** texts, where information is being exchanged, the interpersonal relationship between the encoder and decoder is asymmetrical: the encoder is the 'knower'; the decoder, the receiver. **However**, in **process** texts, the encoder is also an expert in her field on whom the decoder depends to achieve her goal which is often a non-verbal one like making a cake or assembling a piece of furniture. In **narratives**, hearing the verbal story is the goal; **whereas**, in **process** texts, the text is merely a means to a non-verbal end

(Malcolm p. 196)

Cause and effect

Cause / effect can also be used as a rhetorical strategy within an individual sentence or more broadly, as the organizational criteria for an entire article. In some registers the semantic *causes* of an effect might dominate a register, and the *effect* appear as a final conclusion. If a team loses an important game, an editorial might reflect on the reasons or causes for the loss (the effect). In other registers, a team of experts might speculate on the effects of new legislation (the cause). Either way, speculating on unknown effects, or reflecting on possible causes will involve choices of cohesive devices and syntax that encode this logical strategy: causal conjunctions, alpha-beta clause complexes. In the following text, the graphology, lexis and syntactic parallelism indicate the *primary* strategy as classificatory, while the *secondary* strategy indicated by lexis, semantics and cohesion is cause-effect. The linguistic features of the primary strategy classification are bolded; of the secondary strategy are italicized (cause is bolded; effect, not).

> **QLT Phototherapeutics:** *QLT shares surged 380.2 per cent last year [effect]* **on rising excitement over its Visudyne photodynamic treatment for age-related macular degeneration [cause]**, a major cause of blindness among older people. The treatment has been approved in Switzerland, and Vancouver-based QLT is awaiting a green light from regulators in the United States.
>
> **Celestica Inc.**: A spinoff from Onex Corp, Celestica has become a market darling over the past year. The Toronto-based computer and telecommunications maker has benefitted from **the growing trend among high-tech companies to use outside manufacturers [cause]** *to reduce costs and get products to market faster [effects]*. About 20 to 25 per cent of the $500 billion (US) **electronics manufacturing business was forecast to be outsourced in 1999 [cause]**, *and it's expected to grow 25 per cent a year [effect]*. Celestica's shares gained 327.5 per cent last year.
>
> **Nortel Network Corp.**: Nortel Networks was the story of the TSE last year, **soaring 272.7 per cent[cause]**, *driving up the stock affiliate BCE Corp. and accounting for the lion's share of the Canadian market's advance [effects]*. The Brampton, Ont.-based telecommunications giant rode higher in tandem with other telecom companies.
>
> (Northfield, 2000)

Problem / Solution

Like the last few rhetorical strategies, **problem / solution** can organize a single sentence or an entire letter as the following texts illustrate. The focus may be primarily on the *problem(s)* or the *solution(s)*, or both might be manifested equally. If the problems are common knowledge, but the solutions are not, the solutions, as new information, will likely receive the focus. If the problems are not adequately understood, they may need to be developed themselves, before possible solutions can be explored. Problem-solution seems to carry an important semantic dimension to it that is encoded in the lexis, the lexical appraisal, the conjunctions, possible alpha-beta clause complexes and so on. In the following two texts, problem-solution is not the primary rhetorical strategy (dialogue), but the secondary strategy exhibiting a logical coherence between nearby sentences. In both texts (spoken and written), passages pertaining to problem-solution are italicized, (problems are bolded; solutions, not).

(a transcription of a text between two 20-year-old female university students)

"C – *I need a summer job* **[problem]**

R – *so* where have you applied?

C – *I applied at um at GM*   [potential solutions follow with company names]

R – mmm

C – *Bell Canada um oh social services in Oshawa* they're like you know day camp

R – mmm sounds like good jobs

C – and what was the other place? Some kind of government job or something so . . . *but **I never heard from any of them** **[problem]** but* last year the same thing happened **I didn't have a job** right? **[problem]** I finished school like I was finished early April 23rd *Luckily* I finished early or I'd never got then a job *but I bussing tables?*[solution] at the Holiday Inn? *so* I did that for a couple of weeks.

I am uncomfortable with the responses that are made to my questions about the Board **[current problem]**. When I ask a simple question, the response is usually **minimal, vague** and **evasive** **[problem]**. I remember when a manager at the Global Conference last year suggested that certain information was restricted, **people from all over the world were very upset**: they noted how it strengthened the insider / outsider, we / them, illusions that are **not** our principles **[past problem]**. One man demanded a full disclosure be made to fellow leaders the next day, and *it was* [past solution].

I need to know who was asked to be on the board, who was turned down, and who declined the offer, obviously because these are appropriate national volunteers **[problem]**. I have no interest in gossip, only in doing my work: helping to find new national volunteers. **It has been challenging at times to be the 'third man out', so to speak; the only one without the relevant information** **[problem]**. *I hope in the future relevant information will be shared more openly, patiently, and regularly [proposed solution]*.

Argument

The purpose of **argumentation** is quite different from the earlier strategies. In this case information is selected, organized and explored to persuade the reader to agree with the point of view advocated. In order to promote a particular point of view, the encoder may *appeal* to the decoder emotionally (pathos), ethically (ethos) or legally (logos). In addition, the encoder may use various *topoi* to strengthen her position, for example *testimony, authority, size, statistics, past / present, analogy, anecdote*. In terms of organization, the argument may include a progression from the weakest to the strongest supporting evidence. In addition, it may include an alternation between contrary points (cons) or opposition to the point of view that is promoted, and points that support the argument (pros). The 'pros' and 'cons' of an argument can be organized using the *slice* method, echoing debate format, or *chunk* method, as long as the pros complete the argument in the strongest way possible. Because of the possible debate format and the importance of opinion in this rhetorical strategy, adversative extension and lexical appraisal are some of the linguistic patterns usually featured.

In the text that follows the encoder urges readers to advocate for stronger handgun control laws using a variety of *rhetorical* **appeals** (emotional, ethical, logical) and *topoi* (testimony, authority, size, statistics, anecdote). Some of the linguistic features that are common to this strategy are first person Subject, lexical appraisal, statistics lexical sets, mental processes making the appeal (bolded) with action processes encoding the narrative event and frame that motivates the rest of the argument (see italicized). This argument uses problem and solution and narration as embedded strategies.

> *Seven years ago John Huckley pulled a $29 revolver from the pocket and opened fire on a Washington Street. He shot the President. He also shot my husband.*
>
> I'm not **asking** for your **sympathy**. I'm **asking** for your **help**.
>
> I've **learned** from my **own experience** that, **alone**, there's only so much you can do to stop handgun violence. **But** that **together, we** can **confront** the mightiest gun lobby – The N.R.A. – and **win**.
>
> I've only to look at my husband, Jim, to remember that **awful** day . . . the **unending** TV coverage of the handgun firing over and over . . . the **nightmare panic** and **fear**,
>
> It's an **absolute miracle** nobody was killed. After all, **twenty thousand** Americans are killed by handguns every year. **Thousands** more – men, women, even children – are **maimed** for life.

Like **me**, I know you **support stronger** handgun control laws. **So** does the **vast majority** of Americans. **But** the National Rifle Association can spend so much in elections that Congress is **afraid** to pass an **effective** national handgun law.

It's time to **change** that. Before it's **too late** for another **family** like **mine** . . . a **family** like **yours**. . . . (Handgun Control Inc.)

This chapter introduces analysts to the potential value of rhetorical strategies as a research tool, when linguistically defined. There is much to learn, such as:

Are there other rhetorical strategies that encode a predictable tri-functional and tri-stratal assortment of linguistic features?

How do the broader, logical organizing strategies organize the others in particular registers of discourse?

What registers of legal discourse use argumentation as a primary strategy?

To what extent does argumentation use the other non-literary strategies as secondary strategies of development?

What registers of scientific discourse involve process, description, argument?

The more each non-instantial rhetorical strategy is understood linguistically, the better tool discourse analysts will have when considering instantial examples of discourse.

Already rhetorical strategies have been used fruitfully when comparing forensic texts. Many other areas of research would benefit from their application.

Further reading

Asp, E. (2001). 'How to Do Different Things with Words'. In *Communication in Linguistics* de Villiers, J. and Stainton, R. (eds.) Toronto, Canada: Editions du Gref. pp. 1–32.

8 Phasal Analysis

In the early 1980s in an analysis of one of Hamlet's monologues, Michael Gregory noticed that his semological, syntactic, cohesive and lexical analyses related in particular ways. It seemed that there was a momentary consistency in tri-functional and tri-stratal choices, which was then replaced by a new combination of semological, syntactic and lexical patterns a moment later (1995, pp. 113–28). The entire text was *structured* by these chunks of consistency.

During that same period, Gregory and I were analysing several conversations spoken by six-year-old children. As we completed our several analyses, we noticed the same spontaneous structuring phenomenon that Gregory had noticed in the Hamlet text. We wondered if all texts were structured in this way. It was not a contrived, static, topic-focussed structuring like a paragraph in written discourse. Nor did it resemble the structuring formed by turns, adjacency pairs, moves and exchanges (cf. Stenstrom, 1994, chapter 2). When writers and speakers encoded these chunks of consistency, they facilitated both encoding and decoding processes spontaneously without being aware of it. Language choices did not change continuously, but rather, intermittently, more or less together as if one change motivated another. The patterns of consistency were *multi-stratal*, in the sense, that potentially syntactic, semological, graphological, lexical and cohesive patterns were involved, and *multi-functional* in that these patterns represented not just experiential, but also interpersonal and textual choices.

The chunks of consistency that were revealed in our analyses, we called **phases** (cf. Gregory and Malcolm, 1995/1981; Gregory 1985; Malcolm 1985*b*). This means that in a few lines of a text (from spoken or written discourse), experiential, interpersonal and textual systems are realized in a momentarily consistent combination of tri-stratal patterns before shifting to a new, equally consistent, but different, chunk of tri-functional and tri-stratal realizations

(Malcolm, 2005). Phases are most transparent, perhaps, in examples of children's discourse like the following.

> L – nobody's out there
> K – there is so ..oh well have you been in this here before?
> L – yeah you had to sit here didn't you?
> K – yeah
> L – and the teacher was right here getting blocks and stuff
> K – and you were sitting there?
> L – the teacher was sitting here and I was sitting there
> K – and I was sitting there
> L – that's where I was sitting
> K – where? You were sitting here and I was sitting there
> L – oh
> K – I think I was sitting here but

(Malcolm 1985a)

The consistency in this brief segment of discourse is obvious as the interlocutors remember a previously shared experience and explore their memories of it in their linguistic choices. What is not so obvious is the nature of the consistency maintained throughout the passage. In terms of the actual *situation*, the participants, events and circumstances involved in the experience remain consistent throughout the passage (field); the informal relationship between the interactants (personal tenor) remains consistent, and their choice of spontaneous spoken face to face exchange (mode) remains consistent. The functional consistency in the communicative event is reflected in the systems of the language which encode these relationships in the *discourse*. In this instance of the *polyregister* known as casual conversation, the same conceptual sets are explored throughout the text lexically: *sitting, here / there, I / you / teacher*, and the same relational circumstantial processes are manifested semologically *I / you was / were sitting here / there* realizing the experiential component of the message. Tense is consistently past, aspect continuous. Mood choices are declarative or interrogative throughout, and modality choices are absent: both reflecting interpersonal continuity. And there is a consistency in the choice of unmarked experiential theme, with numerous examples of the textual theme, encoded by additive extension throughout the passage.

In a way, *phase* mirrors the same kind of consistency that one sees in *register*, although on a micro level. Whereas, register reflects the relationships which are typical of a single recurring communicative situation, phase reflects the micro-registerial shifts within a single instantial register in a single discourse. At this micro level phases capture the ever-changing nuances in relationships between interactants, experiences and purposes in as single instantial register and discourse. Ever changing, yes, but not *constantly* changing. Over the years, analyses of both literary and non-literary texts, both spoken and written, have confirmed that all discourse is dynamically structured, moment by moment, in chunks of metafunctional consistency known as phases. Phases do not change continuously, but ***intermittently***, the patterns that encode each function of language changing not independently, but ***interdependently***. Perhaps, the best way to illustrate this point is by examining the passage of children's talk which immediately follows the preceding one.

> L – give me the black one
> K – is this one OK?
> L – no, I want the black one.
> K – the big one?
> L – yes
> ..2 seconds
> L – you do the roof
> .. 10 seconds
> K – I need a red

(Malcolm 1985*a*)

   As soon as L says *Give me the black one,* the analyst realizes things have changed. The girls no longer share and question a common past, now they turn their attention to their non-verbal activity, lego, and their discourse follows this shift in experience. This explains the seconds of silence in this phase, where the focus is on building lego, not conversing. The verbal communication that is manifested serves the non-verbal behaviour *give me, I want, you do, I need.* As the processes indicate, this phase describes an action-oriented discourse, experientially. The interpersonal choice of command by L using the imperative *Give me the black,* and later, indirectly, by K using the declarative *I need a red* indicates a shift in power as the girls order one another around as a perfectly acceptable part of their play. And the numerous exophorically related substitutions *one* for lego piece, as well as the exophorically referring participants *I / you,* show a discourse that is less cohesive than coherent, connecting the verbal behaviour to the non-verbal situation, rather than binding the text internally to itself. All in all, this second passage is very different from the first in terms of the choices made in the systems reflecting all three functions. And yet, the second passage is consistent in itself, in a similar, but different way than the earlier passage. The analyst describes the second passage as a second phase, with its new combination of tri-functional consistencies.

Actually, phases are seldom as transparent as these. In *children's* discourse, parallelism and repetition (not just lexical) account for much of the consistency within a single phase. A shift in the relationships within the situation, from a verbal to a non-verbal focus where language plays a secondary role, means a change in all linguistic systems selected, described as a separate phase. The phases which capture the dynamic structuring of *adult* discourse are not so clear, largely because the adults' phases are often longer, more complex, and much more varied (Malcolm, 1988). Adults generally use more predications, more complex alpha-beta clause complexes and a greater variety of sentence types and semological roles than six-year-olds (Malcolm, 1985a, 1988). Adults seem more likely to use questions than children, and less likely to use imperatives (both age groups chose declarative mood 80% of the time (ibid.)). Adults are more likely to use endophoric cohesion than exophoric coherence. These findings relate to the specific nature of the interlocutors' situation in terms of register, communicative purpose, and their equal / symmetrical relationship as peers.

Both adult and child encoders occasionally use transitions to introduce the new patterns which develop into a new phase. Six-year-olds often rely on such formulaic **transition ins** as *D'ya know what? What?* to change topics and phasal consistencies. Adults also use **transitions** to introduce the patterns described as a new phase gradually. In addition, both adults and children use **transition outs** sometimes to conclude the patterns that characterize one phase, before introducing the next. Often these transitions represent a different speech act than the phase proper. For example, transition outs are often comments to phases that employ a brief narrative strategy. Some **transitions in** and **out** both complete the patterns of consistency of one phase and gradually introduce the beginnings of the next phase. Transitions are generally very short: only one or two turns in length. If they were longer, they would likely be described as new phases rather than transitions. Many transitions are marked by a change in tense, mood, primary participant, lexis, and / or cohesive device from the previous phase (cf. Malcolm, 1991).

Phasal analysis is the process of analysing a text tri-stratally and tri-functionally in order to reveal phases, sub-phases and transitions (Malcolm, 1985a). Phasal analyses have revealed not only the distinctions between the discourse of interlocutors of different social provenance (age), but also between adults of different interpersonal relationship: between *friends*, who have shared prior communication and experience, and adult *strangers*, who have not. Strangers are more likely to explore topics available to them in their immediate situation than friends who may bypass such superficial, non-controversial experiences as a consequence of their shared past (Malcolm 1985*a*, p. 252). Strangers are also more likely to explore these topics in a more explicit and less demanding way than friends: transitioning between phasal consistencies. Strangers tend to develop their noun groups more, use more secondary predications, use generalized nouns rather than proper nouns: they seem to take the gnostological 'gaps' of their decoders into account. The discourse of strangers is more cohesive than that of friends.

The noun groups used by friends are seldom developed. The lexis they use is specific and often evaluative involving both involvement and appraisal. Little circumstantial detail is encoded, and endophoric cohesion is limited (ibid.). The phases of adult friends are not as complete as those of strangers nor as long; there is a greater tendency to jump from one group of phasal consistencies to another. An encoder who shares past experience and communication with the decoder is less fearful of communication breakdown and misunderstanding. In a discourse where interlocutors assumed they were strangers, only to find out later that they shared a friend, their entire discourse changed as a consequence, from 'stranger' features to those of 'friend' (Malcolm, 1998).

The phasal analyses of lengthy ***extended texts*** of casual conversation reveal an additional difference. In the discourse of strangers distinct phases evolve gradually, naturally, in a **continuous phasal string**, still tri-functionally consistent, but at a more general degree of delicacy than the individual phases involved. Continuous phasal strings facilitate decoding. Friends who worry less about accurate decoding are more likely to structure their discourse using completely **isolated phases** that jump from one set of tri-functional consistencies to another, like children. Or they may structure their discourse in a discontinuous way: where one set of phasal consistencies ends, only to return moments or even days later as interlocutors revert to much the same linguistic repertoire, as they return to the next instance of the 'same' discussion. Such quick shifts and returns of phasal consistencies are called **discontinuous phasal strings** (Malcolm, 1985*a*, *b*, 1988). Phasal analysis, specifically the idea of phasal strings, reveals the spontaneously encoded dynamic *structure* of a discourse.

Phases are *not* part of the synoptic realizatory code, in terms of communication linguistics theory. Unlike register and rhetorical strategy, they have no non-instantial equivalent stored in the gnostology. Each phase is *only* instantial, occurring simultaneously as encoders manifest their discourse in a communicative event. Hence, as the structuring 'unit' of the dynamically and instantly oriented central plane of experience, phase occurs in the discourse plane only. The existence of phases may be predictable as a cognitive necessity; the linguistic character of a phase is not. In other words, all verbally communicative intentional behaviour is encoded in phases, but nothing more can be said about the nature of phase until the discourse is manifested in its communicative situation. Then the spontaneous structuring of the discourse can be revealed through phasal analysis.

Phasal analyses have revealed much concerning the experiential, interpersonal and textual relationships involved in particular registers. It also reveals micro-registerial shifts within a register from moment to moment as communicative purposes change even slightly. In poly-registers such as casual conversations, interlocutors gossip at one point, share a recipe the next, persuade one another to go shopping a moment later, compare cars the next, and then tell stories. Phasal analysis not only captures such nuances, but also shows very precisely how one register transitions into the next, and the one after that, dynamically, spontaneously, and completely unconsciously. Phasal analysis also reveals the subtle shifts in any one of the relationships involved in a single register: for example, an increase or decrease in interpersonal intimacy. Still, there is much to learn about phase and from phase. Phasal analysis uncovers a dynamic, spontaneous evolution of discourse that would remain unnoticed without it. Phasal analysis reveals whatever self-structuring principles the discourse manifests in that particular instance, whether predictable in a given register, or unpredictable in an interrupted and changed instance of that register, or in a polyregister where discoursal structure cannot be detected without phasal analysis because of continuous, albeit intermittent, fluctuations (Malcolm, 2005).

Phasal analysis methodology

Phasal analysis correlates all the forms of analyses introduced in a very specific way. To prepare for phasal analysis, complete all the individual forms of analyses described in earlier chapters. However, when you intend to analyse a text phasally each form of analysis is adjusted somewhat to consider *sequence*. Phasal analysis maps the *evolution* of style as it happens in time, not just the final cumulative frequencies described in earlier chapters. When you have mastered individual analyses, you take the next step of tracking the position of each linguistic pattern as it emerges. This is done by identifying each sentence or turn by a number, and then describing its features on two summary sheets. On the *Codal Summary* you describe all the linguistic features of the sentence / turn in an abbreviated form (see Step 2b). When you have all the relevant syntactic, semological, cohesive and lexical analyses on one or more page(s), you are ready to look for chunks of tri-stratal consistency. Once you have an idea of where the phases are, you refine your hypotheses using the *Discourse Plane* sheet where you consider the tri-functionality of each 'chunk' or phase of consistency. As you reconsider the linguistic features and boundaries of each phase, you also determine possible sub-phases and transitions. This enables you to begin to uncover the discourse structure of the text involving isolated phases, continuous phasal strings and / or discontinuous phasal strings.

Step 1. Preparation

With written texts, simply number the graphological sentences, whether they are complete independent clauses or not. This may not be as straightforward in spoken texts with no punctuation to guide you. In this case, **number** each speaker's turn (e.g. J253 = Jay's turn #253), and if there are several sentences (sentence level elements including Pp/ic) in a single turn, **letter** each one (a–d).

> *J253*. *a*. / and you know what / *b*. like that boat's great / *c*. it's got a, a seventy-five gallon / *d*. it's got a VW uh gas tank in the front /

Step 2a. Sequential lexical analysis

Phasal analysis requires a conceptual lexical analysis that follows the sequence of occurrence of each item and set. To do this write the sentence / turn number to the left, and then list the lexical / conceptual sets for that sentence only. Continue to do this with each sentence / turn adding new lexical items from the current sentence to other items in earlier sentences forming columns of lexical sets. Make sure that the items you add are positioned in the correct sentence horizontally, while they are added to the appropriate conceptual taxonomy or lexical set vertically. When a new lexical set begins, simply begin a new column to the right of established sets, and then continue with the next set as usual. The only change this makes to suggestions in Chapter 4 is that repetitions of a lexical item are repeated in the appropriate sentence rather than simply adding a count / stroke to the first instance (see 'cat' beside Sentence 1, 2 and 3 rather than cat lll). Additional strokes are only made to a lexical item if it is repeated in the same sentence / turn.

E.g. S. 1. cat   sat   roof
     2. furry
         cat
         meowed   moonlight
     3. cat   dog   chased

A sequentially arranged lexical analysis opens the doors to determining phasal boundaries.

Step 2b. Analysis: Codal summary – describing patterns *sequentially* and *tri-stratally*

Once you have completed your lexical analysis, complete the other types of analyses (syntactic, semological, phonological, cohesive and graphological) as usual specifying the number of sentence / turn as you proceed. Record the findings from your analyses on the **Codal Summary** (CS) keeping the description of each sentence / turn and each clause beside its designated number or letter.

Codal Summary

Passage from _____ Page _____

1	2	3	4	5	6	7	8	9	10	11	12	13
S/ T #	# I C	# D C	S. El	M	M D	A V P T	n M H Q	A	Morphosyntax	Semology	Cohesion	Other

Figure 8.1 Codal Summary

Eleven-by-fourteen-sized paper or larger is useful when recording the numerous details. Starting at the upper left, the first column (#1) is used for identifying the sentence number if it is a written text, the turn number (or sentence letter) if it is spoken. You might also want to keep track of the speaker. After the sentences / turns are identified by number in column 1, the next few columns to the right describe the *syntactic* character of the turns:

Columns #1–9

Column 1 – *identify* the independent clause in each sentence / turn by number / letter, i.e. #1, 2a, 2b,

Column 2 – *number* of *independent clauses* (ic) in the sentence / turn;

Column 3 – *number* and type of *dependent clauses* (rc, sc, nfc) in each ic

Column 4 – *number* of *sentence elements* other than the Pp/ic (L, T, Sa, V etc)

Column 5 – *mood* of each ic: declarative, interrogative, or imperative

Column 6 – *modality* of all clauses (use brackets to indicate level) e.g. ability, future

Column 7 – *aspect*: continuous or completed; *voice*: active or passive; *polarity*: positive or negative;   *tense*: past or present

Column 8 – *noun group structure* at S/Co/Cs/, Cv etc.   e.g. S/ng   Cv/ng
                                                                MMHQ/rc   MH

Column 9 – part of speech and number at *Adjunct* e.g. A/sc-1, A/pg - 2

Possible shortcuts

Once you are familiar with the chart, if you have a lengthy text involving several pages of transcription to analyse, you might consider the following:

- Do *not* fill in Columns #8 or 9 unless you are interested in a nominal or verbal style specifically.
- Assume there are no dc (column #3), there is only a Prop (column #4), the mood is declarative (column #5), there is no modal (column#6), the voice is active, the polarity positive, there is no aspect, (column #7), and only fill in columns #3–7 if this is *not* the case.
- With tense (column #7), once you have identified it as *present* or *past*, do not mark it until there is a change. This means that every sentence without an entry is the same tense as the one specified above.

When you are describing the various features of each designated sentence / turn, use all the abbreviations that you know, and write as small as is readable, because the more sentences / turns you describe on a single page of your codal summary, the better for the next step: preparing for the phasal analysis.

If your codal summary includes only three sentences per page, it will make determining phasal consistencies and boundaries very difficult: they may be pages apart.

The *frequency counts* you include on the codal summary are for the single designated sentence / turn only. This is the major difference between the summary sheets suggested in earlier chapters, and the codal summary introduced in this chapter (see Figure 8.1 p. 215) as a requirement for phasal analysis (Step 3). The earlier summaries were for *entire* texts involving several sentences; codal summaries describe and summarize *one* sentence / turn at a time, in order of its occurrence.

> **E.g.** J – 253. a. / *and* you know what / b. *like* that boat's great / c. it's got *uh*, a seventy-five gallon / d. it's got a VW *uh* gas tank in the front /

On your codal summary, to describe this turn, you would fill it in as follows:

column:	#1	2	3	4	5	6	7	8	9
	ID	*ic*	*dc*	*Sent E*	*mood*	*mod*	*asp . . .*	*ng*	*A*
	J253	ic4	–	Lla,H3	Int	–	act	S/pr3	-
				Dec3			pos	S/ngMH	
							act	Co/pn	
							pres4	Cs/aj	
								Cs/ngMMH	
								Cs/ngMMMHQ/pg	

Columns #10–13

Once you have completed describing particular syntactic details in the narrow columns to the left of the codal summary, divide the space that is left in four. Label these large columns from left to right as follows:

> Column 10 – *syntax*
> Column 11 – *semology*
> Column 12 – *cohesion*
> Column 13 – *other / miscellaneous*

When you examine the summaries of syntax or semology in the following example (p. 231), you will see that they are highly abbreviated, using the abbreviations provided in the earlier chapters. In the *syntactic* description particularly, there is no attempt to record every detail, particularly every part of speech, as you did before. The tree is as informative and minimal as is accurate. The structural labels are most important, with parts of speech labels for clause types (rc,sc,nfc) and groups (pg etc.) only. If something is predictable, for example *M/d H/n* in a *S/ng*, you need not record the details. The amount of detail you include depends on your research interest and how much data you have to analyse: one paragraph or thirty pages of text? When analysing a descriptive passage where I want to compare the type of nominal style of this passage with another, I focus on what is happening at Subject, Complement and Adjunct within the noun group, wondering how and where is the description encoded: right or left-hand embedding?

The *semological* summary for a particular sentence / turn includes the process types and circumstances only, with a frequency count beside each, bracketed to indicate level (SP1, SP2 etc.) as suggested in Chapter 6. The semological roles for syntactic Subjects and Complements need not be recorded if they are implicit in the choice of process (e.g. processor and phenomenon, respectively, with a mental process of cognition). If such assumptions are misleading in marked examples, of course, add whatever details are required for clarification.

The *cohesion* column can be narrower than the syntax and semology columns, because generally, there is less information included in this column: only a list of Rp, Ca, etc. identifying the type of cohesion in the sentence / turn, with frequency counts beside each. The value of describing the syntax next to the semology and the cohesion is that the analyst can better appreciate how these various types of patterns and meanings interrelate: reinforcing one another if predictable (e.g. syntactic Adjunct with semological circumstance) or undermining one another if not (e.g. Complement with processor rather than phenomenon). By the time you have completed all but the last column of the codal summary, sentence by sentence, you will have a very detailed and comprehensive picture of the evolution of the entire text.

The last column(#13) labelled *other* includes whatever information is considered relevant but is not included elsewhere. In this column you might record *lexical* boundaries (where major lexical sets begin and end), or *graphological* and / or *phonological* highlights (complete analyses are elsewhere): punctuation marks or special visual or sounding affects depending on the medium of expression (spoken or written). This is also the column where you note particular *rhetorical* features: alliteration, simile, seriation and so on. Whatever features of the text are relevant to your description, but have not been recorded elsewhere can be added to this column. If you notice endings or beginnings of new patterns, note this in the last column.

Recording all the details of your analyses on a Codal Summary sheet before you have mastered each form of analysis individually can be overwhelming, and is inadvisable. Until you are familiar with all forms of analyses, phasal analysis is not a good idea. It is wiser to follow the approach outlined in Chapters 2 to 6 when beginning to analyse texts. Even when you are comfortable with all the analyses, the complexity and variability of one, like syntax, might warrant a complete separate analyses before being transferred to the codal summary sheet. If the text is simpler and more transparent, however, it might be possible to analyse the syntax right on the codal summary sheet. The complexity of the particular text determines whether a separate analysis is advisable.

Although the codal summary (Figure 8.1) has proven useful in my research over the years, you might find it useful in your area of research to label the columns somewhat differently. Just keep in mind that phasal analysis requires a record of the sequence of occurrence of each linguistic feature.

Step 3. Determining phasal boundaries: looking for *shifts* in patterning

Once your codal summary and lexical analysis are complete, the next step in phasal analysis is to determine the **phasal boundaries** in the text. This is done by observing where the *changes* are in each detail of the analyses. In your lexical analysis, look for and record points where particular lexical sets begin or end. On your codal summary, look down (from top to bottom of) each column from left to right and notice and record where there are shifts. In some texts, where phases are relatively unvaried and consistent, such moments of change may be quite clear. In more complex and internally varied texts, they may be harder to decipher. However, analyses have shown that the phases are still there, although the shift from one range of codal variety to another may be subtle. When all the shifts in patterns are brought together and compared, the analyst discovers that many multi-stratal and tri-functional patterns shift at the same points. These points of change are *phasal boundaries,* and the sentences / turns between these points make up a **phase**. Some phasal boundaries may be obvious; others less so. The process of determining phasal boundaries is *not* complete at this point. If you have questions after your preliminary hypotheses, note them, and refine your analysis using Step 4: the Phasal Summary (see Figure 8.2 p. 221), where you describe each phase tri-functionally.

To determine phasal boundaries, then, you check the patterns in each analysis for passages of continuity and points of change. You want to discover where experiential, interpersonal and textual patterns establish themselves in chunks of momentary consistency, before changing or evolving into the next chunk of consistency. Once you have correlated all the shifts in patterns throughout the text, you should have a basic understanding of how the encoder has unconsciously structured the text by the evolving chunks of consistency that comprise its phases. Although phasal consistencies are tri-stratal and tri-functional, consecutive phases are not necessarily completely different from one another. In some texts, textual patterns may be consistent from phase to phase, while experiential and interpersonal patterns evolve and change intermittently. Experiential and interpersonal criteria, then, would be primary in determining phasal boundaries in such a text.

Phasal analysis reveals the unique dynamic instantiation of registerial consistency in each text. Phases are encoded spontaneously and unconsciously in the moment the discourse is manifested. There is no non-instantial, gnostologically remembered, version of phase.

Step 4a. Refining analysis: Phasal summary – describing each phase *tri-functionally*

Once you have formulated *hypotheses* concerning phasal boundaries based on your observations of the shifts in different patterns (step 3), test and adjust your hypotheses as you complete the **Phasal Summary** (see p. 221). On the right hand side of this summary sheet, number each phase, and note your hypotheses concerning its length in terms of the number of sentences / turns it includes. On the rest of the page summarize the experiential details within the particular phase, then the interpersonal details, then the textual details. The systems which realize each metafunction are described in each of the analyses chapters (2 to 6) under the section called *Metafunction*. Lexical and semological analyses are particularly important in revealing *experiential* information. Lexical appraisal and the syntactic analyses of mood and modality describe *interpersonal* information. Analyses of cohesion and information structure (new / given, theme / rheme) encode *textual* features.

Once you have completed recording all the details that describe the first phase according to each metafunction, do the same for each phase that follows. Often, as you reconsider the details of each phase, you refine the phasal boundaries.

Phasal Summary

Passage from _____ to _____ Page ___

1	2	3	Experiential 4	5	6	7	8	Interpersonal 9	10	11	12	Textual 13	14	15	Other 16
Phase turn #	t	i	pa	eve	cir	lex	oth	m	md	lex	oth	th	coh	oth	

Figure 8.2 Phasal Summary

On the **Phasal Summary** there are sixteen columns. The first three *identify* the phase and sentence / turn. Columns #4–8 describe *experiential* information: the participants, events, and circumstances that represent the experience. Columns #9–12 record *interpersonal* information: the ways language encodes features pertaining to the interactional, the relationships between the interlocutors. Columns #13–15 record *textual* information: the way language is enabled and highlighted in a given medium. Column #16 is available to make whatever notes you feel have been missed.

Columns #1–16

Column 1 – *identify* the **phase** by **number** and **sentences** / turns which are included.

Column 2 – *identify* any **transition(s)** (see following for introduction) operating between phases.

Column 3 – *identify speaker initiating* the phase if spoken.

Column 4 – *describes* the **participants** included in the phase.

Column 5 – the **events** in which the participants are involved in the phase.

Column 6 – the **circumstances** surrounding the events described in the phase.

Column 7 – *summarizes* the **lexical conceptual sets** which are developed in the phase.

Column 8 – *other experiential information*: number and type of clause, tense, aspect, voice etc.

Column 9 – *mood choices* encoded in the phase.

Column 10 – *modality* choices in the phase.

Column 11 – instances of **evaluative lexis, jargon, expletives** used in the phase.

Column 12 – *other interpersonal information*: Sa, H, V, Q (sentence level), negative polarity.

Column 13 – *describes* instances of **marked theme**.

Column 14 – *cohesive repertoire* / style of the phase.

Column 15 – *other textual information*: rhetorical highlights, marked phonological / graphological choices.

Column 16 – *describes* details pertaining to **strategy, register, exchange structure** (See Eggins and Slade, 1997, Chapters 5 and 6).

This following example of a Phasal Summary includes a great variety of information that is relevant to the determination of phasal boundaries. As with the Codal Summary, however, adjustments can be made in the design of the summary to suit personal research styles.

In some texts, particularly those by children, one phase may replace another phase, one set of consistencies another, in quite obvious ways. Resist deciding phasal boundaries on experiential, particularly lexical criteria alone. Phasal analysis is tri-functional: it goes beyond topic analysis. Delineating phases prematurely is worse than 'taking a shot in the dark'; it could lead to 'cooking your data': finding evidence that supports your hypothesis, while ignoring details that would seem to contradict it. Hypotheses concerning phasal boundaries should consider *all* the information in a complete analyses. If you follow the recommended procedure, you will be able to determine phases in both simple and consistent texts and the most complex and internally varied ones.

Step 4b: Identifying transitions and sub-phases

Once you have delineated and described individual phases, you will have discovered how the text fluctuates from one chunk of consistencies to another. At times, even though the tri-functional consistency of a phase is clear, at a more *delicate* level, you may notice that there are different sub-sections, also tri-functional potentially, *within* a single phase. When a green leaf is seen beside a red or an orange one, its green colour will look consistent and distinct. So it is with different phases. However, without the red and orange leaves nearby, one may notice that the green leaf is actually different shades of green: a brighter green towards the tip of the leaf, a darker green towards the stem. So too, with phases. *Within* a single phase, the analyst may notice sub-sections in terms of phasal characteristics, once the more noticeable contrasts between completely different phases are no longer the focus. What is important and what is not always easy to determine is that the same degree of delicacy is maintained throughout the analysis. First, phasal boundaries are determined. Then, a more *delicate* description of individual phases may be pursued as the analyst looks for (i) *transitions between* phases, introducing or completing the patterns of the phase proper and / or (ii) a limited number of *sub-phases within* a particular phase.

Variation and complexity are not the only challenges to discerning phasal boundaries. Most encoders do not 'jump', from one set of phasal consistencies to another, forming a series of **isolated** unrelated **phases.** Often, encoders may change a feature even after one set of tri-functional patterns has been introduced and achieved a measure of temporary consistency. This change may lead to subsequent changes, until an entirely new set of phasal consistencies has evolved. If it takes a few clauses to create the tri-functional consistency of a new phase, these clauses are called a **transition in** to the phase proper. Some encoders also **transition out** of their phases signalling the completion of phasal patterns. Other encoders **transition out** of one phase and **in** to another in just a few clauses.

Research using phasal analyses has revealed that there are particular shifts that often signal phase boundaries (Malcolm, 1991, p. 56). In children's discourse a choice of interrogative mood as in the formulaic '*D'ya know what?'* often signals a transition into a new set of phasal consistencies. Often something as simple as a shift in tense signals the beginning of a new phase, or a shift in Subject / pronoun from first person to third. Sometimes, one phase has Adjuncts, the next does not; one phase has sentence level elements, the next does not; one phase includes certain modals that the next does not; lexical relations give way to conjunction in a second phase. A shift in one pattern triggers shifts in more patterns until a whole new phasal consistency has emerged. One of the ways of transitioning out of a phase, particularly one developed by a narrative strategy, is to shift the speech act from storytelling to comment in a Speaker's Attitude, for example *When she awoke, she was home in her own bed,* **which was lucky**. Some transitions are quite predictable and formulaic; others are quite innovative and unique. And in the complexities and varieties of adult discourse, transitions are not necessarily obvious.

Once a complete analysis has been made of the phases at a consistent degree of delicacy, it is important to increase the level of delicacy and look within individual phases to check whether it is truly as internally consistent as phasal boundaries suggest. Whether an encoder has used transitions between her phases becomes apparent as you complete the phasal summary. If some sentences or clauses seem to belong to one phase in some ways, and to another in others, this may indicate a transition. You might also find that the phase is divided in half by one or two features. Although the phase is consistent overall at a certain degree of delicacy, at a greater degree of delicacy the phase might be described more accurately as two *sub-phases*. A **sub-phase** exhibits the characteristics of the phase at a certain degree of delicacy, but when considered in greater detail, it is subtly different than the other sub-phase(s) which comprise(s) the entire phase.

Maintaining a consistent degree of delicacy throughout your analysis may be challenging, but it is crucial. That is one reason why it is important to complete each step of a phasal analysis at one sitting. You should determine all phasal boundaries, before refining your analysis by looking for transitions and sub-phases. It is also important to know your strengths and weaknesses as an analyst. Some students get so immersed in the details of an analysis, they begin to think every new linguistic choice means a new phase. Such students need to 'come out' of the detail a little, to a slightly more general perspective. Other students may find the appropriate degree of delicacy to distinguish phases, but then have difficulty making more subtle distinctions. It takes experience to move in and out of the details of a text, from general to specific and then back to general, meanwhile staying consistent at each degree of delicacy. But these skills are vital to the analyst working with phase. Phases are not arbitrary. Phasal analyses need to be replicable by different analysts.

Filling out the phasal summary involves continued observation and contemplation as you refine your hypotheses concerning phasal boundaries, transitions and sub-phases. Once you feel that you have accurately mapped the dynamic instantiation of tri-functional consistency throughout the text using phasal analysis, you are ready to consider the discourse structure of the text revealed by the *progression* of phases in your text.

Step 5: Discourse structure: *the progression of phases*

Once you have reached decisions concerning your final description of a text's phases, transitions and sub-phases, you are ready to use your findings to discover more about your text, particularly more about its ***discourse structure***. Are the phases which follow one another related?

My analyses of children's discourse, particularly between children who do not know each other very well, suggests that each phase is usually quite distinct, quite different from the next (cf. Malcolm, 1985*a*). Six-year-olds seem to make quite abrupt shifts in their discourse. In the discourses I have analysed, this was particularly true as the children used language to support them in their non-verbal lego play at times, and then suddenly shifted to use language to explore very different purposes and situations, completely unrelated to their activity. To make these shifts, they often used questions as transitions in such as *you were sitting here? do you remember Riley?*, or the more generic *do ya' know what?* The respondee is then obliged, in most situations, to answer *no, what?*, thereby giving the initiator permission to end what has been, and continue with a new topic, often characterized by an entirely new combination of codal resources. Using this type of transition means that the phases themselves need not be related, need not evolve gradually from one to another. They are interpretable even if they are a series of unrelated **isolated phases**. Research has shown that children are most likely to encode their discourse in isolated phases (ibid.).

A phasal analysis of adult discourse, particularly that of adult 'strangers' who do not share a history of verbal and non-verbal situations before the instantial discourse, illustrates a different phenomenon. Rather than depend on the ritualized formulaic transitions of the children, adults seem to develop their discourse gradually. Everything is complete, explicit; changes are gradual: anything to facilitate decoding. (This is assuming, of course, that the interactants are more interested in cooperating with one another than confronting each other in the situation.) In the discourse of adult strangers, the phases often seem more consistent, less varied, more complete, and longer than those describing the discourse of interactants with prior experience with one another, adult 'friends' (Malcolm, 1998, p. 299). And the phases of strangers often seem to *relate* to one another in a way unlike the isolated phases of the children. There is a greater likelihood that a sequence of separate phases will have something in common, seeming to evolve one from another. Such phases, related by some codal strand, comprise a **continuous phasal string** or block (Malcolm 1985*b*). Sometimes these continuous phasal strings illumine how interactants develop one topic in a gradually evolving way. However, this need not be the case; tri-functional phasal boundaries indicate more than experientially defined topic boundaries.

The discourse of adult 'friends', who share a history of experiences: linguistic and otherwise, has revealed another possible 'structuring', or organization, of phases. People who know each other well are likely familiar with each other's linguistic repertoire also. They may have developed such 'insider' talk that 'outsiders' are not able to interpret it. Part of the linguistic freedom within this constrained range of negotiated choices means that a friend can drop one set of phasal consistencies and begin another completely unrelated set of features without fear of misinterpretation from her well-experienced decoder. And it is quite possible that a friend encoder might re-introduce the selections made earlier, and described as a phase, later in the same discourse with no change in tri-functional consistency. In other words, the same phasal consistencies introduced early in the converstation might reappear. When this happens, the aforementioned phases form a **discontinuous phasal string**. Discontinuous phasal strings, then, are characteristic of the discourse between friends who do not need to be either complete or explicit in order to communicate. This is not to say that the discourse of friends can automatically be described as such interweaving chunks of phasal consistency. Friends also 'risk' the occasional isolated phase too, with or without a transition-in, because interpretation is not deemed a problem.

Phasal analysis enables the analyst to determine larger structuring principles at work even in the sometimes chaotic polyregister of casual conversation. Some discourses are structured in very discrete chunks: *isolated phases*. Others, evolve in a very gradual way, which can best be described as a series of related phases forming a *continuous phasal string*. And still other analyses have revealed that phases can reappear some time after they were first introduced and then replaced by other phasal consistencies. These re-occurrences constitute a *discontinuous phasal string*. These dynamic structuring tendencies may coincide with topic or exchange structural boundaries occasionally. However, phasal analysis tells much more than how the discourse is structured. By examining the discourse structure revealed by phasal analysis, research has proven that phasal analysis can map the subtle shifts of interpersonal relationships, the allocation and reallocation of power, and / or the progression of topics and complete registers in lengthy exchanges (cf. Knight 2010).

In my research over the years, I have found the idea of phasal strings a very useful tool for discovering the broader dynamic structuring of extended discourses. Such phasal strings are the mainstay of spoken discourse, particularly casual conversation, and of it dramatic facsimile where discontinuous phasal strings often carry the linguistic combinations that characterize and distinguish interweaving themes throughout a play (Malcolm, 1991). Phasal analysis of extended texts of written discourse can also reveal how an author builds suspense by a careful alternation of rhetorical strategy that regulates the pacing of the decoder's reading of the text in artful and effective ways. There is much to discover using the phasal analysis of both spoken and written discourse particularly of lengthy texts which are too cumbersome to analyse without such a systematic, sequential and cumulative way of approaching extended texts.

Step 6: Drawing conclusions from your phasal analysis

As you have seen, then, phasal analysis, particularly the phasal analysis of extended spoken texts can reveal subtle structuring principles at work that otherwise might never be noticed. Once you have examined the progression of phases in a text to discover whether the phases are isolated, form continuous or discontinuous phasal strings, your phasal analysis is complete.

Now it is time to write the conclusions to your analysis. As you prepare to summarize your findings, it is useful to revisit and reformulate your earlier hypotheses in light of all your data or evidence, in preparation for developing a *working* **thesis** from which to organize your findings. The purpose of the working thesis is to point you in a fruitful direction of looking and wondering. It will likely be somewhat broad and general at this point. If your analyses were motivated by a particular agenda or hypothesis, your **working thesis** might be a rewording of your intention: *To use phasal analysis to reveal the discourse strategy of the text in order to better understand the encoder's assumptions about the intended decoder* (of course, the more specific to the text under consideration, the better). The **final thesis**, which you cannot write until you have completed a draft of your conclusions, is different: it is the final focus, the most specific focus, the most conclusive and interesting statement that your analysis has revealed. A final thesis will require several rewrites until it is word perfect. When you have found the precise wording of your final thesis, then you are ready to return to your draft and refine it. The final thesis is the one you must commit to throughout the writing of the final draft of your conclusions / paper.

In the conclusions of earlier chapters, you were asked to **describe / summarize** your findings, and then **interpret** them in light of the author's purpose, register, situation, audience, and so on. However, as mentioned previously, in these analyses sequence and the evolution of the text were not considered. If you have decided that your text warrants a complete phasal analysis, because you have seen that it is neither static nor consistent throughout, but rather dynamic, progressive and cumulative, then your conclusions will be somewhat different. In order to capture the evolution of style the encoder has selected and the progression of the text in time, it is best to talk about the text sequentially, from the beginning to the end. What is important, then, is that the findings of the first part of your analysis are described and interpreted, before the next part of the analysis is described and interpreted. And so this continues from beginning to end. One way of doing this is simply discussing the tri-functional character of each phase before interpreting it in terms of relationships, strategy, register and purpose. Once you have considered each individual phase, then you will need to talk about the whole text, the progression of phases, how and why you believe the choices made in the text most effectively fulfill the encoder's communicative purpose.

While doing this, you need to find a balance between generalizations, statistics and specific examples. There is no point talking about a particular sentence without quoting that sentence. There is no point having counted all frequencies of occurrence of a feature unless you use these statistics as evidence to support your generalizations. Generalizations are only credible if they are supported by analysis. Both are required in a scholarly paper.

Step 7: Situating your findings in their scholarly context, and writing an article

If your conclusions are to be turned into a publishable article, there are two further steps to your analysis. Once you have completed the phasal analysis of your passage, and come up with at least a draft of your conclusions, it is important to situate your research in its scholarly context. The way you do this is by:

    a. comparing your analysis of this particular passage to other analyses that are relevant (by the same author, from the same register, exhibiting the same special effect, etc.). This is challenging for analysts who are just beginning such analyses; however, sometimes analyses by fellow classmates can be used as such a body of comparative data.

    b. searching the library / internet for related work by other scholars.

Once you have explored these secondary sources, it is time to reformulate your thesis and rewrite your conclusions, incorporating whatever research is relevant to your own original analysis. It is important that you revise your conclusions with a new audience and new communicative purpose in mind. The register of your own writing has changed. Conclusions, as they have been discussed, are written reports to inform the reader about the findings of your analyses and what you make of them: how you understand them, how you have deduced they serve the encoder of the text you analysed. A published paper is more than a report. It introduces as well as concludes, and it develops an argument using a variety of types of evidence: examples, statistics, comparative data from other research, and relevant quotations from experts in the field. A scholarly paper includes an argument of some sort, a discovery of something that is new and whose significance is more far-reaching than the immediate situation and context either theoretically, procedurally or in terms of the register of which the text is an example. A published paper offers insights to support other scholars in their research. In the ideal scenario, scholars build on one another's research, not necessarily agreeing with each other, but engaging with each other's ideas, testing each other's hypotheses in related areas, and extrapolating from them to come up with new ideas that will improve the theory, methodology and so on. A published paper can be boring and unmemorable, or it can be fascinating, entertaining as well as illuminating. Even important observations and insights may be forgotten, perhaps not even heard, if they are not artfully presented in a way that engages the audience.

Example
Step 1. Preparation

Text   *Experience the Exchange District*

1. In the centre of the City of Winnipeg, the famous corner of Portage and Main is the gateway to the Exchange District. 2. Established at the turn of the century, the Exchange District National Historic Site is the original centre of commerce and culture in Winnipeg. 3. The arrival of the railway in 1881 marked the beginning of an economic boom that would last for four decades and bankroll the construction of office towers, warehouses, banks, hotels and theatres. 4. The legacy of those early years is the Exchange District's exceptional collection of terra cotta and cut stone architecture that is unrivalled in Canada. 5. Together with cobblestone sidewalks and streets, the buildings create an atmosphere growing in popularity as the background for period movies.

6. Expect to be entertained in the Exchange. 7. Attend the theatre, visit the museum, relax in a late night lounge, a traditional pub, or the newest shops and boutiques, galleries and furniture stores. 8. Discover antiques and second-hand furniture stores, curio emporium and merchandise wholesalers.

9. Experience the foods of the Exchange District, from side-walk cafes, lavish meals in fine restaurants, exotic or continental cuisine to one of the funky diners that dot the district. 10. History and architecture are the backdrop for a vibrant business and arts community that is the Exchange District.

Step 2a. *Lexical analysis* (Conceptual set labels – underlined)

position

1. centre	city	streets	famous	exchange
corner	Winnipeg	Portage		
gateway	district	Main		beginning time

2. turn   district   turn   original   exchange established century historic art & culture
   centre   site   commerce
            Winnipeg
   national   bldg.

3.   construction   railway   economic arrival   1881   1881
            office   boom   marked   beginning   #
            towers   bankroll   last   four
            warehouses   1881
            banks   banks   decades
            hotels
            theatres

4.   district   exceptional   exchange   early legacy   collection
      Canada   unrivalled   materials   years
                architecture   terra cotta
                                       cut stone   architecture

5. together sidewalks   streets   cobblestone   together
   background streets   growing   create
            buildings   opularity   atmosphere   create
                                            period   movies

6.   Exchange   exchange   expect
                                                        entertained

7.   bldg. / tourist attractions
            theatre   attend   late   traditional
            museums   visit   night
            lounge
            pub   relax
            shops   newest
            boutiques
            galleries
            furniture stores   stores

8.   furniture stores   merchandise   antiques   discover
            emporium   wholesalers   curio

9.   Exchange   foods   exchange   experience
            district 11 meals lavish
            sidewalk   cafes fine
            cafes   restaurants
            restaurants cuisine exotic
            diners   continental
                         diners funky

10.   architecture   history
   backdrop   vibrant business   architecture
            Exchange   exchange   arts
            District   community
                                                exchange

Comments

- *general city* set evolves throughout passage, from general to *bldg*, to *tourist attractions*, to *shops*, to *restaurants*, to *general*
- *exceptional* set throughout except S. #3,8   full of appraisal
- *history* and *culture* sets all but S. # 1, 5
- *commerce* set through most
- *food* set only S. #9
- no explicit *people* set until S. #10

Step 2b

Codal Summary   **Text: *Winnipeg tourist pamphlet***

1	2	3	4	5	6	7	8	9	10	11	12	13
S/ T #	# I C	# D C	S.E I	M	M d	A V P T	n M H Q	A	Morphosyntax	Semology	Cohesion	Other
1	1			D		p	**		A/pg S P Cs/ng	SP1 rp:r	L	Q/pg-ASC
2	1	1		D		t	**		A/nfc SPCs	SP1 rp:r SP2 mp:cr	Lr	ng ASC
3	1	2		D	h		**		S P Cs/rc	SP1 rp:i SP2a rp:r	Lc (CaEn)	seriation
		1							SPCs + Pco	SP2b *ap:r		*ng *Q
4	1			D			**		S P Cs ng (Q/rc)	SP1 rp:i SP2 rp:a	Lr	appraisal
		1							SPCs			
5	1			D		m	**		A/avg S P Co/nfc	SP1 mp/cr SP2 ap:e	Lc	
		1							P Cp A			
6	1			I		pa			P Co/nfc	SP1 mp:c SP2 :mp:r	Lr	imperative
									PA			
7	3			I					P Cp; P Cp;	SP1a ap:e SP1b ap:e	Lc	compound
									P Cp (5x)	SP1c ap:e + cont:p (5)		seriation
8	1	1		I					P Co (4x)	SP1 mp:p + phen (4)	Lc	seriation
9	1			I					P CoA CoA Co +Co/	SP1 mp:p SP 2 *ap/ rp	Lr Lc	seriation
									ng Q/rc			
		1							SPCs			
10	1			D					S P Cs/ng Qpg Q/rc	SP1 Rp:i SP2 rp:i	LrLc	summary
									SPCs			

Figure 8.3 Codal Summary of Example

Step 3a. Determining phasal boundaries:
hypotheses from *lexical analysis*

Phase 1 sentence #1–2   *city general, position, commerce, history, culture, exceptional,*   # sets

Phase 2 sentence #3–6   *city general* less important, *bldg.*, more *arts & culture, exceptional* set

Phase 3 sentence #7–8   P.3a – S. #7 *tourist sites*; P.3b- S. #8 *stores*

Phase 4 sentence #9   *food* and *food bldg*. & big *exceptional* set, other sets missing

Phase 1 sentence #10   generalized again: balance between *city, position, business / commerce, history, culture exceptional + community*

Step 3b. – Determining phasal boundaries: hypotheses from *codal summary*

Patterns and Shifts

major **shift** in mood sentence #6 and #10

theme marking S.#1,2,5

major noun groups with lots of Q/pg at A, S & C;

rc/nfc all in C S.#1-4 rp:r/i at SP1, with variety at SP2;

S.#6,8,9 mp:c/p, with ap in S.#7, S.#10 return to rp:i

lexical collocation: main cohesive device throughout

significant seriation S. #3, 7–9

compounding S, #4, 10

hypotheses   (without lexical information included)

Phase 1   S.# 1–2   rp, all D, theme marking, major ng with Q/pg(pg) in A,S,C

Phase 2   S. # 3–5   D, past tense (#3),Co/nfc, series in #3, mp & theme in #5 only,

Phase 3   S. # 6–9   Imperative mood, often simple / compound sentences, major seriation

Phase 4/1   S. # 10   Return to major ng (pg & rc), rp, compounding at S

Comments: Questions

Should sentence 9 be called a separate phase on experiential grounds only: *food* lexical set?

Should sentence 10 be called a new phase (P.4), or a return to phase one?

Step 4

Phasal Summary Sheet   *preliminary* version

			Experiential						Interpersonal			Textual			Other
1	2	3	4	5	6	7	8	9	10	11	12	13	14	15	16
phase	t	i	pa	eve	cir	lex	cir / oth	m	md	lex	oth	th	coh	oth	
P1 S.1-2			n-a	rp:r/i pres.		city,posit hist,com cult	A time / place	D	appraisal			th	Lr & Lc		nominal style description
P.2 T- in#3 4-5				past pres mp# 5		bldg. com		D	appraisal			-	no th		seriation
									less appr			-	Lc		
P.3 T-				mp:r ap		tourist		I	appr#9						verbal & nominal style

⇨

in#6 S.7-9			mp:r pres	cite shops food									seriation narr & descript
P.4/1 S.10			pres rp:i				D	appr			-	Lr	
				city,hist, cult,com									

Figure 8.4 Phasal Summary of Example

After reviewing the Phasal Summary, I am unsatisfied by my description of sentence three. Although sentences four and five are more specific lexically than sentences one and two, they are not that different from what I have called phase one. They return to the present tense, theme marking returns in sentence five, and they are still declarative and dependent on lexical relations for cohesion, not just repetition. The problem is sentence three, with its different tense, extensive *building* set that is seriated, its end of theme marking and its move to more specific lexis. It makes me want to reconsider the *delicacy* with which I have examined the text. Is sentence #3 as different from S.#2 as it is from S#6 or 7? No, it is not.

So, I surrender my earlier hypotheses and refine my description of the text by calling sentences one to five, the entire first graphological paragraph, a single phase. Determining sub-phases within this phase reveals the progression from general to specific and back to general:

Phase 1

    a. sub-phase 1(S#1–2) general city lexis, history, culture, commerce and position, declarative, theme, present tense, extensive noun groups, appraisal, lexical repetition, rp;

    b. sub-phase 2 (S#3) past tense, no theme, specific building lexis, seriation, appraisal, declarative, appraisal;

    c. sub-phase 3 (S#4–5) present, declarative, lexical collocation, end of building set, ng, rp (mp in S#5).

Determining sub-phases in phase one, makes me wonder about determining sub-phases in phase 2 (S#6–9). Sub-phases would allow me to capture the lexical distinctiveness and importance of appraisal in sentence #9, the action orientation of sentence #7 with its *tourist site* lexis; the *shopping* lexis of sentence #8. But this does not feel right for two reasons: one, it is too experientially based, and two, if I am using sub-phase to reproduce sentence boundaries only, there is no point. It is not necessary to determine sub-phases in phase two.

The idea of sub-phase is particularly useful in the analysis of extended texts where single phases might be up to twenty turns in length, and sub-phases, themselves, up to seven turns in length.

Revised **Phasal Summary**

			Experiential					Interpersonal				Textual			Other
1	2	3	4	5	6	7	8	9	10	11	12	13	14	15	16
Phase turn #	t	i	Pa	eve	cir	Lex	oth	m	md	lex	oth	th	Coh	Oth	
P.1a. #1,2			City	rp pre	pla tim	city, com, hist,cult		D		appr		th	Lr		nominal style
P.1b #3				pas		buildings							Lc		seriation
P.1c #4,5				pre		com, hist, hist, mat				appr		th	Lc		
P.2 #6			you	mp		entertain		I					Lr		nom / verb styl
#7						tourist site				appr			Lc		styl
#8						shopping				appr			Lc		seriation
#9						food				appr			Lc		seriation seriation
P.1 #10			hist com.	rp		hist,cult, commun				appr			Lr Lc		nom style

Figure 8.5 *Revised* Phasal Summary of Example

Step 5: Discoursal structure

The brief return to phase one (S#10) suggests the discontinuous phasal strings of adult friends. However, there is not enough evidence to say more than this.

Step 6: Conclusions

The following conclusions were written by a student who had not yet learned about sub-phases and reoccurring phases. For this reason, his analysis is more closely aligned to my preliminary phasal summary than my revised summary. He divided what I have called phase one into two phases (two of the three sub-phases I described in phase one), and calls the return to phase one in sentence ten a fourth phase. I admire both his lively writing style and the way he uses his analysis to talk about the contextual matters of audience and purpose. He also describes the graphological appearance of the original text which is meaningful, but unfortunately not available to the reader of this book.

> A collage of overlapping photos and images, in muted pastels, adorns the cover of this tourist brochure below the heading '1999-2000 Visitor's Guide' and

subheading 'the Exchange District,' the tiny pale letters of 'National Historic Site' – with their perhaps limp connotations of dutiful museum-going and officialdom – sensibly inconspicuous. The history theme dominates the visuals: turn-of-the-century towers and manhood, not to mention handholding cherubs, loom over the contemporary human figures, a childless couple shopping (the fun side of commerce) and a guitarist (the cool side of culture); and the District's logo features a Chaplinesque silhouette. Flowers and a tree stand by to 'green over' any sense of a concrete jungle. From the appeal to nostalgia, the rather bland colours and the appearance of the people, both typical and (for the marketers) hopefully prototypical, we can assume a target readership in the over twenty-five age range, with the stress on the thirty-and forty-somethings.

The tourist or visitor (or, in my own case, the long-absent native) who picks up this brochure at the Forks, the airport or downtown, may already be interested in closing an information gap, but if his attention is not piqued he will put it back on the rack in favour of another. Competing 'products' might include leaflets about 'Folklorama' or 'The Parks of Winnipeg'. Thus, while not requiring a hard-sell approach, the message must be clear, concise and attractively presented. There is no 'captive audience' (as there is, say, on a subway stop platform) whom one can tease and dazzle with language games and lengthy narratives. For our visitors, English may be a second, distant third or magical language, so 'standard English' ought to be the rule; 'regionalisms' and slang in general should be avoided, and the tone neutral, midway between the formal and the informal. Nor is the Exchange District a household word like Nike regarding shoes, requiring an innovative approach to capture a product-savvy consumer. What readers want to know, in simple terms, is *What's in the District?, Where is the place* and *What are the names, addresses, opening / closing times, telephone numbers etc.?*

Turning the first page, the first word the decoder reads is 'Experience.' And then the visitor's eye, I believe, will skim and scan down the page past the chubby cherubs, who were, no doubt, selected in order to lighten still further – or 'cutesify' – the brief history lesson below (or possibly even to appeal subconsciously to the high-spending childless couples). If this is not a productive 'experience,' the leaflet will be cast to the winds, its mission aborted. The text on *this* particular page must therefore answer the crucial 'personal' questions *Is there anything in here for me?* For the brochure's ultimate goal is simply to get people into the area, preferably people with money to spend – yuppies, swinging singles, wealthy seniors and the like. That spending is its chief *raison d'etre* is indisputable; not only are shoppers portrayed on the cover, but shopping also comes first on the list of contents below the logo (and presumably the encoders, the Exchange District Biz, represent local businesses).

The exhortative invitation to 'Experience' seems like a solid start: all-embracing, a blend of action and mental processes, it suggests more than mere transaction, sightseeing or being passively entertained. It is a buzzword, and a resonant one in a culture of empowered individualism – the world is there to provide *experiences* for you. The imperative is straightforward but not aggressive, perhaps partly because of a funky font that hints at Oriental calligraphy.

Examining what I consider to constitute the first phase, sentences one and two, we find one of the key queries (Where?) answered immediately in the theme-marked adjunct: the Exchange District is alliteratively *In the centre of the city near Portage and Main*. Now, if our visitor knows anything at all about Winnipeg, he will probably have heard of this windy corner, so the encoder is cleverly 'anchoring' new information to what the decoder may already know. The ambiguous syntax of the first sentence – the subject could be *the famous corner* in which case there is a comma splice after *Main*, or equally *the gateway* (i.e. ASPCs or CsPS) – will not disconcert the reader, I would argue: *In the centre of the City of Winnipeg the famous corner of Portage and Main, is the gateway to the Exchange District*. The roving eye instead alights upon the key noun groups, the chunky informative bits suitably separated by commas, and gains a 'knowing' satisfaction. *Gateway* has a romantic history in frontier mythology, connoting 'to the West'. Thus, when collocated with *to the Exchange District* it neatly marries adventure to civilization, two concepts which we tend to think of as antithetical. The cherubs, too, serve to signify a quasi-European cultural sophistication miraculously flowering in the middle of the prairie.

Again, in sentence two, we find theme-marking *Established at the turn of the century* answering another important question (when?), and once more a simple copula 'is' predication leads on to info-laden noun and preposition groups (e.g. *the original centre, in Winnipeg*). The non-finite clause '*Established . . .*' is used to convey historical data concisely, while the less stilted present tense dominates the primary predications throughout and gives the text its casual dynamism lexically. We learn the District's full name, which runs to an impressive five capitalized words, *the Exchange District National Historic Site*; the encoders must have calculated (rightly, I think) that the high prestige of *National* outweighs the 'dutiful museum-going' effect that it might produce on the younger crowd. Of psychological interest are the reiteration of *centre*, where arguably we all wish to be, and the choice of *original*, which always goes down well in a culture with a thirst for the authentic, the genuine article. The decoder may also be positively affected by the growing chain of hyperbolic adjectives, from *famous* to *original* and later to *exceptional* and so on. Finally, two principal and alliterative motifs are rhythmically sounded: *commerce and culture in Winnipeg*.

The first phase, then, is characterized by simple relational predications of identity and numerous noun and preposition groups, significant ones of place and time theme-marked. This is a descriptive style well-geared to inform the skim-reader, who will likely spot *centre . . . Winnipeg . . . Portage & Main . . . Exchange . . . National* and *commerce and culture*, which seem to promise something for everyone. Alliteration, assonance, for example *corner of Portage* and dramatic lexis *gateway, famous* spice up the broth.

With sentence three, we have the transition to a new phase. For the first and only time, the past tense is used together with an exact date *1881*, for Canadians, an impressively early one. The shift to a non-theme-marked syntactic style and the rather 'active' relational process *marked the beginning* give this one-sided history lesson some pace and drama, further heightened by the nifty hypothetical modality *would last . . . and bankroll* and the explosive lexical choice *boom*. The rather adventurous verbalization *bankroll* seems to have been chosen in the same spirit – the alternative *pay / finance* might have sounded dull, technical and / or workmanlike, depending on the reader. As we might expect, prepositional groups of time *in 1881, for four decades* keep the lesson clear and simple. The necessarily crude narrative (this is not the place for a debate or inquiry) points to a clear causal relationship between trains and the *economic boom*. Putting *The arrival of the railway* first appeals both to the North American visitor's notions of *the birth of the nation*, *progress* and so on, and to the association most foreigners make between Canada and its mighty, spiral-tunnelling, transcontinental railway.

The sentence ends with a rhetorical device characteristic of the whole text – the congerie, or 'heap of words', in this case a long list of buildings *office towers, warehouses, banks, hotels and theatres*. The congerie works cumulatively to wow the reader and convey a sense that 'you name it, we got it'. As I have said, our visitors are likely to be scanners, some with faulty English. Another advantage of the congerie is that there is no confusing grammar, no decoding to do at all, apart from the basic semantics.

Sentences four and five, the main body of phase two, cleverly shift back into the present tense through the use of *legacy*, concentrating on the concrete results of past events – the here and now – which, after all, constitute the 'real' attractions of the District. Again, in sentence four, simple relational processes at the primary and secondary levels of predication function as descriptive noun group carriers. *Those early years*, referring back to the *four decades*, makes the text more cohesive and comprehensible, while *exceptional* and *unrivalled* add more links to the chain of superlative appraisal. The somewhat technical terms *terra cotta and cut stone architecture* sound impressive, whether we understand them or not, and seduce the sightseer. And just as sentence two featured *National Historic Site*, sentence four ends with *unrivalled in Canada*; thus, the encoders are using a rhetorical climax, from *District* to *City* to *Canada*, to build excitement and a sense of importance.

The personified verb in *The buildings **create*** (S#5), like *The arrival ... **marked*** (S#3), dynamizes the inanimate. The lexical cohesion used throughout the text continues with *the buildings* referring back to the congerie in three and the *collection* in four. The return to theme-marking *Together with. . .* serves to highlight *cobblestone* (a rare thing in Canada) as well as to avoid having to cobble together too many noun groups after the verb. Intriguingly, the non-finite clause *growing in popularity* constitutes a quasi-mental process of which the processors are general, which leads nicely, as we shall see, into the next phase. That its *growing popularity as the background for period movies* is considered worth mentioning may well have much to do with the current retro-mania: retro clothing, screen adaptations of historical novels, etc. This idea of visiting a sort of film set adds a dash of fantasy to the appeal.

To sum up, phase *two* is a lexically cohesive, noun-heavy history lesson that, in spite of its content, manages to focus dynamically on the visibly real, by keeping the tense present and the topics tangible. Ingeniously, the story is sketched in terms of a 'creation myth' – *gateway, arrival, the beginning, construction, create* – which carries the reader away, and it must be said, conveniently *leaves* out any troubling references to alternative views such as those of First Nations peoples.

Phases one and two add up to a rather long paragraph, but the cherubs graphic effectively sets the first phase apart, and the lack of complex constructions (only one ic per sentence) makes it an easy read. The dark purple bar of colour down the left side of the page, below the cherubs, demands our speculative attention. It seems to me to be a way of 'walling in' the reader so that the only way out is to the right, the new, farther into the brochure. Be that as it may, so far 'the Exchange District Biz' has largely got it right: no big surprises or experiments, just a great deal of pertinent information in fairly plain language, nicely gauged to the target reader I have described.

The second paragraph, but third phase, starts off with an imperative reminiscent of the invitation at the top to *Experience*.... Suddenly the focus is on the reader; history class dismissed. *Expect* is an undemanding mental process; the processors are people in general, so *all* readers are being addressed. Again, the imperative succeeds in coming across as an invitation *rather* than a command, perhaps because *to be entertained* in the servile passive voice, suggests that one will have the right to be the object or centre of others' efforts.

The nominal ellipsis – just *the Exchange* instead of its full name – is a fascinating rhetorical device. Clearly the encoders are attempting to make the decoders feel like 'insiders' who can already understand local abbreviations and diminutives. And with entertainment as the new topic instead of history, calling it *the Exchange* subtly alters the mood from the relatively sober and didactic to the convivial and expansive. Also striking in sentence six are the alliteration, assonance and rhythm: *Expect to be entertained in the Exchange* has a vibrant ring to it which suits the new theme admirably. This mood is maintained in sentence seven with three more imperative invitations. *Attend . . .visit . . . relax. . . .* These are action processes, but like *experience* there is much of the mental in *relax*, the reader does not feel pressed to do more than his desired amount of rat-racing around. Although we do have three independent clauses here, as usual the syntax, with its punchy paratactic parallel structures *Attend the theatre, visit the museum,* makes few demands on the readers, who may skim and scan to their hearts' content without coming to semantic grief.

Yet again, the Biz employs congerie, which leads us to believe that there is absolutely no wish that cannot be satisfied in this amazing District. The long list of both commercial and cultural amenities, which coheres with sentence two: *centre of commerce and culture* interestingly and appropriately, includes *boutiques* and *pubs*, which connote European white-collar establishments rather than American blue-collar 'bars'. This accords well with my hypothesis about the well-heeled audience (and who but the well-off can afford to be tourists?) targeted by the visuals on the brochure's cover. *Traditional* contrasts nicely with *newest*, strengthening the all-encompassing effect of the congerie. The next sentence, too, consists of an imperative *Discover. . .* followed by a congerie *antiques and secondhand furniture stores, curio emporium* and *merchandise wholesalers.* Notably, the cultural dominates the commercial until the latter half of the paragraph, as if to cloak spending in the guise of entertainment.

The fact that the next sentence (#9) *follows* the same pattern as the previous one, imperative plus noun groups, indicates that the decision to start a new paragraph was probably made simply in order to make the last two paragraphs look balanced, but perhaps also on the basis of the new but related topic: food. This time the imperative is *Experience* which, as I have said, is richer in suggestion than most of its alternatives – in this sentence, *taste, try,* or *sample* – which largely lack the mental element.

By now, it comes as no surprise, at least to the analyst and perhaps to the reader, that every sort of food under the sun seems to be available. The adjectives *funky* and *exotic* add appeal to the younger generation, while *lavish* and *fine* might be said to matter to the rest. The wide-reaching *from . . ., to . . .* prepositional group format in effect amplifies the congerie. Once again, all readers are being addressed: the message is that all tastes can be catered to. Alliteration *continental cuisine, dot the district* and the unusual verb *dot* contribute to the 'funky' flavour of this sub-phase.

To summarize briefly, while phases one and two focus on the District itself and a certain view of its history, phase three appeals directly to the reader with imperative mental and action processes. The quick-fire invitations to a litany of activities and places are well-calculated to interest the widest possible range of readers.

It remains to examine the fourth and final phase: sentence ten. One notices at once the return to *History and architecture* and relational processes. This is clearly an attempt to summarize and recapitulate the principal themes, commerce and culture, now written more casually as *business and art* to carry through the familiarity established in phase three. The adjective *vibrant*, which is what all cities try to be, completes the chain that began with *famous. Backdrop* fits in with the earlier relevance to *period movies,* again, carrying with it a whiff of the theatrical. And *Exchange District* features at both the beginning and the end of the paragraph according to the advertiser's rule of 'repeat the product name'.

At the bottom of the page there is another framing device *for more information*, in bold type, the same purple as the 'wall' of colour down the left. Its function is less to enable people to contact the Biz than it is to take responsibility for the text, to 'validate' it with a name, an address, numbers and that signifier of hip modernity: email.

Having analysed the text and graphics in some detail, we are now in a position to return to our introductory remarks regarding the rhetorical 'bottom line'. Will it get people to spend money in the District? In short, I believe it does its best. It is attractive. It invites rather than begs or commands. It deals with the key questions: *what there is* and *where it came from*. Its nominal, predictable style *is* conducive to skim-reading, and does not intimidate the foreign visitor; here, the cliché is at home. The division into phases allows us to see more clearly the shifts from the District to the reader and back, and the way the shorter opening and closing phases serve to sandwich the 'meat' in between, while lexical cohesion holds them all together. And if, in addition, we consider the paragraph as a graphological unit, we can add that each one contains a congerie, and that the number of words and phrases to do with history diminishes exponentially from nine to three to one, leaving the reader fully 'present'.

Finally, returning to the cover, it may be that the pastels are muted, and the images washed out, to the point of merging into a smudge, at least seen from a distance. But, as I have said, a certain amount of interest on the visitor's part is given: this clearly-labelled *Visitor's Guide* self-selects for the information-deprived. Assuming that the cover succeeds, then, the scanners, whether it be for historical data, for shopping opportunities, cultural events, or any combination of these, will find their 'thing' in a congerie somewhere on the first page. And the text will have fulfilled its function to propel them into the rest of the brochure, and the Biz would hope into the District, wallets bulging!

(Dawes, 2000)

Conclusions

A **phase** is a momentary stretch of tri-functional consistency which may be consistent for two turns or twenty. It appears to 'structure' every discourse in a dynamic way as it is manifested, whether written or spoken, whether casual talk or formal legal discourse. Encoders are unconscious of their tendency to encode discourse in chunks of tri-functional consistency, and yet it is not that surprising that they do. It certainly supports their decoders' process of interpretation, that there are intermittent moments of codal consistency, and not a continuous, arbitrary and random shift of one pattern and then another. And it likely supports the encoding process as well, that there are moments of consistency before there is change, and that changes often happen together in an interrelated way.

One might expect that as one changes the topic from one experience to another, it is quite natural that interpersonal and textual relationships change too, and these changes are manifested in changes of mood, modality, theme and cohesion. This would be assuming that experiential choices are the prime motivating principle in terms of discourse selections. And no doubt, sometimes they are. However, you have all experienced discourse, where the topic being explored is irrelevant; instead, what is happening interpersonally is the driving force behind the discourse. This happens all the time when you meet someone on a bus, or waiting in a line; where you establish a relationship through an exchange of neutral non-confrontational experiences like the weather, before taking the greater interpersonal risks of exposing personal opinions and values.

Sometimes, a single experience is explored in several phases, where interpersonal and textual shifts account for the phasal boundaries. At other times the cohesive style might be quite consistent throughout the text, and interpersonal and experiential shifts determine the phases. Phase is not the same as topic or exchange (cf. Knight 2010). The distinguishing feature of phase is its tri-functional character, and this is what it has to offer the analysis of discourse. Such a descriptive tool as phasal analysis helps us understand the interdependent and intermittent dynamic structuring principles inherent in the encoding and decoding process.

In registers that are highly unmarked / predictable, phasal analysis will reveal the schematic structure that is predictable in terms of the genre / register and situation. In addition, if there is any interruption of registerial characteristics in the actual instantial discourse, that reflects a minute shift in relationship between the interlocutors involved in the communicative situation, phasal analysis will also capture that shift. As a moment-by-moment description of the dynamic shifting of metafunctional consistency, phase reveals both predictable generic schema and unpredictable fluctuations in the same. Phasal analysis, then, reveals whatever discoursal structure the discourse manifests in that particular instance, whether a predictable one in a given genre, or an unpredictable one in an interrupted and changed instance of that genre, or in a poly-register where schematic structures cannot be detected without phasal analysis.

In its stylistic predictability, consistency and in its organizational capabilities, rhetorical strategies are not unlike the idea of *phase* and *phasal strings*. However, rhetorical strategies and phasal strings are very different in many important ways. Rhetorical strategies are both non-instantial and instantial: they do not occur as, and because, the text is manifested in time. Rather, they are static resources that fulfill particular purposes in particular registers. They give a cumulative sequence in texts involving *process*, they organize the similarities and differences that facilitate *comparison* in texts involving that strategy, they organize the evidence in *arguments*.

Rhetorical strategies, like the non-instantial version of register that language users use continuously although unconsciously to guide their expectations, interpretations and comparisons, are not like the phases of phasal analysis in communication linguistics. There is no gnostological non-instantial phase. Phases are *instantial* only: they are a dynamic structuring device that happens unconsciously and simultaneously in the process of encoding and decoding. They describe the cognitive and physiological tendency to make patterns of metafunctional consistency that facilitate encoding and decoding.

There is no phase until a discourse has been manifested in an instantial situation. Phasal analysis can then determine the dynamic instantiation of metafunctional consistencies through micro-analysis. Once phasal boundaries are ascertained, they can then be used to determine larger discoursal structures, in a replicable and precise way (Malcolm, 1985*a*, *b*, 1998). Such continuously evolving or intermittent phasal strings will enable the analyst to determine the precise way the encoder has employed rhetorical strategies to organize, embed and / or configure particular registers in order to achieve her purposes.

Of course, not all analyses using phasal analysis as a research tool are designed to focus on the phasal description itself. Phasal analysis may be nothing more than a place to start in analysis when considering another research focus (cf. Young 2001, Knight 2010 using phasal analysis in her investigation of humour in conversation). In such papers, the characterization of individual phases might not be the point. Rather, phasal analysis is used to show the evolution of a particular phenomenon in the discourse.

There is so little research on phasal analysis, so few analysts are familiar with this research tool, that it is difficult to know the range of variables which affect this inherent structuring principle. Research has shown that different strategies, different registers, different aged interlocutors, and different interpersonal relationships between interlocutors all affect the length of phase, its internal variation and complexity, the likelihood of transitions, phasal strings and so on (Malcolm, 1985*a*, *b*; 1991; 1998). However, without the results from phasal analyses describing thousands of texts, from a great range of encoders, directed to a great variety of decoders, from a great variety of registers, temporal, geographic, and social provenances, it remains difficult to understand exactly what phase is, and to assess what affects it and what it affects. Phases, both because they are unconsciously created and sustained, and because they are spontaneously occurring, as discourse happens, can never be completely predictable. Hence, phasal analysis can be an immensely useful tool in the study of spoken and written discourse; as useful as the idea of clause in syntax, which is also tri-functional. And more useful than the graphological units of sentence and paragraph which are limited to the constraints of relatively formal written discourse. Phase is equally adept at capturing the innate 'structuring' principles at work in all types of discourse, no matter what field, mode, or tenor in the situation.

This is not to say that the forms of analyses I have introduced in this book, which culminate in phasal analysis, are the only worthwhile tools of analysis.

Nor are they even the only forms of analysis which will contribute to distinguishing phasal boundaries. A full phonological analysis would add an important dimension to the discernment of phasal boundaries. Martinec assumes that one of the levels of rhythmic waves in his hierarchical model of rhythm captures what I am describing as phase, phonologically (in conversation). And Eggins and Slade's various ways of analysing casual conversation, particularly their analysis of discourse structure, would contribute to the determining and understanding of phasal boundaries and phases in general (1997). It may be that phases are sometimes isomorphic with exchanges in spoken discourse depending on the register. However, this correlation needs to be explored in depth before such conclusions can be drawn (cf. Knight 2010).

Phasal analysis has proven an invaluable research tool with which to probe both individual instantial discourses and gnostologically recorded, and culturally specific, non-instantial notions of rhetorical strategy and register. Up until now, it has been used by few linguists outside Canada; however, it has great potential for describing the subtle structuring principles at work in all texts, particularly extended spoken discourse, where sentence-oriented frameworks are inadequate.

Review of phasal analysis

1. Preparation for analysis

a. **Number** the *sentences*, if the text is written; the *turns*, if the text is a transcription of a spoken text.

b. Complete any **analyses** that are too complex to be done on the codal summary.

2. Description

a. Complete a sequentially organized conceptual **lexical analysis** of the lexical items in your text in terms of the order of occurrence.

b. **Codal summary**: Complete the codal summary sheets in order to correlate your semological, syntactic, and cohesive information (columns for each). You need not include as much detail as you did in your first individual analyses: be purposeful in your selection of what details to include. Include an extra column entitled 'other' to capture relevant lexical, phonological, rhetorical details and the like.

Note: Keep a **comments** page or a written log as you complete the summary sheet to record your insights concerning your analyses. You are never so close to a text as when you are in the middle of analysis or summary. A day later, you may have forgotten some of your most interesting observations and insights.

3. Determining phasal boundaries

a. Look on your sequentially organized **lexical analysis** and note at what sentence / turn certain conceptual sets appear and others disappear. Note beginnings and endings, accounting for lexical *shifts*, and on a **comments** page begin to form hypotheses of text structuring or chunking.

b. Look from top to bottom of each column of your **codal summary** to see where there are stretches of codal consistency and where there are changes in this consistency. Note where each *shift* is, and in your **comments** correlate different shifts, adjusting prior hypotheses from your lexical analysis with phasal boundary hypotheses from your codal summary.

4. Phasal summary

a. *Identify phases*: Fill in your **phasal summary** in terms of the hypothetical phases you have come up with in step 3. Now you are no longer describing what happens sentence-by-sentence, but you are combining using frequency counts all the details from all the sentences in a single description of the specific phase. Summarize all the information for one phase, and then do the same for the next phase and the next. Remember, to fill in your phasal summary you need to consider both the lexical and codal description summaries of step 2. If there are a few sentences that you are not sure about (which phase they belong to), you might describe them separately at this point. Once you have completed your phasal summary sheet, write a short description of each phase in prose, organizing your description in terms of experiential, interpersonal, textual and other information.

b. *Identify transitions*: Based on your phasal interpretation and what you have learned from step 4 thus far, reconsider your hypothetical phasal boundaries. Are there **transitions in**, **out**, or **out** and **in** of your phases that facilitate the encoder's shift from one set of consistencies to the next?

Identify sub-phases: Reconsider your phasal boundaries once you have ascertained any transitions operating between phases. Do you still consider them valid, or have you changed delicacy somewhere along the way? If so, you need to re-evaluate your boundaries.

Are there **sub-phases** within your phases that you did not notice originally?

5. Discourse structure: the progression of phases

a. Is each phase distinct in which case you would call each an *isolated phase*?

b. Does one phase seemingly gradually evolve into the next in which case you would consider a number of such related, evolving phases, a **continuous phasal string** or block?

c. Does one set of phasal consistencies disappear only to reappear at a later point in the discourse? If so, you would call it a *discontinuous phasal string*?

6. Conclusions to your phasal analysis

a. Develop a few **working theses** to help you focus and structure your conclusions.

b. Describe the text in terms of the phases of consistency that your analysis has uncovered.

This may be organized sentence-by-sentence, phase-by-phase, or thematically.

c. Interpret your findings in terms of whatever seems most significant, in terms of your working thesis. What do phases reveal aside from the intricacies of their tri-functional character? **Speculate** why these choices have been made:

1) Do they shed light on the temporal, geographical or social provenance of their **cultural context** (CCC)?

2) Do they tell you more about the relationships within the generic **situation** (GS): the field, mode, personal or functional tenor?

3) Do they tell you more about the linguistic reflection, the **register**, associated with the reoccurring situation of the discourse.

4) Do they further explain the **interpersonal relationship** between the encoder and the decoder?

5) Do they reveal how certain effects like **suspense** and **humour** were created?

6) Do they show how the **linguistic context** of the text affected the discourse?

7) Do they tell you about the encoder's **purpose** and **intention**?

8) Do they reveal more about the **encoding-decoding process** itself?

9) Do they show you how certain **rhetorical strategies** have been used to develop and structure the text?

10) Do they tell you more about the nature of **phase** itself, or the **discourse structure** revealed by the phases, or more about the methodology **phasal analysis**?

d. Assess how an analysis of the phases has helped you understand the text more than if you had not uncovered the phasal consistencies.

e. Develop a **final thesis** based on the draft of your conclusions, and refine your conclusions having committed to the precise wording of your final thesis.

7. Situate your findings in their scholarly context, and write for publication

Contextualize by

a. additional related analyses and

b. research of secondary sources.

Revise your conclusions with the communicative purpose and shift in register that a scholarly paper entails. From your final thesis, come up with an introductory paragraph which not only introduces your topic and text, but also the theoretical and descriptive framework. Further develop the body of the paper by describing and interpreting the phasal consistencies your analysis has revealed. Finally, draw your conclusions of the text, as well as what you have learned theoretically and methodologically. You have now contributed to the development of phasal analysis as a research tool. Thanks!

Further reading

Knight, N. (2010), 'Laughing our Bonds Off: Conversational Humour in Relation to Affiliation.' Doctoral Dissertation. University of Sydney, Australia.

Works Cited

Asp, E. (2001). 'How to Do Different Things with Words'. In *Communication in Linguistics* de Villiers, J. and Stainton, R. (eds.) Toronto, Canada: Editions du Gref. pp.1–32.

Becker, B. and Malcolm, K. (2008), 'Edwardian Postcards as an insight into the Edwardian Mind and Community', in M. Harry et al. (eds), *Atlantic Provinces Linguistic Association*, 59–65.

Bonvillain, N. (2003), *Language, Culture and Communication*, (4th edn) New Jersey: Prentice Hall.

Chothia, J. (1979), *Forging a New Language*. Cambridge: CUP.

Chrysler Group LLC. (1973), 'Wanted: Men who can handle a real road machine. Dodge Challenger Rallye'. Advertisement, Chrysler Group LLC.

Couper-Kuhlen, E. and Selting, M. (1996), 'Towards an interactional perspective on prosody and a prosodic perspective on interaction', in E. Couper-Kuhlen and M. Selting (eds), *Prosody in Conversation*. Cambridge: CUP.

Dawes, M. (2000), 'Experience the Exchange District'. An unpublished undergraduate essay. Winnipeg, Manitoba: University of Winnipeg.

de Villiers, J. and Stainton, R. (eds.) (2001). *Communication in Linguistics*. Toronto, Canada: Editions du Gref.

Dinneen, S. (1978), *An Introduction to General Linguistics*. Washington: Georgetown University Press.

Dondis, D. A. (1973), *A Primer of Visual Literacy*. Cambridge, MA: MIT Press.

Downing, A. and Locke, P. (1992), *A University Course in English Grammar*. London: Prentice Hall.

Eggins, S. (1994), *An Introduction to Systemic Functional Linguistics*. London: Pinter Publishers.

Eggins, S. and Slade, D. (1997), *Analyzing Casual Conversation*. London: Cassell.

Epps, A. (2009), 'So what better thing to ask a professional interviewer about than what makes a good interview?' *The Uniter*. Winnipeg: University of Winnipeg Press. 13 August 2009.

Exchange District Biz National Historical Site. (1999), '1999-2000 Visitor's Guide: the Exchange District'. Winnipeg, Manitoba.

Finegon, E. and Besnier, N. (1989), *Language*. New York: Harcourt & Brace Jovanovich.

Firbas, J. (1972), 'On the interplay of prosodic and non-prosodic means of functional sentence perspective', in V. Fried (ed.) *The Prague School of Linguistics and Language Teaching*. London: Oxford, University Press.

Firth, J. R. (1957), *Papers in Linguistics*. Oxford University Press.

Fleming, I. (1988), *Communication Analysis*, vol. 2. Dallas: Summer Institute of Linguistics.

Gregory, M. (1981), 'The nature and use of metafunctions in systemic theory', in *The Eighth Lacus Forum*. Columbia, SC: Hornbeam Press, 67.

—. (1985), 'Towards Communication Linguistics: a framework', in W. Greaves and J. Benson (eds) *Systemic Perspectives on Discourse*. Norwood, NJ: Ablex.

—. (1995/1981), Hamlet's voice: Aspects of text formation and cohesion in a soliloquy', in J. Cha (ed.) *Before and Towards Communication Linguistics*. Korea: Sookmynung Women's University, 113–28.

—. (1995/1982*a*), 'Clause and sentence as distinct units in the morphosyntactic analysis of English and their relation to semological propositions and predications', in J. Cha (ed.) *Before and Towards Communication Linguistics*. Korea: Sookmynung Women's University, 212–21.

—. (1995/1983), 'Propositional and Predicational analysis in discourse description', in J. Cha (ed.) *Before and Towards Communication Linguistics*. Korea: Sookmynung Women's University, 222–8.

Gregory, M. and Carroll, S. (1978), *Language and Situation*. London: Routledge and Kegan Paul.

Gregory, M. and Malcolm, K. (1995/1981), 'Generic situation and discourse phase: An approach to the analysis of children's talk', in J. Cha (ed.) *Before and Towards Communication Linguistics*. Korea: Sookmyung Women's University, 154–95.

Halliday, Michael. (1994), *An Introduction to Functional Grammar* (2nd edn). London: Edward Arnold.

—. (1978), *Language as a Social Semiotic: The Social Interpretation of Language and Meaning.* London: Edward Arnold.

—. (1973), *Explorations in the Functions of Language.* London: Edward Arnold.

Halliday, Michael and Ruqaiya Hasan. (1985/89), *Language, Context and Text: Aspects of Language in a Social Semiotic*. Oxford: OUP.

—. (1976), *Cohesion in English*. London: Longman.

Handgun Control Inc. 'A $29 handgun shattered my family's Life', The Brady Campaign to Prevent Gun Violence.

Hummel, M. and Ray, J. (2008), *Caribou and the North*. Toronto: Dundurn Press.

Hyundai Sonata Advertisement. (2001), In *Parenting*. New York: Time Inc. Sept. 2001, 65.

Knight, N. (2010) 'Laughing Our Bonds Off: Conversational Humour in relation to Affiliation', Doctoral Dissertation, University of Sydney, Sydney, Australia.

Kress, G. and van Leeuwen, T. (1996), *Reading Images: The Grammar of Visual Design*. London: Routledge.

Labov, W. (1966), *The Social Stratification of English in New York City*. Washington DC: Center for Applied Linguistics.

Ladefoged, P. (2001), *Vowels and Consonants*. Oxford, UK: Blackwell Publishers.

Lemke, J. (2002), 'Travels in hypermodality', *Visual Communication*, 1 (3), 299–325, October.

Malcolm, Karen. (2005), 'What Communication Linguistics has to offer Genre and Register Research', in H. Gruber et al. (eds) *Folia Linguistica. Acta Societatis Linguisticae Europaeae. XXXIX/1–2 2005*. Berlin, Germany: Mouton de Gruyter. 57–74.

—. (2001), 'A language of innuendo and avoidance: Hemingway's Hills Like White Elephants', in R. Stainton and J. DeVilliers (eds) *Communication in Linguistics*. Toronto: Editions du Gref.

—. (1998), 'The language of friends and strangers: only their phases show for *sure*', in Sanchez-Macarro, A. and Carter, R. (eds) *Linguistic Choice Across Genres: Variation in Spoken and Written English*. Amsterdam: Benjamins, 291–300.

—. (1991), 'Prose dialogue and discourse', in E. Ventola (ed.) *Approaches to the Analysis of Literary Discourse*. Abo, Finland: Abo Akademi Press, 39–62.

—. (1989), 'Description and narration with a difference: the participle', in *The Sixteenth Lacus Forum*. Hornbeam Press, 420–9.

—. (1988), 'Casual conversation: A message focused register', in B. Greaves and J. Benson (eds) *Systemic Functional Approaches Perspectives to Discourse*, vol. XXVI. Norwood, NJ: Ablex. 73–8.

—. (1987), 'Woolf's Descriptive Style', in *The Fourteenth Lacus Forum*. Norwood, NJ: Hornbeam Press.

—. (1985a), The Dynamics of Casual Conversation: From the Perspective of Communication Linguistics. Doctoral Dissertation. York University.

—. (1985b), 'Communication linguistics: A sample analysis', in B. Greaves and J. Benson (eds.) *Systemic Perspectives on Discourse*. Norwood, NJ: Ablex, 136–51.

—. (1984), 'Situational and gnostological exophora', in *The Eleventh Lacus Forum*. 263–73.

Malcolm, K. and Becker, B. (2008), 'Edwardian Postcards as an insight into the Edwardian Mind and Community', M. Harry et al. (eds) *Atlantic Provinces Linguistic Association*, 59–65.

Malcolm, K. and Becker, B. (2008b). 'Suspended Conversations that intersect in the Edwardian Postcard'. In Systemic Functional Linguistics in Use. Nina Nørgaard (ed.). Special issue of Odense Working Papers in Language and Communication, Institute of Language and Communication, University of Southern Denmark. 2008.

Martin, J. (1992), *English Text*. Amsterdam: John Benjamins.

—. (1985), 'Process and text: two aspects of human semiosis', in Benson, J. and W. Greaves (eds) *Systemic Perspectives on Discourse*, vol. 1. Norwood, NJ: Ablex, 248–73.

—. (1984), 'Language, register and Genre', in F. Christie. (ed.) *Children Writing: Reader*. Geelong, Vic: Deakin University Press, 21–9.

Martin, J. R. and White, P. R. R. (2005), *The Language of Evaluation, Appraisal in English*, London & New York: Palgrave Macmillan.

Martinec, R. (1999a), Rhythmic hierarchy in monologue and dialogue. (Draft)

—. (1999b), Rhythm in multi-modal texts. (Draft)

Northfield, S. (2000), 'The TSE's winners and losers of 1999', *Globe and Mail*.

Pike, K. (1945), *The Intonation of American English*. Ann Arbor: University of Michigan Publications.

Pike, K. and Pike, E. (1982), *Grammatical Analysis*. Summer Institute of Linguistics: University of Texas.

Prest, A. (2003), 'Hot winger, sharp goalie *snip* Blades', Sports Section. Winnipeg, Free Press.

Rist, C. (1999), 'The physics of singing', *Discover* Aug.

Saeed, J. (2003), *Semantics*. Malden, MA: Blackwell Publishing.

Sebba, M. (1986), 'London Jamaican and Black London English', in D. Sutcliff and A. Wong (eds) *Language and the Black Experience*. Oxford: Blackwell.

Stillar, G. (1993), *A Communication Linguistics Perspective on the Structuration of Ideology in Discourse*. Master's Thesis. York University, Toronto, Canada.

Sweet, H. (1877), *A Handbook of Phonetics*. Oxford: Clarendon.

Thompson, P. and Davenport, P. (1982), *The Dictionary of Visual Language*. Harmondsworth: Penguin.

Ventola, E. (1987), *The Structure of Social Interaction: A Systemic Approach to the Semiotics of Service Encounters*. London: Pinter.

Warren Commissions Hearings. vol. 19. p. 467, taken 22 November 1963.

Watt, D. (2001) 'Intonational Cohesion and Tone Sequences in English' In *Communication in Linguistics* de Villiers, J. and Stainton, R. (eds.) Toronto, Canada: Editions du Gref. pp. 361–378.

Young, Lynne (2001) 'Second language Acquisition: Learning How to Mean' In *Communication in Linguistics* de Villiers, J. and Stainton, R. (eds.) Toronto, Canada: Editions du Gref.

C.P.R. v. Murray, (1932) S.C.R.112; (1932) 2 D.L.R. 806; 38 C.R.C. 298.

http://www.realhistoryarchives.com/collections/assassinations/jfk/origwit.htm

http:www.440magnum-network.com/info/ads/1973dodgechallenger1.shtml

Index